The Literary Universe of
Jack B. Yeats

Jack B. Yeats, by Harry Kernoff, from the collection of the author

The Literary Universe of
Jack B. Yeats

Nora A. McGuinness

The Catholic University of America Press
Washington, D.C.

Library of Congress Cataloging-in-Publication Data
McGuinness, Nora A., 1936–
    The literary universe of Jack B. Yeats / by Nora A.
    McGuinness.
        p.   cm.
    Includes bibliographical references and index.
    1. Yeats, Jack Butler, 1871–1957—Criticism and
    interpretation.
    I. Title.
    PR6047.E3Z74   1991
    828'.91209—dc20
    ISBN 0-8132-0737-1 (alk. paper)
    90-2536

To the AEM's, MJM, and KAM

Contents

Acknowledgments

My greatest debt is to Ruby Cohn, who suggested I work on Jack Yeats, who supervised the doctoral dissertation out of which this book grew, and who has been a mentor and friend since I began my work. I am also indebted to Anne Yeats, who generously gave me much firsthand information about her uncle, access to primary materials, and hospitality during several stages of this investigation.

I also wish to acknowledge the help of my colleagues. At the University of California, Davis: Peter Hays and David Robertson read early drafts; Robert Crummey and Dale Rogers Marshall, as Associate Deans of the College of Letters and Science, helped make it possible for me to read portions of this work at professional meetings and gain helpful insights; and Eldora Synhorst, Gerry Baker, Judith Ryan, and Carol Beck did typing, wordprocessing, and photocopying of many drafts. In the American Conference on Irish Studies many have given both information and support. At the Catholic University of America Press: anonymous readers, director David McGonagle, and editors Cynthia Miller and Susan Needham have given invaluable assistance.

My final debt is to my husband Arthur and my children—Anne, Michael and Kathryn—whose pride and encouragement sustained my efforts.

Introduction

My analysis of Jack B. Yeats's writings approaches his literary universe thematically, by isolating motifs that persist throughout his writing. My purpose is not so much to examine individual products of Yeats's literary imagination as to explicate his universe.[1]

In Yeats's universe, the characters to be emulated learn to abandon systems of rational thought and attempts of the conscious will to control events. In his attitude toward the power of reason and the will, Yeats reflects mysticism, showing characters obtaining release from consciousness and gaining entrance to a visionary state in which they perceive the futility of human attempts to struggle against the spiritual forces of the universe, forces larger than the individual. The ideal Yeats character accepts what comes. His tragic protagonists are persons of good will who attempt to intervene in human events, often to improve the lot of their unheeding communities.

Striving to unite with a universal force is the most important activity in Yeats's fictional and dramatic worlds. Yeats's "artists" are profoundly aware of the spiritual and of the unconscious; they strive to attain vision by utilizing the unconscious, to share their visions of the universal with others, but rarely to act in the attempt to make the world around them attain closer congruence with the visionary world. In his conception of the artist, Yeats exhibits Romantic ideals. Since strivings to attain and communicate vision are the most significant human actions possible in Yeats's universe, they give inherent dignity to the artist.

Yeats's concept of individual consciousness and personal identity is Modernist. The shifting of names in his narratives expresses his sense of personal identity in flux. Yeats's emphasis on the subject of consciousness as a construct, as a locus of relations, rather than as a stable form, does not reflect classical rationalist presuppositions about human nature—that it is an intelligible entity and that human experience and knowledge, human thought and language, are identifiable.

Yeats's main theme, the first precept for human conduct which his work embodies, is that all humans should engage in the attempt at union with the universal. A corollary precept is that the artist, because he engages seriously in this beneficial pursuit of spiritual union and then shares his insights, deserves the respect of society. Yeats's second theme is that the artist must himself respect the limitations of the human mind to encompass, and language or painting to express, the symbolic order of the unconscious. The totality of the vision cannot be shared because of the limits of the medium. The corollary to this second precept is that while the artist must pursue his private vision to arrive at artistic authenticity, he must not allow his vision to obscure ordinary reality; he must be true to his private vision while remaining in touch with the public world, achieving balance.

In examining a body of writing, one may gain insight through a new paradigm, because the new model enlarges or re-focuses what older approaches had left obscure or had taken for granted. By exploring Yeats's literary universe through his themes, I believe that I offer a more complete picture of his work than has emerged from previous analyses. Robin Skelton's metaphysical approach to the drama of Jack Yeats, Brian O'Doherty's mythic approach, and Marilyn Gaddis Rose's use of his writing as a way of understanding his painting all put Yeats's work in plausible contexts. The references to his written work in Hilary Pyle's biography and Martha Caldwell's dissertation on Yeats's painting supply useful background materials. James Mays's comments on Yeats's writing and John Pilling's explication of one fictional text, *The Charmed Life*, illuminate aspects of Yeats's writing, but they do not contribute to an understanding of his literary "universe" and of the extraordinary internal coherence of his work. John Purser's work, done after my own, was published too recently to be of use in my study. Although I have profited from earlier analyses, my pursuit of Yeats's themes causes me to argue for more complexity and subtlety in the form of his writing, and for more seriousness in his social criticism, than earlier critics have granted it.

I also argue that Yeats is a nationalist writer in many important ways. Previous critics have overlooked the relation of Yeats's writing to Irish events which had a strong influence on his work. Yeats was an Irish nationalist, at once a contributor to the Irish Rising and one of its victims. Both before the 1922 Treaty and after it, Irish nationalism affected Yeats's writings. Although he rarely wrote essays, journal articles, or tracts, he did try to express his nationalism by sharing his vision of Ireland, as he thought an artist should. Before the 1916 uprising, he edited and illustrated a ballad collection, *A Broadside* (1908–15), to contribute to the nationalist consciousness-raising. About the time of the Treaty he made a speech to the Irish Race Congress which shows the influence of his political ideals on his aesthetic ideals. After the Treaty and the Troubles put an end to the Republic of his hopes, Yeats wrote narratives and plays to express his vision of Ireland, commenting obliquely on the actual world through the portrayal of an ideal world, or gently satirizing the actual state for failing to live up to his visionary one.

Yeats was a social critic who maintained aesthetic distance from events in order to permit artistry in dealing with them. In the early chapters of this study, I examine distancing factors in his personal and cultural life, and look at Irish socialism and nationalism as they provided perspective for his attitudes. In later chapters I consider how the collapse of the Irish revolutionary nationalist ideal further distanced Yeats, forcing him to pursue the private vision more intently and to search for new methods of relating to his society and of expressing that relation. I show how motifs found in the *Broadside* ballads begin to structure the themes of his fiction and how these themes function in the drama, where Yeats's social criticism is most apparent.

In examining Yeats's literary universe, I find mysticism, romanticism, and a modernist sense of the discontinuity between experience and knowledge, thought and language, at the same time that I find a longing for integrity and universals, a hope that, in spite of his own fragmentary experience, somewhere absolutes do exist. Pursuing the themes in his literary work, I try to help the reader enter the universe of a gifted artist, Jack B. Yeats.

The Literary Universe of
Jack B. Yeats

1. The Spear Head

Jack B. Yeats wrote to his brother W. B. Yeats on 31 October 1925: "You say that my painting is now 'great'. Great is a word that may mean so many different things. But I know I am the first living painter in the world. And the second is so far away that I am only able to make him out faintly. I have no modesty. I have the immodesty of the spear head."[1] From among the controlling metaphors Jack Yeats provided for his life, the "spear head" most clearly indicates both the vision and the narcissism which characterize his literary universe. He forged ahead, in his writing and in his painting, testing the limits of form, always in search of a medium adequate to the expression of his private vision. From his earliest days, Yeats seemed convinced of the validity of his vision. He also seemed, even to his family, to be distant, like the "outsider" of his painting and writing. William Murphy, whose massive biography of Yeats's father—John Butler Yeats—furnishes information on Yeats's life, testifies to the impression of isolation and determination he made on his own family. Murphy himself describes Jack as "distant and private" and quotes his sister Lollie (Elizabeth Corbet Yeats) as writing to their father about Jack: "He goes his own way, and apparently sees his own road clear before him."[2]

In his epitaph, Yeats provided a similar metaphor, describing his life as travelling an outsider's path, one chosen for its distance from the middle-class norm: "I have travelled all my life without a ticket . . . . When we are asked about it all in the end, we who travel without tickets, we can say with that vanity which takes the place of

1

self-confidence: even though we went without tickets we never were commuters."[3] This metaphor of the traveller without a ticket is useful for understanding Yeats's work. The traveller motif was clearly important to him for both personal and nationalist reasons; the significance of being "without a ticket" is less clear. Judging from the spear head passage, written when he was in his fifties, Yeats saw himself as an artist who did not have the reinforcement of a community validation, as one who left the ordinary, communal way to pursue truth on his own. David Lynch, in his penetrating study of familial influences on the poetry of W. B. Yeats[4] (hereafter WB), gives a picture of the Yeats household as one that would encourage in its youngest member the feeling of being without a ticket. Other sources corroborate. The personalities and upbringing of Yeats's parents contributed to this family situation.

Yeats's father, John Butler Yeats (hereafter JBY), the eldest son of a Church of Ireland rector, was educated at Trinity College and intended for the church. Finding while he was at university that he had no religious belief, JBY abandoned theology and studied law. From his childhood, JBY seems to have perceived his father as his "friend and counsellor" and his mother as his "conscience"; she was, he recalls, "not very sympathetic toward my artistic strivings."[5] JBY's perception of this split in parental functions, and of his mother's attitude, was to have a profound influence on his own life and on Jack's life.

Susan Pollexfen Yeats, Jack's mother, was the eldest daughter of a prosperous ship owner and mill operator who was socially ambitious. Susan was so good looking that she was later described to her son WB as the most beautiful woman in Sligo. She was much sought after, and, apparently, petulant and spoiled. When the Yeatses were married, on 10 September 1863, Susan was twenty-two and JBY was twenty-four. They had spent very little time in each other's company. Murphy says of their wedding day: "The Pollexfens . . . must have watched with pride and satisfaction as their eldest daughter was married to an authentic Irish landlord, a descendant of the Ormonde Butlers, of respected Irish clergymen, and of men of power in the [Dublin] Castle, who was moreover a rising star in the King's Inns and well connected throughout Dublin. It was an auspicious marriage for a family on the rise, yet it was virtually the last time they would be pleased with John Butler Yeats."[6] However auspicious the marriage seemed in prospect, in actuality it left much to be desired by both parties. The "authentic Irish landlord" had too few lands to support his lifestyle. Three years after his marriage, JBY was admitted to the Bar, but became disillusioned with the triviality of law cases and the amount of time "wasted" on them. He was also depressed by the number of unemployed barristers he met, although, as a result of his brilliance, his own prospects were good. Helen Vendler characterizes JBY's reaction to this situation as that of an "exemplary passive-aggressive"; he entered the profession of the law in obedience to his father's wishes, but "simply refused to practice it."[7] He moved to London, giving up the status of Dublin barrister, and became an art student.

JBY suffered guilt at not being able to live up to his wife's expectations of their life together. Having regarded his mother, who was not very sympathetic to his artistic endeavors, as his conscience, he assumed Susan's disapproval of his art activity was correct. Again, he acted a passive-aggressive role. He did not argue with her; he went his own way, but with guilt and lack of self-confidence. In *Prodigal Father,* Murphy speaks of 1871, the year Yeats was born, as "the most dismal period" of the Yeats family's first residence in London.[8] If Murphy is correct, Yeats was not born into a welcoming environment. Soon after his birth, after eight years of a marriage which had produced five children, his parents separated, his mother refusing to return from Sligo to London. Lynch succinctly describes the situation between Susan and JBY: "The quiet and docile daughter made an austere, melancholy, and hypochondriacal wife; the charming law student and Butler heir was an unreliable and improvident husband. Either one would have been difficult for anyone to live with, and an open, if not openly acknowledged, breach soon formed between them. . . . They did not live together again for five years."[9]

The resulting, prolonged parental separation probably contributed to Yeats's feeling that he was a person without a ticket. Given the apparent condition of Susan Yeats at the time of his birth—alienated from her husband, disappointed in her life, chronically anxious about money and harassed by her five young children—it is hard to imagine that she gave what psychologists would consider the "proper" maternal response to her youngest son. JBY, in a widely quoted letter to John Quinn, wrote of Susan that she was not sympathetic. The feelings of people about her did not concern her, he said, since she was not aware of them, but was always in an island of her own. Their father worried principally about the emotional stability of Willie and Lily, but it is unlikely that Jack escaped the effects of maternal deprivation that Lollie so clearly and WB observably exhibited in later life. One of the speakers in a late narrative, *And To You Also,* a speaker who bears resemblances to Yeats himself, speaks of maternal love in a way that might be autobiographical: "I was never loved more than a little and never for very long" (177).

It is not surprising that Yeats's sense of reinforcing community was weak, as his use of the traveller metaphor indicates. In fact, granting this state of maternal deprivation, even narcissism would not be surprising. Psychologists might term his inability to perceive the second "living painter in the world," as indicated in the spear head passage, an extreme form of narcissism. Yeats's tendency to use orphans, wanderers, and travellers as central characters in his fiction and drama might be considered further evidence of his feelings of extreme isolation.

Since all of the elder Yeats children later recorded having been unhappy at their grandfather's house, Merville, where their mother stayed with them after Jack's birth, it cannot have been a very nurturing atmosphere for the young child. Their father worried about the effects on his children of the instability of the Pollexfen aunts and uncles, several of whom suffered from manic depression and had to be institutionalized. The prevailing gloom of Merville must have increased, and Jack must have been further isolated, at the deaths of his closest siblings, Bobbie and Jane Grace. Bobbie, one year older than Jack, died when Jack was two. Jane, born on Jack's fourth birthday, died less than ten months later. Most of those who record personal impressions of Yeats mention the deep reserve he projected, a reserve that might have resulted from such early isolation.

The Yeats children, particularly Jack, seem to have experienced not only maternal withdrawal, what psychologists term the "lost mother" syndrome, but also paternal separation, the "absent father" syndrome. Psychologists stress the importance for psychological health and maturation, particularly for forming a reasonable and realistic estimate of the importance and role of the self in society, of an early interaction with the father, termed the "Oedipal event." According to Freudian theory, if the proper relation of infant to mother and father has not been established, the individual may experience difficulty relating to the larger community as well as to the self. The absence of any true relation to the community for most of Yeats's protagonists, in drama and fiction, may reflect his own psychological situation and be a result of the second cause of narcisissism, the "absent father" syndrome.

Yeats's separation from his father was prolonged. Susan Yeats remained separated from her husband and kept her youngest son with her, for the most part in Sligo, from his birth until he was five. He was only occasionally visited by, or visited, his father. After the death of Jane Grace, Susan returned, with Jack, to London and her husband. But after three years, because of the decline of her psychic health, Jack was sent back to Sligo, at the age of eight, to live with his Pollexfen grandparents. He was isolated again, this time from father, mother, and surviving siblings. It seems very unlikely that a five-year-old would have had a chance to establish a good relation with his father in such a brief period, especially in three years so marked by his father's financial and marital problems. Later, when the sixteen-year-old boy was sent back to his father's house after the failure of his grandfather's business enterprises, JBY was remote and psychically "absent," feeling guilty over his wife's recent stroke, an affliction which removed her almost entirely from communication with her family. Vendler states that JBY became "ever less domestically attached, shifted the care of his wife onto his daughters and housekeeper, and lived a quasi-bachelor existence in his studio."[10]

Probably as a result of these family dislocations, Yeats exhibits some of the characteristics of a child psychologically stranded in the world by withdrawn or absent parents. He was essentially a private person, attentive to his own inner vision and singularly un-influenced by the community of artists, yet not unworldly. JBY's portrait of Jack as a boy shows what Hilary Pyle calls a "shy, fair-haired boy, his head bent at a typical angle; he is carried away in a dream on his own, and yet alert at the same time to what is going on before him, inquiring, without giving anything away."[11] As in the case of the characters he creates, Yeats's own inwardness and attention to the private world did not preclude an awareness of what was going on outside. He seems to have been aware that both worlds were important, and the necessity of the artist's keeping balance between the visionary and public worlds became one of his prevailing themes in fiction and drama. However, he was deeply reserved and not in the habit of speaking, or writing, directly about things that affected him. We, therefore, know very little from the usual sorts of records about his inner life. Before his death he destroyed all diaries and journals, leaving only his sketchbooks.

JBY, however, left many records, and in them we find the genesis of some social attitudes we see in his son's work. For example, JBY tried to convince his children of a connection between earning money and coarseness. JBY once wrote a semi-autobiographical narrative in which the hero described himself in the following terms:

I have been denied also the practical businesslike energy by which many men, inferior to me as I know and believe, have been enabled to procure for themselves a state of happiness and goodness. . . . It may be charged against me as a fault that I have not cultivated a habit of practical energy. . . . I want those coarse instincts which set the practical energies of other men in operation.[12]

In this description of his fictional surrogate we see elements of JBY's attitudes toward money and success which had considerable influence on his youngest son. In the internal debate reflected in *A Broadside*, Yeats's ballad collection, over the proper relation of the artist to the art-buying public, we find traces of JBY's values and ideas of propriety. JBY described an artist with whom he shared a studio, one who had become successful, as having abandoned serious painting "to spend his life selling water-color drawings, . . . a tradesman and not an artist."[13] Another of JBY's biographers, Douglas Archibald, asserts that JBY's neighbors in Bedford Park approximated a society of *poor* (emphasis in original) gentlemen, the kind of gentlemen JBY professed a preference for, saying they were more interested in life than in achievement. Archibald says that JBY's companions were "congenial and interesting near-failures,"[14] not the successful and famous figures of late Victorian London. Since JBY came to the attention of Browning and Rossetti and did not take up the opportunity to know them better, and since he scorned artists of his acquaintance who did achieve recognition, for being too devoted to "getting on," he seems to have been as little inclined to pursue success as to pursue money.

Yeats himself did have "practical businesslike energy," as his friend Synge testified, and as his shrewd marketing practices for his prodigious output of drawings, paintings, and writing show. Although Yeats did not pursue commercial success, attaining recognition as an artist only in the last decade of his long life, he procured for his wife and himself a limited amount of money, partially by using these energies. Yet he seems, as his use of the word "commuters" in his epitaph shows, to have retained some of JBY's feeling that practical energies were set in operation by "coarse" instincts. Through his own fiction, for example, Jack cautions against concentration on getting on. His fictional portraits of those who sacrifice their own "finer" instincts to achieve commercial success, as in *Sailing, Sailing Swiftly,* show them to be very limited people, while some of the more congenial characters who turn up in the fiction exhibit JBY's attitudes toward money and success. Bowsie of *The Charmed Life* and Oliver Gaw of *The Careless Flower*, particularly, show the best side of Bedford Park bohemians.

JBY frequently held forth to his sons on the "natural" way of life of their landed Yeats ancestors, expecting them to behave like his family rather than like their mother's trading family. Ambition was to be controlled. Their father contrasted for his children the two ancestral families, castigating the Pollexfens for their pursuit of money and success. Yeats ambivalently portrays characters like the ones his father valued, but keeps his comic distance from them, gently satirizing their pretensions while sympathetically portraying the best aspects of their "natural" way of life. James Gilfoyle of *The Amaranthers,* Ambrose Oldbury of *The Old Sea Road,* and the heirs of *Rattle,* for example, share JBY's wish to pursue the "natural" life while someone else, presumably someone with "coarse" instincts, supplies the money they depend on but are loath to pursue.

Aristocratic in his disdain for procuring the necessities of life, JBY considered himself an Irish landlord who was above worrying about money or earning it. He resisted all attempts of family and friends to help him to financial self-sufficiency. From his inherited lands—even after the subtraction of mortgages, his mother's join-ture, and estate expenses—JBY had, early in his marriage, an annual unearned income of £200. Since this was a large sum for the time, a man of ordinary financial prudence could have managed, but JBY was not such a man. Household expenses were modest, but JBY never kept accounts and may have frittered away much of his income.

Clearly JBY had the education and intelligence to manage his finances, but he scorned "getting on." To have managed his money efficiently would have been to place too high a value on it. Unable to earn much from his portraits, he lived on "loans," often disguised gifts, in a very hand-to-mouth fashion. He would have been hard pressed to support his children without the help of the Pollexfen in-laws he held up to scorn.

There are less ambivalent Pollexfen values in Jack's attitudes toward things other than money and success. He rejected his father's religious skepticism, for example, in favor of his mother's and grandmother's devout religion. Susan and JBY had quarreled often over church attendance and prayers of their children, but Jack attended church every Sunday. There were, apparently, no quarrels about it; Jack simply went his way and did not discuss his actions. Pyle says: "Jack kept his views to himself, mulled over them and reproduced definite and mildly quizzical statements which no one could parry. He saw ideas in their final stages, and not as matter for theoretical discussion."[15]

The adolescent Yeats exhibited the aloofness of the traveller. Although Pyle comments that he never seems to have had any difficulty settling down in London with his family, and asserts that "he was accepted: he had been ever present, only physically absent,"[16] she may overestimate the ease with which he settled down. He was in transit for several years, continuing to live a fragmented family life. He spent summers with his grandparents in Sligo, alternating between the Yeats and Pollexfen value systems. He was welcomed back to London, but he was, for Lollie at least, a distant figure; she refers to him in her diary for 1888 as a "comical boy" although she was not much older than he.

Jack was not close to WB either, although as the only boys they shared a room and did projects together, like painting a map on the ceiling of the study. Murphy attributes the distancing action to WB, saying:

With Jack, Willie was less than brotherly, regarding him as a perpetual youngster and seldom showing enthusiasm for his paintings, just as later he would look down on his writings. Yet there was apparently no specific origin for his behavior beyond his "lack of ordinary good nature". Papa liked to think there was affection between the brothers but was never quite sure.[17]

Murphy acknowledges, however, that Jack was distant to all, relating that JBY was never sure about Jack's affection for his father either, saying that Jack was polite, and that he had a gracious manner. Later correspondence reveals a distance between the adult Jack and JBY that his correspondence with his other children does not indicate: "JBY's letters to Jack from America reveal a cautious affection, a kind of toe in the water. Had Jack responded with enthusiasm he might have received as many letters as the other children. But he wrote seldom, though always politely and respectfully."[18]

Not having been as intimately involved with his older brother and sisters as they were with each other, either in childhood or in adolescence, Jack preserved his outsider status in the family all his life. He married young, unlike WB, who married late, and the girls, who did not marry at all. As a married man he became, Vendler asserts, "rather out of touch with the rest of the family."[19] In contrasting the relationship between JBY and Jack with that of the relations between JBY and the other children, Murphy says: "Papa told Lily he thought Jack possessed an impenetrable reserve that made him, though so outwardly friendly and amusing, virtually inaccessible. 'I sometimes think that while Jack is fond of his friends, he does not allow himself to be as fond of them as he would like *because he always thinks that they are not fond* of him'"(emphasis in original).[20]

A more accurate description of a narcissistic personality would be hard to frame. This defensive distance toward the "other" can be a result of early isolation. According to David Lynch's analysis, the victim of a narcissistic disorder feels himself "an outcast from the feast of life, emptier, lonelier, and more like 'nobody' than most."[21] It would be difficult to think one's friends were fond of one under such circumstances.

JBY was convinced that Jack's distance was defensive. In one of his frequent exhortations to WB to attempt to become closer to Jack, JBY created a third apt metaphor for Jack's life. Urging WB to visit Jack in Devon, hoping this visit would narrow the gap between them, JBY said: "In Jack is an *unsunned* well of affection. He won't let the light get down into it" (emphasis in original).[22] This unsunned well metaphor reflects an accurate observation on JBY's part. During the course of his life, Yeats seems to have been close to few people—his sister Lily, his wife Cottie, and four writers: John Masefield, John Millington Synge, Samuel Beckett, and Thomas MacGreevy. Though he had many friends, most describe him as reserved.

Jack exhibited a reserve more Pollexfen than Yeats. Although he was outwardly like the Yeats family—optimistic, charming, amusing, and friendly—yet Pyle attributes Pollexfen traits to him: "Many traits of the Pollexfens were in their grandson, the silence, the independence, the reserve, the calm elusiveness and puckish humour."[23] JBY believed that the crucial strain in Jack came from the Pollexfens.[24] When one considers JBY's statements about the Pollexfens (for example his remark about Susan's living in an island of her own or his observation that they "never uttered an opinion about anything"),[25] this is a strong statement about his youngest son's reserve. When he lectured WB on his fraternal responsibility to Jack, JBY never seemed to doubt WB's basic feelings. About Jack's fraternal affections Murphy records JBY's reservations: "I am perfectly certain Willie is very fond of Jack and I suppose Jack has an affection for Willie."[26] One is reminded of JBY's statement about his wife, that "her affection was a matter that one *inferred*. No one ever saw it or heard it speak"(emphasis in the original).[27]

Jack was reserved and did not record his deep feelings. After his mother's death he uncharacteristically ceased his work for six months. Whether abstaining from the artistic work his mother had not approved of in his father was a voluntary penance, or whether he was simply too grief stricken to paint, is not clear. Pyle finds the silence characteristic: "There is no comment from Jack Yeats anywhere, he was characteristically silent, but his sketchbooks cease for a while and do not commence again until the summer of 1900, and not in number until the year after that. He never made a direct comment on a matter about which he felt deeply."[28]

He was equally reticent about his relation to his wife, but JBY, at least, believed that Cottie, who was a few years older than Jack, was very loving, extending to him uncritical, undemanding love. Pyle records that JBY once attempted to persuade Jack to return to art school and improve his practice of drawing from life. (Yeats worked without models, apparently with more care for expressing his private vision than for reproducing outside reality.) JBY tried to enlist Cottie's aid, with little success: "I have taken Cottie aside and talked to her, but she always believes whatever Jack wishes her to believe."[29] She was quiet and shy, and to resist JBY's notable powers of persuasion Cottie must have had a strong belief that Jack was right.

Their marriage was by all accounts an exceedingly happy one. If JBY thought Cottie was too adoringly uncritical, he recognized that his son needed some human connection and that she represented it. In writing of Jack's "unsunned well" of affection he added: "I fancy Cottie knows all about it. There must be somebody to whom Jack unbosoms."[30] Pyle states that "their long devoted relationship . . . was a rewarding one."[31]

Some early family experiences, then, contributed to Yeats's sense of isolation: lack of loving maternal attention in his early childhood, the absence of his father for a large part of his infancy and childhood, isolation from his siblings by the early deaths of two of them and a long physical separation from the others. These factors made Yeats an essentially reserved person, a detached social critic, and a somewhat narcissistic artist. His painting is described by one of his admirers as having "a certain individualist detachment, as though seen by the eye of a spectator who is nearly, but not quite, at home."[32] The same might be said of his writing.

Later family experiences in his happy married life kept him from disabling narcissism through national and personal crises and protected him from that depressive collapse which affected his mother and haunted her family. Cottie's support and his own inner resilience and conviction gave him the basis he needed to nurture his imagination and to develop through solitary experiment the techniques for refining expression, both in fiction and drama, of his private and his social vision.

2. A Sense of Place and Past

Psychologists claim that a healthy identity is not simply a matter of the psyche in isolation or in the family. The connection one has with one's culture both encourages aspiration and provides means for effective action. Yeats's connection with his culture and his sense of wholeness both required the achievement of a sense of place and past. His sense of integrity of personality was, perhaps, incompletely developed because of the withdrawal of his mother and absence of his father at crucial points in his early life. His pursuit of artistic integrity and the formulation of his own aesthetic required a search for social integrity, for a sense not only of who he was but also of how he might overcome his isolation and fit into a community. To understand the aesthetic that shaped his literary work and the social attitudes expressed in it, we must examine both his own explication of his aesthetic and the elements in his national and cultural milieu which, by first including and then excluding him from community, shaped this aesthetic.

Because he wished to be an Irish artist, Yeats had to come to terms with his country's struggle for cultural identity—no mean feat during the first two decades of the twentieth century. Yeats's friends were also involved in this struggle. Samuel Beckett, one of Yeats's friends, is alleged to have told a story of representatives of various nations writing an essay on "The Camel." The Frenchman's essay was entitled "The Camel and Love," the German's "The Camel and Metaphysics," and the Irishman's "The Camel and the Fight for Irish Freedom."[1]

Other artists of the "celtic revival" shared Yeats's sense that not only past but place was important in art. Ann Saddlemyer has contrasted the celtic revival with other "folk spirit" movements of the late nineteenth century by its concern for place: "But the new element in the 'celtic revival' was a sense of *place* as opposed to a vague atmosphere" (emphasis in original).[2] John Millington Synge, also Yeats's friend, found connection with place and past an extremely important aesthetic criterion, stating that a sense of "a particular time and locality and the life that is in it" gives a work its artistic value.[3] So, for aesthetic as well as psychological reasons, Yeats sought to locate himself in his place and past.

Every Irish artist developing his aesthetic during the "Irish Renaissance" or "celtic revival" had individually to define what it meant to be an "Irish artist." Living in England from 1887 to 1910, but returning to Ireland every year, Yeats was inevitably caught up in a national identity crisis. As an Anglo-Irish writer, an outsider in both countries where he at times resided, he was in a very ambiguous situation. What was said of WB applies to Jack as well: "In London he was an Irishman among Englishmen, in Sligo a Protestant among Catholics, at Merville a Yeats among Pollexfens. . . . He was destined never to become a member of the majority no matter where he went."[4]

In order to appreciate the influence of this ambiguity and cultural minority status on Yeats's motifs and themes, particularly as they reinforced his sense of being a spear head, it is necessary to understand the identity crisis of nationalism itself over the nearly six decades (1890s to 1940s), during which he wrote. The early decades of this century saw the establishment of an Irish nationalist aesthetic, and during these years Yeats's values were in tune with those of the nationalist movement. He achieved a sense of place and past and, temporarily, a sense of community. The nationalist aesthetic changed after 1922, however, and the community excluded many Anglo-Irish artists. After a decade of silence, Yeats began in the 1930s to write major narratives showing full development of the themes implicit in his earlier work. The forms of his narratives developed in the direction of Modernism, reflecting his renewed sense of isolation from an increasingly conservative Irish society; his 1925 spear head self-identification indicates both his isolation and his sense that the community itself was fragmenting.

Richard Loftus provides a useful overview of the changing relation between nationalism and art in Ireland during the first half of this century. In his view, the years preceding the Easter Rising of 1916 saw political hysteria envelop the Irish cultural movement and make it difficult for an artist to maintain his integrity.[5] Yeats tried hard to avoid political hysteria; like his brother, he felt that his "mission in Ireland" was "to serve taste rather than any definite propaganda."[6] After the Civil War the nationalist movement changed, and many artists then found it difficult to reconcile their aesthetic beliefs with their allegiance to the movement, since nationalism soon became narrow and reflected the values of a middle-class society. Nationalists in the later 1920s and the 1930s demanded that the artist "respect the forms of conventional morality and taste" and "play the role of craftsman,"[7] reflecting the mores of the conservative Catholic majority in the new state. As early as the days of *The Nation,* in the mid-nineteenth century, nationalists had built up such an idealistic concept of Ireland that social criticism almost automatically implied a denial of nationalistic values. Irish artists of the 1930s and 1940s found it difficult to maintain integrity while writing about their national life without offending many of their countrymen.

Even as recently as 1989, some nationalists demanded politicization of all art. Those who form what David Krause has called "The De-Yeatsification Cabal" attacked WB, and by extension, contemporary writers who were not sufficiently political in their art. In his era's confrontation between "political hysteria and poetic gaiety," WB, according to Krause, avoided polemic by using allusive images and correspondences. Jack attempted to use the same sorts of images and correspondences, in painting and writing, also to avoid polemic. However, this mode does not serve the ends of some critics:

The recent anti-Yeatsians are a loosely organized cabal led primarily by a group of neo-nationalist critics who insist on judging not only Yeats but all Irish poets according to a political ideology: the poet's work must first of all be relevant to contemporary Irish problems and particularly the historical situation of political unrest. . . . A poet might be sympathetic toward the oppressed people . . ., but if his poems are not, even indirectly, related to that tragic grievance, they are suspect and irrelevant. . . . [These critics] want an unashamedly utilitarian literature, a poetry that serves the struggle.[8]

Jack Yeats's mode did not serve the struggle enough for some critics of his writing and painting; much of the later criticism of his work reflects the attitude described in this quotation. The general relation of his work to nationalism resembles that described in Loftus's overview.

Yeats had been concerned with raising patriotic consciousness, particularly in the 1908–15 *Broadside,* but later he became critical of the narrowness and complacency that patriotism had assumed in the 1930s and 1940s and concerned about their consequences for the artist. In *Sailing, Sailing Swiftly,* a fiction written in the early 1930s, Yeats shows the decline of an artist who allows himself to reflect social mores and become a "craftsman"; in a later play, *Apparitions,* he shows society's rejection of the artist who resists or exceeds societal expectations. Yeats's refusal to play the craftsman or propagandist led many who had praised his early art to reject both his later paintings and his writings. This rejection renewed his early sense of isolation and had significant effects on his narrative and dramatic forms.

Yeats's isolation in the 1930s was so deep that by 1945 Edward Sheehy, an art critic writing on the belated loan exhibition of Yeats's work, describes his distance from the nationalist community thus: "When politics ousted patriotism, collaboration ceased and the artist was thrust back into himself and his own past."[9] Feeling it necessary even to defend Yeats as a national painter, Sheehy goes on to say that though Yeats came from the Ascendancy, he was the most national of Irish painters.

To understand the significance of Sheehy's defense, one must be aware of the severity of the Irish literary "Ascendancy-phobia" of the late 1920s and the 1930s. Exclusivist attitudes had been growing since the turn of the century, and these attitudes focused on Modernism, a movement seen as Anglo-Irish. Roy Foster describes the conflict in these terms:

> But the symbolic confrontation between the modernists at the Abbey and the outraged "Irish Irelanders" has been seen as the drawing up of armies in a "battle of two civilizations," since the unacceptable views of Yeats [WB] and Synge were identified by their opponents as the result of their Anglo-Irish background. . . . Thus the emotions focussed by cultural revivalism around the turn of the century were fundamentally sectarian and even racialist. To a strong element within the Gaelic League, literature in English was Protestant as well as anti-national; patriotism was Gaelicist and spiritually Catholic. This enforced a complex censorship, ironically defined by G. B. Shaw: "To satirize the follies of humanity is to insult the Irish nation, because the Irish nation is, in fact, the human race, and has no follies and stands there pure and beautiful and saintly to be eternally oppressed and collected for by the Clan. [na Gael]"[10]

This sectarianism is reflected in Daniel Corkery's two books *The Hidden Ireland* and *Synge and Anglo-Irish Literature*. David Greene goes so far as to maintain that the Ascendancy writer became "a casual but inevitable victim of the new nationalism with which Ireland was aflame."[11] By the 1930s Jack Yeats's writing became unpopular in mainstream Ireland. Sean O'Faolain, in 1941, included Yeats's fiction in *The Bell*, a periodical Foster describes as "the record of an alternative culture."[12] Yeats had become a victim of the cultural nationalism he had helped to foster.

His relegation to "alternative" status was due not only to Yeats's Ascendancy origins and his political stance on the far left, but also to his experimental modernist approach to writing after 1922. During this year of crisis in Irish nationalism—the split between pro- and anti-treaty forces—Yeats began working in a new style. Ironically, his work was seen as too visionary by the conservative, philistine element which came to dominate the Republic founded by three poetic visionary martyrs—Pearse, MacDonagh, and Plunkett. Although the patriot O'Leary had protested in the 1890s against "the right of patriots to perpetrate bad verses," the wish of Yeats's generation of nationalists—to create a society of the intellect—had not motivated those who later took control of the movement.[13]

Writing in 1945, Ernie O'Malley, one of Yeats's anti-treaty friends, an IRA executive, and a guerilla war hero, spoke of Yeats's "philosophic isolation" in the new state and his "contemplative detachment," trying to express his artistic vision to a public which resented the new directions of his work. This Irish art world had become complacent, and did not wish to risk disturbance.[14] Even in the 1930s, Mairin Allen had noted the hostility to Yeats's experimental paintings: "The conservatives stop short in their wholehearted approval of what they have learned to call Mr. Yeats' 'middle period.' And their plea is that they no longer know what he is painting; they want pictures to be clear and intelligible. They will pay the piper, provided they are allowed to call the tune, a tune they can understand."[15]

In the 1940s Yeats created a character in "The Green Wave," the prologue to *In Sand,* who represents this wish for intelligible art and speaks in almost these words. The artist in the dialogue resists this call for easily understood art, as did Yeats himself. Because they could not understand the tune of his writings, however, many critics did not like the drama and fiction Yeats wrote in the 1930s and 1940s any better than they liked his painting.

Yeats, however, was an independent artist and had always marched to his own tune. Although he undoubtedly had played a significant role in the formulation of a nationalist aesthetic before 1922, and that aesthetic, in turn, had a significant effect on his literary universe and personal aesthetic, he was always his own man, a nationalist with a difference. Constantine Curran links Yeats's early work with that of nationalist writers like Douglas Hyde, Synge, and Padraic Colum, first calling Yeats "one more name in that sudden output of Irish genius" revealing that "there was beauty in the ordinary life of the Irish people," but then asserts Yeats's independence of nationalism.[16] A difference between him and lesser nationalist artists was that Yeats was truly a spear head. His work went beyond the movement.

After May of 1923, with the failure of the Republican cause in the Civil War, Yeats turned consciously from popular ideals of nationalism toward a private vision. The novelist Benedict Kiely said that the "terrible beauty" of a poets' rebellion had given birth to "a grocer's republic," and that the new Ireland, which had been described by visionaries in metaphors of "the dawn, the Spring, the rose tree blossoming, the young girl with the walk of a queen," turned out to be "severe, pious and frumpish."[17] In the 1930s, when the promise should have matured into achievement, the ideal began to disintegrate. According to Brian Inglis, the community of writers began to disintegrate with it; many "lapsed into alcoholic garrulity, or introverted resentment, or hack work. . . . The home market was so limited that Irish publishers would not venture on any but established authors" and, as a result, "hopes of further development of a distinctively Irish literature in English were dashed."[18] Finding themselves victims of the complex censorship ridiculed by Shaw, as well as that of the official Censorship Board, many Irish writers emigrated or began to write almost exclusively for the English or American market.

Yeats was sufficiently independent to persist in his experimental, often modernist writing. By turning inward, by seeking forms to express his vision, he transcended the despair that the revolution's failure to create a new Ireland might have induced. His primary theme became the need to transcend present reality, to accept change, chance, and randomness by uniting oneself to the spiritual forces of the universe, those larger than the individual. He was responding to a personal need as well as to a need of his society, a need to assert wholeness even in the presence of fragmentation, a fragmentation of which his friends among the Modernist Irish writers, like Beckett, were all too aware. Like them, he turned against conventional, realist narrative and drama and shaped his own forms.

It might be thought that Yeats turned from political commitment to aestheticism. Seamus Deane, for example, sees much of Irish literature veering between these two poles.[19] Yet Yeats's work, no matter how private and inward turning it seems at first reading, continues to have a political subtext. His literary universe is remarkably integral, and he used the distance his sense of isolation in the 1930s and 1940s induced to make himself a good social critic, one who could be of use to his nation even when nationalism, as Loftus and others point out, had ceased to be a powerful force for most Irish artists and writers.

Motifs which pervade Yeats's socially critical narratives and drama often appear in his earlier writing. Yeats's tendency to repeat motifs and themes in his graphic work has been recognized by Martha Caldwell: "The main constants in Yeats's art, however, have to do with themes and with the development of a thematic idea over a long period of time. . . . [Themes] tend to become broader in scope and richer in terms of association as his art develops."[20] AE (George Russell) noted the transformation of motifs in Yeats's painting of the early 1920s, the period just after the rupture over the treaty and subsequent Civil War: "All the creatures of his early work are here again, in some way transfigured and made more poetical and mysterious by that technique of broken color, which suggests that they do not exist by themselves, but are part of the procession of things in which sky, earth, men and animals are blended and have no true existence apart from each other."[21] Their "transfiguration" by broken color is the result of Yeats's search for what structuralists would call "the transcendental signifier." Turning inward, he developed his power of immersing himself in the spiritual forces of the universe and then expressing his universal vision. This growing power has become apparent in his "middle period" paintings.

Certain motifs used in his early writings, transformed in his major works by his powerful vision and his use of experimental forms, also reflect this growing power of a great artist to universalize his subjects, to see that disparate things do not "exist by themselves, but are part of the procession of things." Yeats's discovery of this universalizing power might never have occurred had not the rise of revolutionary nationalism, and then the failure of its Republican ideals, influenced his literary work. The effects of this transformation of motifs and creation of new forms are both positive and negative. The positive effects are seen in his fiction. Had his ideal of nationalism triumphed, had he not felt increasingly isolated, had he not turned inward to his memories and private mythology, he might never have developed the new forms and mature style that make his fiction powerful. The negative effects of isolation on his creation of literary form are more clearly seen in the drama. His loss of a sense of oneness with his community resulted, at times, in his creation of dramatic forms that do not take sufficiently into account the audience's difficulties in decoding. Perhaps the spear head in as ephemeral a form as a performance runs greater risks than a spear head in painting or fiction, where the viewer or reader has more time to absorb and puzzle out the new and unfamiliar.

The persistence of some motifs, from the drawings and poems of *A Broadside* through the drama and fiction written some thirty years later, shows both the continuity and the importance of Irish nationalism in Yeats's work. Through similarity of motifs, the political subtext of *A Broadside* is re-echoed in the political subtext of the drama, and, to a lesser extent, of the fiction. The few critics who have written about Yeats's fiction and drama have not perceived this subtext, and have not detected its unifying force, perhaps because they did not look at his early work carefully enough. The best way to understand the fiction and drama is to start with *A Broadside*, the collection of ballads published by the Yeats family's Cuala Press as a periodical from 1908–15, and then to look at Yeats's early aesthetic pronouncements. (The 1902–3 *Broadsheet* done with Pamela Colman Smith and the 1936–37 *Broadside* are less useful for gaining this understanding, because Yeats did not have artistic control of these publications; they cannot be said to reflect his vision.)

The 1908–15 ballad collection, of which he was editor, does reflect his emerging nationalist attitudes toward art, including attitudes toward language and race. One would not ordinarily expect nationalists to concern themselves very much with theories of art, since aesthetics and revolutionary politics make strange bedfellows. In Ireland at the turn of this century, however, because of events in the previous four centuries, the nationalist revival had a more cultural than political character. WB's nationalism, for example, has been seen as part of his much larger vision of art. As Douglas Hyde, Eoin MacNeill, and the others involved in the Gaelic League conceived it, nationalism meant a struggle for the cultural survival of a race, not merely for the political emergence of a nation. Utilizing what Foster calls "the rhetorical continuity of 'literary Fenianism' and the long tradition of Celtic antiquarianism," these two men founded, in 1893, a league "to revive the use of the Irish language, and to introduce it into the educational curriculum at all levels":

Hyde's famous lecture of November 1892, 'On the Necessity for De-Anglicizing the Irish People,' is inevitably and correctly seen as a vital statement; [sic] though he was preoccupied by an Anglo-Irish rather than a Gaelic idea of 'Irish' literary tradition and his 'de-Anglicization' meant, most coherently, anti-materialism. . . . An idealization of the lifestyle of the west became the theme of Gaelic League zealots: where Balfour's administrators saw an economic disaster area, the League saw the remnants of a Celtic 'civilization' that implied a spiritual empire far greater than England's tawdry industrialized hegemony. Psychologically, this may have been an important counter to generations of West Briton condescension.[22]

For the last four hundred years of their occupation of Ireland, the English had not only condescended, but had attempted to wipe out the native culture, using economic as well as military weapons, and the Irish had resisted. "Complete military subjugation of the country as a necessary precondition of its conversion to the reformed faith"[23] was a Tudor ideal. After the Reformation, the capacity of the Gaelic civilization to accommodate itself to invasion and disruption diminished. After the unsuccessful rebellions culminating in the Battle of Kinsale (1601), the flight of the earls (1607), principally O'Donnell and O'Neill, spelled the end of the authentic Gaelic civilization as a form of "high culture." Lughaidh O'Clerigh, O'Donnell's biographer, laments the loss thus:

There were lost there all who escaped of the noble freeborn sons of Mil, valiant, impetuous chiefs, lords of territories and tribes, chieftains of districts and cantreds; for it is full certain that there will never be in Erin at any time together people better or more famous than the nobles who were there, and who died afterwards in other countries one after another, after being robbed of their patrimony and of their noble land which they left to their enemies in that defeat. There were lost besides nobility and

honour, generosity and great deeds, hospitality and kindliness, courtesy
and noble birth, culture and activity, strength and courage, valour and
steadfastness, the authority and sovereignty of the Gaels of Ireland to the
end of time.[24]

The later punitive campaign of Cromwell, with its declared intent to drive the Gaelic Catholics "to Hell or Connaught," and the
penetration of the "New English" (who increased from less than 2
percent of the population in 1600 to 27 percent in 1700) dominated
the history of the seventeenth century, a century which ended with
the Williamite wars of the 1680s and the subsequent Penal Laws.
The struggle for cultural control—the attempt, for political ends,
to eradicate, or to prevent the eradication of, the indigenous culture—has been described by Marxist critics such as Terry Eagleton:
"Literature is an agent as well as an effect of such struggles, a crucial
mechanism by which the language and ideology of an imperialist
class establishes its hegemony or by which a subordinated state,
class, or religion preserves and perpetuates at the ideological level
an historical identity shattered or eroded at the political."[25]

The Irish of Gaelic stock, who were left without the leadership
of their native aristocracy and scholar class—and who were restricted by the Penal Laws in property owning, inheriting, bearing
arms, seeking education, and participating in professional and public life—became less able to perpetuate an identity at the political
level. Recognizing the power and material well-being of the New
English, or of the Anglo-Irish Ascendancy, many native Irishmen of
the eighteenth century sought to attain for themselves what was
clearly a better way of life by abandoning the "old ways": by flocking
to the cities, by imitating English manners and mannerisms, and by
adopting the English language. Remnants of the Gaelic civilization
survived beyond the eighteenth century largely in the oral tradition, in the underground poetic tradition, and in the minds of anti-
quarians.

In the nineteenth century, institutions such as the National
Schools encouraged the spread of the English language and culture
among the Gaelic-speaking people remaining in the country as
well as among the urban, more Anglicized Irish, continuing the

conquerors' attack on the native culture. Social mobility, economic prosperity, and even political reform depended on accepting English as a substitute for Gaelic culture, to the extent that the native Irish came to regard their own language and traditions as marks of social inferiority. Both Daniel O'Connell's political movement for Catholic Relief, which encouraged use of the English language, and the emigration of Gaelic speakers after the famine contributed to the linguistic and cultural demise of Irish Gaelic in the nineteenth century. Although O'Connell's own first language was Irish, he considered it a drawback in the modern world. At the end of the century, Douglas Hyde related a poignant story of conversing in Irish to a country girl on a railroad platform until her brother shamed her into turning the language of conversation to English. Hyde was convinced that the essential cultural foundation upon which any valid claim to independent nationality would have to stand had been so badly undermined that its restoration was the highest national priority.

Cultural nationalism, as Yeats came to understand it, meant not primarily the struggle of Irish politicians against English politicians, but the vital struggle of Irish against English culture, the struggle for de-Anglicizing Ireland. Gaelic Leaguers thought that "language revival would inevitably bring political autonomy, in itself 'an accidental and an external thing.'"[26] For them, Irish identity was closely tied to the Irish language. In 1896, the publication *United Ireland* began a regular column, "Irish Language Notes." The tone was set by a lead quotation from Tacitus: "The language of the conqueror in the mouths of the conquered is the language of slaves."[27]

The perpetuation of this kind of rhetoric evidently persuaded Yeats to learn Irish, though he was no scholar. Studying this difficult language represented a significant commitment for one whose secondary education consisted of a few terms of art school. He went to Kerry in 1913 to further his studies, and there he saw a slogan which he approved: "A country without a language is a country without a soul."[28]

Although socially ambitious eighteenth- and nineteenth-century

Irishmen had ignored the Irish language and the Celtic past, many twentieth-century Irishmen, Yeats among them, wished to restore their cultural distinctiveness and make Irish a meaningful element in their lives. The speaking of Irish acquired political implications. Sean O'Faolain equates the experience with speaking a "runic language," saying that the old language of Ireland became the symbol of a larger freedom. Maire MacEntee, a modern poet who writes in Irish, is more explicit: "For, no mistake about it, the culture to which Irish is a key is, in our time, a revolutionary culture. It is a culture of the oppressed, the almost legendary dispossessed. It is impossible to know it without being caught up in the great wave of historical indignation that informs the world-wide social revolution of today."[29]

Yeats was caught up in the social revolution to which Gaelic speaking provided a key. Many of the ballads selected for *A Broadside* reflect his social bias. Thomas Davis's attacks on the "philistine utilitarianism of English civilization and the contrasting spirituality of the Irish"[30] had influenced JBY and both his sons. For Yeats, cultural hegemony and nationalism in Ireland had become inextricably linked. The nationalists of Yeats's generation and persuasion felt that they had to raise consciousness of an Irish aesthetic. The political and economic conditions in the first decade of the twentieth century, when Yeats began producing *A Broadside*, were right for restoring the language and the cultural foundation for nationalism. Since the 1830s, a native Irish, urban middle class, capable of appreciating its heritage and acting to restore it, had been growing. Many Catholic Gaelic speakers, deprived of land, had moved from rural isolation into towns and cities, and by the twentieth century had created a respectable bourgeoisie, hitherto unknown. Peter Costello asserts: "Before the emergence of this new middle class, the literary and social revolution at the turn of the century would have been impossible. The modern prosperity of the country had brought about an increased literacy, and this increased the appetite not only for Irish literature, but also for self-government."[31]

Yeats, like other twentieth-century cultural nationalists, appealed to this new middle-class audience. The leaders of the movement wished to reestablish Irish cultural hegemony, to control not only what language would be spoken and written but also what subjects would be treated and in what forms this national literature would be cast. Even those who wrote in the English language consciously avoided "English" verse forms and "English" subject matter. Their aesthetic preferences had a profound impact on Yeats's writing of fiction and drama.

The nationalists exhibited a strong sense of difference from their conquerors, a difference both racial and linguistic; this sense of difference also influenced Yeats. Speaking on "The Necessity for De-Anglicizing the Irish People," Hyde told the National Literary Society in Dublin, in 1892, that sentiments of nationality involved "the half unconscious feeling that the race which at one time held possession of more than half Europe, which established itself in Greece and burned infant Rome, is now—almost extirpated and absorbed elsewhere—making its last stand for independence in this island of Ireland; and do what they may the race of today cannot wholly divest itself from the mantle of its own past."[32]

These cultural nationalists believed that the true spirit of this race survived in the countryside, particularly in the Gaelic West, and that the dark men of the Western Gaeltacht were the direct descendants of the aristocratic race of Mil. Loftus finds an almost Nietzschean nationalist concept of racial superiority and purity accepted in Ireland.[33] Yeats was sufficiently influenced by the racial aspect of the nationalist aesthetic to illustrate his *Broadside* with dark men of the West, proud and free. In his study of Irish literature of the 1890s, Wayne Hall lists characteristics ascribed by Stopford Brooke to the true Gael; these characteristics are reflected in Yeats's portrayal of the man of the West as "undaunted by defeat, tenacious and unchanging, fiercely individualistic, passionate, sensuous, yet always yearning for something immediately beyond the senses."[34]

All the Yeatses shared the belief that the Irish were a superior race. In his biography of JBY, Archibald cites a passage from the elder Yeats's *Early Memories*, claiming that JBY's family believed that "an Irishman, whether a Protestant or Catholic, was superior to every Englishman, that he was a better comrade and physically stronger and of greater courage." Archibald finds this a characteristic family attitude: "There are expressions of it in the Reverend Yeatses of Drumcliffe and Tullyish; it appears throughout [WB's] *Reveries over Childhood and Youth* and (in a different key) in Jack's *Sligo* and in the subject matter and feeling of many of his paintings."[35]

Yeats's graphic work of the period earlier than *A Broadside* supports the case for the ballad collection's political subtext, showing that Jack believed in the superiority of the Gael as he believed in the language movement. His illustrations of Irish textbooks such as Norma Borthwick's *Ceahta Beaga Gaelige* (Irish reading lessons) helped spread use of the language in those early years. He also supported AE's and WB's attempts to spread the knowledge of Gaelic literature by illustrating *Irish Fairy Tales* (1892) and *New Songs* (1904). Jack entered so fully into the movement to spread Gaelic culture that AE published an article about his work entitled "An Artist of Gaelic Ireland" and said that he saw in Yeats's painting "for the first time . . . something which could be called altogether Gaelic."[36]

Yeats's *A Broadside* was an appeal for consciousness of the Gaelic culture and race in all the Irish, an attempt to show the dignity of their heritage to the Anglo-Irish as well as to the native Irish. By presenting his view of Ireland to a largely unsympathetic or indifferent audience, Yeats hoped to convert it to a more appreciative attitude toward Gaelic culture. When it became clear that cultural nationalism could not, by itself, prevail (Hyde himself resigned from the Gaelic League in July 1915 because his movement had been taken over by political extremists of the Irish Republication Brotherhood), Yeats stopped publishing *A Broadside*.

The subtext of *A Broadside* was influenced by politically revolutionary ideas. Hilary Pyle points out the early effect on Yeats of the 1898 IRB-dominated celebration of the rising of a century earlier:

The 1898 celebrations made a profound impression on Jack Yeats as they did on many others. His romantic emotion and affection for Ireland had been an inspiration . . . but now the first stirrings of nationalism occurred within him. His brother was President of the English committee of the Wolfe Tone Memorial Association, and Jack B. must have heard much talk about Tone before the celebrations; but visually he had stumbled upon something new, and the excited uplifted crowd, and the colorful ceremony appear to have had a more immediate effect on him, and activated a bias which grew stronger and deeper with the years. Home Rule would never be enough for him.[37]

Yeat's sympathy with the revolutionary wing of the nationalists is most apparent in the *Broadside* ballads about, and drawings of, such revolutionary heroes as Napoleon, Tone, and Emmet. The Fenian John O'Leary, himself a revolutionary hero after his release from British prison, came often to the Yeats home while Jack was still living there. O'Leary's influence on WB was enormous, and it would be extraordinary if Jack escaped his charisma.

The shattering of the revolutionary ideal, and his own compassion, made Yeats depressed and emotionally ill when the 1916 Easter Rising failed. The signs that this crisis was developing are clear in the last few volumes of *A Broadside*. Jack did not want, as WB did, "a terrible beauty" out of which to create new art; he wanted a better life for real people in the real world. Hilary Pyle comments, "The insurrection was not a triumph for Jack Yeats as it was for his brother. For him [its failure] was the still-birth of all that was real." She goes on to describe his patriotism as "of a deeply emotional nature," and asserts that it "had nothing to do with war or the practicalities of the situation, but was rather a dedication to perfect life, without blemish, where no man was subject to another."[38]

If such a life was not literally possible in Ireland, then Yeats would create it in his art, a "perfect life" where there were no evictions and no political injustices. Seamus Deane notes in Irish literature a "consistent fascination with the discrepancy between the Irish world as imagined and the Irish world as it is. . . ."[39] Yeats's narratives and drama highlight the discrepancy between contemporary Irish society and the romantic revolutionary ideal. The raw materials out of which he built his private ideal can be found in his early work: the plays for the miniature stage, the children's books, the periodical fiction, but especially the ballads and drawings of *A Broadside.*

Yeats's use of the hero reflects the pervasive effect on his literary universe of his idealistic revolutionary nationalism. The heroes, mostly outsiders, portrayed in *A Broadside* and in the utopian universe he created in his later work tend to fall into several types associated both with the heroes of his personal life and with the culture heroes of the revolutionary nationalists.

His treatment of the pirate exemplifies the way a personally significant heroic figure reinforced by nationalist aesthetics can become a generalized heroic figure. At the personal level, the pirate can be linked to Yeats's maternal grandfather, William Pollexfen. Pyle speaks of Yeats's bond with his grandfather: "Local memory recalls the pony trap driving down the main street of Sligo with the young boy sitting upright on the seat beside the old man, wielding a dinner bell to clear the road before them; and the bond, never openly expressed, was, one suspects, always close. . . ."[40] WB said of his feelings for his grandfather and their use in his art, "I often wonder if the delight in passionate men in my plays and in my poetry is more than his memory."[41]

In an earlier era, "Grandpapa," a man of great physical strength and courage, might well have become a pirate. After running away to sea (he told WB he had gone to sea "through the hawse-hole"), Pollexfen had become a commercial success in Sligo. He inspired affection as well as admiration in his favorite grandson, but not, apparently, in many others. Although he was admired for his larger than life qualities, Pollexfen was not an accepted member of the Sligo community. WB tells us that he was solitary and silent, with few friends; that he disliked his neighbors; that he was fierce and had a violent temper. Apparently Grandpapa, who kept a hatchet by his bedside for dealing with burglars, provided Jack with an early model of violent and unconventional behavior, coupled with that gentleness and affection toward beloved children which even JBY, who rarely saw anything to admire in his in-laws, acknowledged. Both sets of qualities are present in Yeats's pirates. Memory of Grandpapa Pollexfen gave rise in his younger Yeats grandson's early work to a fascination with pirates, a breed of men who operated as violently and outside the law as did the revolutionary nationalists.

One of the early reviews of Yeats's plays, entitled "Captain Jack B. Yeats: A Pirate of the Old School," emphasizes the use of pirate material and Yeats's connection with the early pirate drama, saying that he was "destined to go down to posterity in Cassells' *New Biographical Dictionary* as the Last of the Pirates."[42] Continuing the pirate metaphor, the reviewer discusses Yeats's use of the work of his predecessors in toy theatres and his preoccupation with pirate subject matter in *James Flaunty or the Terror of the Western Seas*, *The Scourge of the Gulph*, *The Treasure of the Garden*, and an unpublished play, *James Dance, or The Fortunate Ship Boy*. It is hard to overestimate the importance in Yeats's literary universe of the pirate motif; he himself said of his early plays, "I like the piratical ones best."[43]

Literary friendship, as well as family role models, played a part in developing this motif. Just before he began the new *Broadside*, Yeats had been involved with John Masefield in some collaborative efforts. Masefield had done some ballads for the *Broadsheet*, an earlier Cuala Press ballad collection to which Yeats had contributed; Yeats had illustrated Masefield's *A Mainsail Haul*; and Masefield had dedicated ballads in *Salt-Water Ballads* (1903) and the book *On The Spanish Main* (1906) to Yeats.[44] Between them they created Theodore, a pirate named for an actual associate of Jean Lafitte, around whom they built up a myth; Theodore often appears in the drawings of the early *Broadside* issues.

Like pirates, nationalist heroes were often men of action and involuntary outsiders. Ernie O'Malley, who as an "Irreconcilable" might be expected to understand the status of outsider, speaks of the isolation of a small town such as Sligo when Yeats was growing up there and of the role of "outsiders" in such a culture. O'Malley relates outsider status to another figure who assumes heroic stature in Yeats's literary universe, the artist: "Here then in his native town he could see people who were not accepted in a conventional setting. They bore much the same relationship to the tightened

security of bourgeois respectability, ringed by experience which it
fears to enlarge, as the artist does to that life."⁴⁵

The second aspect of Yeats's monomyth was the artist/outsider
conflation. At the personal level, JBY inspired this hero. JBY's unconventional lifestyle and his unexpected comings and goings into
the more staid environment of Merville caused the Pollexfen aunts
and uncles to view their brother-in-law as a déclassé outsider. WB
recalled that an aunt said, when his father arrived in Sligo to take
him back to London: "You are going to London. Here you are somebody. There you will be nobody at all." WB reflected on this statement: "I knew at the time that these words were a blow at my father
and not at me, but it was some years before I knew her reason. She
thought so able a man as my father could have found some way of
painting more popular pictures if he had set his mind to it."⁴⁶

Jack's primary society, his mother's family, closed ranks against
his father, making him an outsider; they saw JBY as choosing bohe-
mia and failure. It must have been clear to so observant a child as
Jack that his father was an "outsider" precisely because he chose
to be an artist. Had he remained a barrister, the profession the
Pollexfens always attributed to him, JBY would have been accepted.
Born "inside" a class structure dominated by land owners, one that
did not permit entry to merchants and ship owners like the Pollexfens, this Irish landlord had thrown away not only his own class
standing but that of his wife and children. His father's rejection of
this Ascendancy heritage was to have profound implications, both
social and artistic, for Yeats.

Growing up "déclassé," Yeats embraced his "outsider" status,
and the outsider remained a prominent motif in his art, one used
in *A Broadside*. He adverts to his mental connection between artist
and outsider, to the artist's exclusion from the "tightened ring of
bourgeois respectability," when he says of his own life, in his epitaph, "we never were commuters." Becoming an artist meant, for
him, becoming an outsider from both Ascendancy standing and
middle class, suburban professionalism. Foster ascribes the adjec-
tive "déclassé" to all of the artists of the Abbey Theatre movement,

including WB and Synge, but stresses their position as permanent outsiders: "No matter how much they learnt, spoke and wrote Irish, or repudiated the ethos of their class and caste [they] would be considered fundamentally un-Irish. The nationalist opinions of the young Yeats [WB] did not count, when the 'un-Irish' pedigree of his suspect artistic productions was so evident."[47] Aligning himself with artists reinforced the personal isolation Yeats felt.

He felt psychologically an outsider, distanced even from his own family. He became socially an outsider by his choice of profession and, within the profession, by his refusal to paint portraits or be a social recorder of historical events. He became politically an outsider, not simply by his own choice of the extremist wing of nationalist politics, but by the newly dominant culture's increased rejection of the Anglo-Irish after the Troubles. He was culturally an outsider from the London-dominated establishment of literature and painting. A review of the first critical book on Yeats's work, Ernest Marriott's *Jack B. Yeats, His Pictorial and Dramatic Art*, states the point bluntly: "Mr. Marriott is not a Londoner. Manchester claims him. He is therefore one of those rare free men of England. If he lived in London he'd never dare write so serious or so enthusiastic a book on such an outsider as Jack B. Yeats."[48]

Yeats's fascination with the outsider motif is clear from his painting as well as from his writing. The art critic Edward Sheehy, writing on the retrospective "Loan Exhibition" of Yeats's paintings, says, "His favorite characters are those of no fixed abode, the jockeys, the tinkers, the sailors, the tawdry denizens of the travelling circus, the pie-sellers and three-card men of the race-course, the rovers and the ramblers of the countryside and the world."[49] This preference for outsiders as subjects is reflected in the fiction and drama whose protagonists are usually lone men, without family or community ties.

Political prisoners seemed to Yeats to be an especially fascinating kind of "outsider," and the political outsider constitutes the aspect of his hero monomyth most clearly reinforced by nationalist aesthetics. Yeats had always been interested in and sympathetic to those political outsiders of his childhood, the released political prisoners. Since he was born just after the '67 Fenian Rising activities, and lived in Sligo during the Land Wars, there were many of these prisoners to observe. Most of these Fenians and Land Leaguers had chosen to operate outside the law to achieve the social justice and political freedom denied them by the colonial system which labeled their activities "outrages." His friend Thomas Mac-Greevy, who asserts that Yeats had "grown up to the heroic approach," records that, as a boy, Yeats attended rallies to welcome political prisoners released from jail.[50] Men similar to those released, who had been arrested for "outrages" during the Land Wars, appear in *A Broadside*.

If one's heroic ideal accommodates violent action, if the pirate, the outsider, and the political prisoner are one's heroes, and if one desires social justice, one might very well endorse violent political action, outside the law where necessary. Yeats personally abhorred violence. When he asked Synge to contribute a ballad to *A Broadside* in 1908, he requested one not too "bloodish," admitting that he personally had a horror of terrible things. Yeats's compassion for the downtrodden may also help explain his acceptance of political violence in certain circumstances and his endorsement, ultimately, of the extremists among the nationalist forces. Long after their utterance, Yeats recalled the words of a local politician who told him, and Synge, how he became a nationalist after witnessing an eviction:

I was but a little child with my little book going to school, and by the house, then, I saw the agent. He took the unfortunate tenant and thrun him in the road, and I saw the man's wife come out crying and the agent's wife thrun her in the channel and when I saw that, though I was but a child, I swore I'd be a Nationalist. I swore by heaven, and I swore by hell and all the rivers that run through them.[51]

Allowing for a grain of political rhetoric, this recounted story describes an all too common event. It may also explain why two Anglo-Irish gentlemen, Yeats the nephew and Synge the brother of a land agent, abandoned their class ties and became both socialists and nationalists. Whatever the cause, Yeats apparently countenanced violence for certain political ends. Murphy, discussing nationalist feelings among the Yeats family, says: "Although the Yeatses were all to a certain extent fervid nationalists, all—except Jack—abhorred violence as a means to achieve independence."[52] Murphy also states that Jack in 1916 "was the most radical politically of the Yeatses. He had become a dedicated Irish nationalist, and since moving to Ireland six years earlier had attended Sinn Fein meetings regularly."[53]

Sinn Fein, whose name in Irish means "ourselves," or "our own things," was a party formed in 1905 from Arthur Griffith's Cumann na nGaedheal. The Cumann had been formed in opposition to the Boer War in October 1900 and it advocated political and economic self-reliance for Ireland by:

(1) cultivating a fraternal spirit among Irishmen; (2) diffusing knowledge of Ireland's resources and supporting Irish industries; (3) the study and teaching of Irish history, literature, language, music and art; (4) the assiduous cultivation and encouragement of Irish games, pastimes, and characteristics; (5) the discountenancing of anything tending toward the anglicization of Ireland; (6) the physical and intellectual training of the young; (7) the development of Irish foreign policy; (8) extending to each other friendly advice and aid, socially and politically; (9) the nationalization of public boards.[54]

Although this platform of 1900 does not sound violent, Griffiths's abstentionist tactics encouraged the violent separatists to join his movement and to gather strength there till 1916, when they surfaced in a much stronger position.

Yeats's six years of documented attendance at Sinn Fein meetings, 1910 to 1916, were roughly the period when he was working on *A Broadside* (1908–15). The cast of outsiders which appears in this work, and in Yeats's paintings from this period, splendidly documents his commitment to the Sinn Fein political and cultural ideology. Yeats hoped that these moving, idealized "characters" might raise the consciousness of the Anglo-Irish, who had for so long scorned or patronized the native Irish, encouraging them to cultivate Irish characteristics and discountenance the anglicization of Ireland. He also hoped his work would make British ballad collectors aware of a nobler Irishman than the "stage Irishmen" they had been presented with in the nineteenth century.

Regarded as an entity, this ballad collection has a political subtext as well as a personally significant text. Showing both familial and nationalist influences, it presents motifs found later in the fiction and drama—Yeats's own, private, interpretation of the revolutionary political ideal, expressed through psychogically resonant motifs. Its values are deeply personal and at the same time reflect the ideals of the Gaelic League, the Gaelic Athletic Association, and other "consciousness raising" organizations attempting to restore respect for the Gaelic heritage of modern Ireland. The authors whose attributed ballads appear in its pages were Yeats's friends or those with whom he shared Sinn Fein, or socialist, ideals. The anonymous verses he took from the public domain and those he wrote to suit the occasion are reflections of his own political and social preoccupations as well as examples of works consonant with the nationalist aesthetic. They may profitably be read to illuminate the later fiction, drama, and painting as evidence of the influence of nationalism and nationalist aesthetics on the themes that appear in the later work. Their "sub-rosa" message to the Anglo-Irish, for example, is echoed in the drama written for what he called the "larger theatre."

Of the collection's "cast of characters" Anne Yeats says, introducing a collection of drawings taken from *A Broadside*:

Jack B. Yeats loved characters, especially romantic characters, as can be seen from the pictures in this book. Characters from circus and fairground, race-course and music hall, from small towns and villages, from the bogs and the lonely country roads, ballad singers and boxers, jockeys, and pirates, travellers and trick o' the loop men, they all fascinated him, and he drew them constantly.

. . . [They were] well suited to his image of the men of the West of Ireland as untamed, fierce-eyed, independent and free. As a child in the seaport town of Sligo, he knew sailors from the foreign ships, and dreamed of far-off romantic places.

. . . But always wherever he lived he remained in love with Sligo, and retained his passionate excitement and childlike curiosity about those travelling people who came and went so freely but so seldom stayed, those people about whom you'd wonder "from whence have they come, and where will they go?"[55]

His niece's comment about the men of the West of Ireland could have been taken from a Sinn Fein description of the "last of the Celtic heroes," yet, as she has said, the fascination existed from Yeats's earliest years. The walkers of country roads and characters from country towns portrayed in *A Broadside*—the shopkeepers, sidecar-drivers, ballad singers, orators on platforms, sailors, maggie-men, and flaming tinkers—manage to give an impression of the wild and free life, the consummate attractiveness of the Gaelic peasants for the cultural nationalists.

Yeats's presentation of these characters in *A Broadside* fits clearly into the aims of his family and friends to present, through the Cuala Press, an idealized Ireland in the hope of raising the self-esteem of the Irish people. Lady Gregory had encouraged this idealized view of the past in *Ideals in Ireland* (1900). From her idealized view the literary movement could readily extract some clear conceptions about the nature of art: "Art should be heroic and passionate. . . . Art should rely on memory and *a sense of past and place*."[56] (emphasis mine).

Yet Jack retained his independence, even from the Cuala ideals. He, not his brother or sisters, all involved in the Press, determined the content of the *Broadside* issues published between 1908 and 1915; he did not control the 1902–3 or the 1936–37 issues. In 1908, his early need for control is made clear in a letter to John Quinn in which he says, "I don't like being responsible for anything that I have not got absolute control of."[57]

At this time there seems to have been little conflict within the Press, as the Yeats siblings were united in their aims. WB figured largely in the formulation of Cuala's ideals as did AE, Moore, Synge, and Horace Plunkett. Their literary manifesto contained a pastoral vision of Ireland, both past and future, slightly socialist in the Fabian vein, contrasting Ireland with a materialist, technological, industrialized England as William Morris and the Bedford Park bohemians had seen it and as Thomas Davis, among other Young Irelanders, had castigated it. In a 1904 speech WB voiced these ideals which Jack espoused:

And this Ireland too, as we think, will be a country where not only will the wealth be distributed but where there will be an imaginative culture and power to understand imaginative and spiritual things among the people. We wish to preserve an ancient ideal of life. Wherever its customs prevail, there you will find the folk song, the folk tale, the proverb and the charming manners that come from an ancient culture. . . . In Ireland alone among the nations that I know you will find, away on the western sea board, under broken roofs, a race of gentlemen keep alive the ideals of a great time when they sang the heroic life with drawn swords in their hands.[58]

Jack's drawing of an idealized Gaelic warrior, the illustration to Ernest Rhys's poem "The Swordsman to His Sword," in the third issue of *A Broadside* (August 1908), exemplifies WB's vision of this race of gentlemen. A heroic swordsman, holding his drawn sword, sits on a lonely beach, outlined against the western sea. The poem's speaker says to his sword: "For her [Ireland's] sake be a brand," "be a flash in my hand and a laugh on the lips of my fame." There are echoes in these words of the "Song of Amergin" and of Cuchulain, who died bound upright and who was spared by the fertility god in WB's play *The Green Helmet* because he laughed and set his life at no price. The same Cuchulain, when told by a Druid he would have a short life, is supposed to have said that he preferred a short life and fame to a long life without glory. These nationalist echoes—being a "brand" for Ireland and dying gladly for fame (as Pearse and MacDonagh later did to establish the revolution by martyrdom)—would have been correctly decoded by many of the subscribers to *A Broadside*.

Many other drawings and poems in *A Broadside* reinforce nationalist ideals. The ballads can be grouped according to classic aims of Irish nationalist poetry. "The Rhymes of the Gitanos," "Where Demons Grin," and "The Rag and Bone Man," for example, tell the complaint of the poor man; "The Lamentation of Hugh Reynolds," "The Ballad of Israel Hands," and "The Deserter's Meditation" tell the complaint of the prisoner condemned to hang; and

"The Gay Old Hag," "The Treason Song," and "Seamus a-Righ" keep alive the memory of old wrongs. Some important ballads like "The Ancient Mare" or "World" contain political allegories of the gathering strength of separatism that produced the 1916 Rising. Some, pseudonymously published over the name "Wolfe T. (or Tone) McGowan," glorify rebel heroes. Yeats identified Native Americans, for example, in their political intransigence against the colonizer, with the native Irish. These "Indians" appear in an untitled poem beginning "Bring wine, and oil, and barley cakes." Other Wolfe Tone McGowan poems present the plight of the exile, as in "Irlanda, Irlanda," or the determination and willingness to use violence of the rebels as in "Die We Must."

Ballads on still other politically important themes were written by contemporary nationalist sympathizers such as Ernest Rhys, James Stephens, and James Starkie (Seamus O'Sullivan) or reprinted from the works of earlier nationalists such as James Clarence Mangan and Thomas Davis.

Translations of the poems of Douglas Hyde reinforce other tenets of the nationalist dogma, such as the respect for bardic powers and the duties of patrons espoused by the earlier Gaelic civilization. Some present satires on unequal marriages, those whereby both young men and girls were sacrificed to their families' hunger for land, a land hunger which nationalists saw as a direct result of the Penal Laws, an old wrong to the Gaels.

As the dates of the issues grow closer to the 1916 Rising, complaints such as "The Boys of Mullabaun" directly protest practices like forbidding assembly and levying curfews. The collection ends with an impassioned promise to fight for and free the "little Rose," Ireland, a reflection of the strength the separatist wing of Sinn Fein had attained by this time.

The 1908–15 *Broadside* is rich as a revolutionary nationalist document and as a personal statement. Some poems and drawings in this collection have important personal echoes useful to isolate for later analysis of the fiction and drama. The drawing "A Youthful Pirate," for example, clearly echoes motifs of the pirate saga of *A Little Fleet* and the early drama, later represented in Yeats's outsider protagonists. In "Tramps" we see a pair of outsiders/travellers, the most permanent and resonant motif in Yeats's work. Often representing the two halves of the artist's personality, these pairs of travellers have great significance in the drawings and paintings and in such fictions as *The Charmed Life*, *Ah Well*, and *The Careless Flower*. As representatives of the nationalist heroes "on the move," the tramps also figure in the political subtext of dramas such as *The Old Sea Road* and *La La Noo*.

The poems selected, as well as the drawings illustrating them, exemplify important motifs. For example, an unsigned Yeats poem, "The Travelling Circus," in the first issue (June 1908) introduces three favorite motifs, the circus ring, the clown, and the female bareback rider, all later to be used metaphorically:

> Trumpets and fifes in the streets, the circus is come to town
> There's a fine blue peacock's plume in the tall white hat of the clown,
> And the piebald horse's feet go sounding
> Sounding sounding round and around the ring
> And the lady leaps the hoops like a swift white bird on the wing
> And the Bandsman's drums go pounding.

The ring stands as metaphor for the artistic life in later Yeats dramas such as *Apparitions*. (Yeats set that play in an arena to call attention to his ring metaphor.) The metaphoric use of the performance ring is central to some issues of *A Broadside*, especially to those in which Yeats is exemplifying his theories of the balance required for true art. The bareback rider, the lady who "leaps the hoops" and has both focus and balance, also assumes metaphoric importance in this context. The clown, like that of Rouault, is often the artist.

Other personal motifs that are to figure prominently in the later fiction and drama need to be looked at in some detail. Two such that can be isolated from *A Broadside* are the motif of the outsider and the related one of the traveller. Throughout Yeats's fiction and drama, the protagonists are single male travellers or pairs of males. Family situations are rarely shown, perhaps because Yeats had no sympathy for familial scenes or wish to portray them. The attempts of a benevolent outsider to apply the results of his acquired wisdom to benefit a community to which his travels take him form the pattern for such fictions as *Ah Well* and *The Careless Flower* and such plays as *Harlequin's Positions*. Sometimes the thematic emphasis of a text is on the experience of learning through travel, as in *The Amaranthers*. Often the learner is an artist, as in *Sailing, Sailing Swiftly*. There may be several discoverers, a pair of travellers, as in *The Charmed Life* or *The Old Sea Road*. The prototypes of these fictional and dramatic characters can be discerned by examining *A Broadside*.

James Guthrie's poem "Of One Journeying," found in an early issue, contains a significant traveller; the traveller's journey is through time, and he is depicted in youth as a Pan figure going the roads. The Pan or eternal youth figure is important in Yeats's creative universe and found in, for example, "the Good Boy" who appears in *And To You Also*, and is often depicted in paintings. Simultaneity and journeys through time dominate *Sligo* and the later tales and fabulations. In Yeats's work there is an emphasis on defeating the aging process similar to that in some of WB's poems.

Nostalgia for times past, a characteristic attitude in Jack Yeats's later work, appears particularly in Volume I of *A Broadside*. The great paintings of the 40s and 50s have a nostalgic quality, as do the writings of the 40s. The first few issues of *A Broadside* published after his return to live in Ireland (1911) feature the same kind of nostalgia that dominates *Sligo*. Two West of Ireland scenes of the kind Yeats loved looking back on, "A Small Fair" and a "Jolly Rake of All Trades," are found in one such issue.

Not all of the memories reflected in *A Broadside* are such pleasant ones. A less happy side of Yeats's early life is shown by a sketch of a little boy going, not too happily, to school. Yeats did not enjoy his school days. He wrote Lady Gregory in 1909 of the Misses Blythe's private school: "Whenever I pass the school, I wish I had the heart to do as a bookmaker's clerk I know of in London, who, whenever he passes his boyhood's 'College for the sons of gentlemen' stoops . . . and gathers up the mud of the street in his hands and spatters all the windows."[59] Yeats had, apparently, often dawdled his way to school, as the child is doing in the drawing. Always preoccupied with sketching, he often chalked pictures on the pavement. Once his uncle, taking him to task for being late to school because of the chalked pictures, was told: "Oh, I only did them as I was running past."[60]

Most drawings of this time, however, do exhibit happier earlier memories. "Hobby Horses" shows three people on roller skates, dressed as American Indians, riding hobby horses (wooden sticks with horse's heads), and going from the wings to the stage of a large hall. Dressed in this way, Yeats may have taken part in a Wild West show at the Olympia Theater in London when he was a teenager.[61]

The "Theodore" pirate material is a very prominent part of this nostalgia motif. A personally important drawing of this period will often feature Theodore. One such drawing illustrates characters from the Theodore saga. All the pirates are labeled: the chaplain, the cabin boy, the cook, and "The Music." The last-named pirate functionary fascinated Yeats, and in the essay "With Synge in Connemara" (which, at the time this drawing was issued, Cuala Press was preparing to publish in *Synge and the Ireland of His Time*) he likens Synge to "The Music": "If he had lived in the days of piracy he would have been the fiddler in a pirate-schooner, him they called 'the music'—The music' looked on at everything with dancing eyes but drew no sword, and when the schooner was taken and the pirates hung ... 'the music' was spared because he *was* 'the music' [emphasis in the original]."[62]

Perhaps this drawing is a tribute to Synge and a farewell to Masefield and their private pirate saga, sailing boats down the Gara. Yeats and Cottie sold their Devon house, Cashlauna Shelmiddy, and moved to the outskirts of Dublin at this time. He had told Synge in a letter of 1905: "I wish I could live in Ireland. Everyone who has any right there should be in it."[63] However, by the time Jack thought he could move back, Synge had died.

Poems written in this period exhibit nostalgia; his days in Devon must have seemed idyllic in retrospect, compared to pre-Rising conditions in Ireland. The last "Wolfe T. McGowan" poem in *A Broadside,* "The Gara River," expresses nostalgia for the days sailing paper boats on the Gara with Masefield:

Oh give me back my ships again
Lonesome Gara, babbling Gara,
My gilded galleons of Spain
Your blue waves sunk, oh bonny Gara.

Give me again the Monte bold
The beaks that dipped, the beams that rolled
The green hulled holy ships of old
That you have foundered, babbling Gara.

Give me my youth to have again
Lonesome Gara, hurried Gara,
Link upon link, a golden chain
That time has plundered, merry Gara.

The green, sweet combes, the setting sun,
The fires we lit, the yarns we spun,
The stately ships launched one by one
And one by one, lost, sunny Gara.

Masefield, for whom the poem was probably written, was regretting "the jolly times" in Devon, now that Yeats was living in Ireland. A poem Masefield contributed to the *Broadside* is equally nostalgic. The speaker, who in Yeats's accompanying drawing watches a toy ship called the "Theodore," says:

O Bill, O Bill, O cousin Jane,
Come out now, never mind the rain,
She's outward bound to Port of Spain.
O Maggie, Sarah,

She's off, upon the starboard tack.
Run up and dip the ensign, Jack.
O ain't it like the old times back
Upon the Gara?

The "Theodore" was the "fireship" of one of Yeats's books for children, *A Little Fleet*. This poem is probably a loving tribute to these times by Masefield, called both the "Fleet Poet" and "The Mate," who contributed short poems to the children's book. Letters in the collection of Anne Yeats (particularly one from 4 August 1911) indicate that Masefield wrote this ballad and gathered, wrote, or restructured many of the other *Broadside* ballads which deal with the sea. When Masefield was made Poet Laureate in 1930, Jack sent him a poem about Theodore, indicating that this private mythology was still important to them both, twenty years after Yeats left Devon.

"Treasure," an unsigned poem which also uses nostalgic Theodore material, is attributable to Yeats because of its similarity, both in rhyme pattern and in use of syllabic rather than accentual rhythm, to pseudonymous poems in the collection. Theodore finds a purse in an old pair of trousers and the poem ends with his cry, "And therefore let's be merry." Perhaps, after the move to Greystones, Yeats wished he could find such a purse and be merry, since the winter had been difficult for two reasons: personally, he had lost his beloved uncle, George Pollexfen, and, aesthetically, he was attempting to paint seriously, in oils, experiencing difficulty working in the new medium and its tradition. James White notes, as did AE, that Yeats's painting becomes more symbolic at this time: "When Yeats turned finally to oil painting around this period he relinquished his role as illustrator and began to experiment . . . now the subjects take on symbolic qualities. . . . Gradually we behold the full artist appearing in a brilliant series of works. . . ."[64]

Another nostalgic poem included in *A Broadside* at this time is connected to pirates other than Theodore: "The Adventurer's Oath from the Cardboard Drama of *Esmeralda Grande*." In the essay on his "Miniature Theatre," Yeats tells us of the importance to him of this oath from his first cardboard drama:

I write them all myself. So what shall I say of them, but that I admire them all but I like the piratical ones best —and always feel very proud of myself when reciting in two voices the Adventurer's Oath in *Esmeralda Grande*; it requires two voices, a deep roar for the captain and a fearstruck wail for the crew which gradually grows feebler as the thing goes on. And now, looking back, I think my audiences liked the oath best of all.[65]

The oath itself is full of Gaelic place names and nostalgic references from his Sligo childhood, written in rhythmically incantatory lines illustrated by these lines of the captain, which are repeated by the crew:

By the wind from Carrick-na-Gat
By the light on the Blennick
By Schule-na-meala,
By Pooldthoya,
By Benbulben and Knock-na-rea,
By the Spanish Main,
By the Old Trade and the merchants of the Old Trade,
We swear to stand by Captain Blackbeard the Second.

In fair or in foul,
In smooth or in breakers,
Until our bones are white
Until our bones are white. Oh-h-h-h-h (shudderingly)

The drawing for this poem is a reworking of the original sketch (done in 1900 when the play was published) with the captain reading the oath to the five pirates on stage.

The drawing that follows this dramatic excerpt, *Romantic Shades,* is a fittingly nostalgic conclusion to the first boxed set of *A Broadside* and prefigures the second set. In it a fantastic collection of characters from Yeats's own plays and drawings—Theodore, Napoleon, Indians, hunters, little boys, jockeys, pirates, patriots, and rogues—watch while an Oriental magician pulls roses out of a hat and drops them in a circle. The magician's acts represent those of the artist and Yeats's reflections on the role of the artist begin to pervade *A Broadside*; they are pursued in the fiction and drama. This year had been a period of intense self-examination, its nostalgia caused by several factors: (1) his return with his English wife to an Ireland that was growing more separatist (2) his uprooting from Devon and (3) the death of his Uncle George which he felt would change the pace and atmosphere of the family firm[66] that had represented security in his childhood. (In the play *Rattle*, heirs are faced with a decision about a similar family firm, and an enigmatic figure drops roses in a mystical circle.)

Yeats shows us in this very significant drawing both the transcending of nostalgia and the results of his reflection on the role of the artist, in a fashion analogous to WB's "Circus Animals' Desertion." The artist-magician pulls his creations out of the hat while the onlookers marvel. Yeats had been impressed at his uncle's funeral by the white and red roses the "Priori Masons" threw into the grave. By the 1920s the rose had become an important symbol in his work, related in his imagination both to artistic inspiration and inability to communicate the entirety of the vision. White, in his introduction to the centenary exhibit catalogue of Yeats's paintings, tells us of the importance of the "sub rosa" delight Yeats took in the practice of his art; he got more delight in this practice than in the communication of emotion that resulted from the finished work. Yeats showed White the pink rose tied to his easel and said that he had placed it there to remind himself of his vow that all his work would be "sub rosa; I would never again discuss the meaning of my pictures."[67]

This summary drawing is Yeats's first published use of the rose symbol, a decade earlier than its acknowledgment, in the context of the artist's relation to his creations. (In the *Broadside* drawing, Yeats's creations watch the artist at his rose strewing somewhat as the creations of Flann O'Brien watch the novelist in *At Swim Two Birds*.) A *Broadside* is the first expression of Yeats's groping toward the meaning of being an artist. He looks at the creatures of his own writings as well as those of his drawings; the two are inextricably related in his own mind and express the one vision. Having begun this set of *A Broadside* with one of his own poems, "The Travelling Circus," Yeats ends it with his very different poem, "The Adventurer's Oath," and closes off the set and the volume graphically, by showing the artist in that mystic circle, the circus ring. The sense of fitting closure that marks the fiction is shown in Yeats's use of this device.

Reflections on the artist's relation to the muse form as important a personal motif in the second *Broadside* volume, as nostalgia had in the first. During the period in which he was composing *A Broadside*, Yeats was moving into what most art critics consider his middle period, a period characterized by a radical change from his early style. His struggles with aesthetic issues are reflected in the *Broadside* drawings. Often an important series of drawings explores a single motif. One of Yeats's favorite metaphors for expressing the artist's relations to the muse was the circus performance. In a drawing called "Circus People" he shows a clown menacing an acrobat while a female bareback rider hovers in the distance. White says that in a later Yeats painting the rider holding a rose symbolized the muse, and the clown represented the artist.[68] In "Circus People," the clown seems to represent the artist struggling for his right to have a relation with the muse.

Yeats was struggling at this time to justify a new relation to his muse: committing himself to being a "serious" artist by switching his medium from watercolor to oil. Given JBY's criteria for serious artistry, and his comment about the friend who "wasted his time" on watercolours which sold, Yeats's decision to stop illustrating and painting watercolors and declare himself as a serious painter must have been a difficult one. Even though he was less dominated by JBY than his brother WB, Jack, late in life, told an interviewer that he became a painter because he was the son of a painter. There was some vestige of the dominating male parent to cope with in declaring his choice of vocation. JBY himself was now far off in New York, where he was to remain until his death in 1922. JBY's removing himself from the Irish scene seems to have liberated both of his sons artistically.

The theme of the proper role of the artist, balanced between his muse and his public, also increasingly preoccupies Yeats. He had been able to support himself and his wife as a "commercial" artist working in England. Did he have the right to commit himself to serious art, eventually working "sub rosa" and ignoring the public, when the results of JBY's similar commitment had been so deleterious to family welfare? Did he have the right, in his pursuit of the muse, to remove his wife from her country? This removal most probably concerned a man whose own mother had resisted so strongly his father's attempts to move her from Ireland, the land of her birth. Moreover, did he have the right to declare himself an Irish artist and pursue his muse in Ireland? Markets for artists were in London; by deciding to leave England, he was abandoning the "practical energies" which had served him so well.

Another drawing using the circus motif, "Tumblers at the Circus," exemplifies Yeats's insight about the artist's role. Here two clowns (artists) perform, one bouncing on a seesaw while the other, rolled up in the air, prepares to come down on a horse's back. Personally, artists must maintain a balance between the two roles and the dual halves of the personality. In *The Charmed Life*, particularly, Yeats explores the artist's need to maintain balance between private vision and relation to external reality. Perhaps the drawing also represents the awareness of those polarities within the self later to be explored in the more visionary paintings such as "That We May Never Meet Again" (1954) or "Glory" (1952), and through the fictive device of Bowsie and Mr. No Matter of *The Charmed Life*, or Jack and the Old Brown Man of *Ah Well*.

This drawing may also make a transference from literature to the graphic arts of the Antaeus myth which preoccupied the nationalists—the idea that "literature needed contact with the soil to maintain its strength, 'Antaeus-like,' and its appropriate relationship to past and place."[69] The clown in contact with the soil sustains his other half, off in the air in a visionary tryst with the muse. These reflections may all be emerging in this end-of-the-year summation to a period of intense self-scrutiny and a choice of new directions.

"The Haute Ecole Act" (January 1913) continues to use the circus motif to explore the proper relation between the artist/muse/public. The same subject was treated in an important painting of 1925, of which Hilary Pyle says: "The subject seems to have remained in his mind because he sketched the painting in a letter . . . about its possible sale in 1938, and later developed the theme in 1943 in "This Grand Conversation was under the Rose."[70] White speaks of the bareback rider in this painting who now seems to represent the performer, not the muse, and who has attracted Yeats by her attention to her performance in the ring and her lack of attention to the effect she was having on the audience. White's observation is apposite to the Haute Ecole drawing as well. Ultimately Yeats became a painter who painted primarily because he was delighted by the practice of painting, secondarily because he wished to communicate his vision. By 1921, he said in a speech to the first Congress of the Fine Gaedhael: "The true artist has painted the picture because he wishes to hold again for his own pleasure—and for always—a moment, and because he is impelled—perhaps unconsciously, but nevertheless impelled—by his human affection to pass on the moment to his fellows, and to those who come after him."[71] The muse calls; the artist shares his "moment" of vision, but must always focus on his experience of the moment, his own pleasure in it, not on those who watch him or will admire or buy the painting. Later, when the majority of his countrymen rejected his vision of Ireland, the Grand Conversation with the muse had to become sub rosa, but in 1913 Jack was still hoping to share the vision with his audience.

His struggles to master the new medium of oils for expressing his vision for his people and country affect Yeats's choice of motifs in this volume. In the 1920s he reflected on this struggle: "The manual skill and the knowledge of his materials are most necessary to the artist, and he cannot be too skillful in the handling of his brushes or know too much about his paints. But these are not the end, they are only the means, and are only of interest to the artist himself."[72] In his struggles to increase his skill in brushwork and to know his paints, Yeats must have been restrained by the memory of his father—who alienated his wife and her family and neglected to provide for his children in his obsession to master technique. Perhaps that is why Yeats used two clowns; the one in the air, visionary and self-absorbed, needs the other, Antaeus-like on the other end of the seesaw, holding on to reality.

An independent artist but not a primitive one, Yeats studied the writings of his contemporaries as well as their paintings. JBY was still thundering advice, now from New York where he had gone in 1908, the year Yeats began A Broadside. He recommended that his son read some theory of painting, for example, Clausen's Six Lectures on Painting.[73] In London, Yeats had learned from the English painters in the Allied Artists Association, like Walter Sickert and William Nicholson, and would probably also have known the work of John Singer Sargent and Augustus John. A nationalist artist but not a fanatic one, he did not reject what he had learned from the English art school or English painters in his efforts to establish an Irish aesthetic; however, he recognized the limits of trying to paint or write by received standards and felt the need for artistic authenticity.

Although Yeats rarely expressed aesthetic opinions (JBY said that the Pollexfens among whom Jack grew up "never" uttered an opinion about anything),[74] he occasionally wrote, in letters to his friends, statements useful in formulating an idea of his working principles. He wrote a letter to Thomas Bodkin in 1921 describing what an artist must do to strike a balance between representation and presentation, and between working for an audience and working only for oneself. Those who tried "to paint only what was: not what they saw" (representation) or who followed "Fancy" (presentation) were equally wrong, he thought. The eternal seesaw must be kept in balance. The worst were those who made "pictures," who kept their eyes on the audience rather than concentrating on their own experience of the moment: "These were the most wretched and very few followed truth. Which is a difficult road for any man, but especially for the painter. As it is necessary for him then to approach that ideal state of a man knowing himself. The painters of the material thing that was, the painters of 'Fancy,' and the 'picture' makers, are often curious and interesting but nothing more."[75]

Yeats extended these aesthetic principles to his writing. He never wrote only of "the material thing that was" even in his early journalistic work, always of "what he saw." His later fiction and drama represent serious attempts to render "what he saw" in the medium of the word. As what he saw became more visionary, he had to find new forms to express it; he tended to mystify his readers in the way he mystified viewers with his metaphoric paintings. In both media, he remained true to his vision, however, to what he termed "clairvoyance." In a 1906 letter to John Quinn, Yeats was discussing the work of "fine painters," saying "men may paint better than they know, I think these things are done by a sort of clairvoyance (for want of a better word)."[76] His struggle to preserve his clairvoyance, to work from what he called "half-memory"—part memory, part subconscious—must have involved him in struggles like those portrayed with the two clowns on the seesaw. Perhaps the one clown on the ground portrays the material thing that was, while the other portrays what he saw. The *Broadside* drawings of these years, particularly those not illustrating ballads, exhibit in the graphic mode aspects of this profound struggle. *Sligo* shows a similar struggle in literature, some twenty years later.

Yeats also published some remarks on aesthetics which help us to understand his attitudes. His first ironic "pronouncement" on aesthetics, an untitled, unpublished booklet in the possession of Anne Yeats, is known informally as *Jack on Jack*. This stenciled, hand-illustrated, octavo volume is hand printed. The cover carries a whimsical self-portrait, in profile, showing the cigar-smoking artist in a broad-brimmed hat. Beneath this drawing are Yeats's monogram and a logo—a drawing of a snail with a tower where his spiral shell should be—of Snail's Castle, Jack and Cottie's home in Devon. On the inside front cover is inscribed "A LIMITED EDITION OF SIX WERE PUBLISHED OF THIS APPRECIATION." Below this inscription, in a different hand, is inscribed "This is No. 6." and below that line his signature and the date, 1902, appear.

The cover and inscription establish the tone for what is to follow and reveal the kind of gentle humor which is to be found in the fiction and drama. *Jack on Jack* opens with a drawing of a figure facing a child's version of a tree captioned "Thinking About a Grandmother." The text begins:

Jack, as his friends call him, for he is the soul of good fellowship, and has a host of friends to each of whom he manages admirably to give a few moments of his very full life–For Jack B. is one of the busiest homme in our great Empire.

In the picture which heads this article, by the way we hope it is his own and not anyone else's Grandmother of whom the figure is thinking—Notice the cleverness with which the darkness under the leaves, which are as the quintessence of Valambrosiusness, is shown with pure ink. And also note the marvelous reticence with which but four lines are used to give the shadow of the hauntingly interesting figure of the man, or is it a woman, on the right of the design.

This sendup of art criticism continues with observations on the sketch "Daniel in the Lion's Den": "Observe how nobly the different ages of the family of lions are shown, and by what brilliant means, i.e. by making them different sizes. . . ." The remarks on this sketch end with a comic deflation of art criticism's pomposity: "We are often asked 'What is Art?' This is Art."

In *Hail and Farewell* George Moore mentions Yeats's boredom in the National Gallery.[77] The next paragraph of *Jack on Jack* travesties the dullness of academy painting and the pedantry of art criticism:

> And now turn to the Portrait of the Dook or as Mr. Yeats catalogued it
> Portrait of A Dook
> as the Masters used to ticket some of their finest pieces:
> Portrait of a Man, or Portrait of a Party.

Yeats goes on to exhibit his love of puns while caricaturing the snobbery and pseudo-lyricism of some art criticism:

> Ah what a marvelous piece of work is this portrait of
> the Dook of all the Dookeries in hunting costume,
> remark how cleverly the artist has hid the Dooks of the Dook.

[The Dook's left hand is inside his coat in the Napoleonic pose, while his right is concealed by his three-quarter frontal stance.]

After a few more travesties of criticism (for example, "with what heaven born intelligence the hunting stick and hat, made apparently of some black material, are painted"), Yeats turns the humor on himself:

Mr. Jack B. Yeats is a great and living Artist. We have known this for some time, and the thousands of orders for portraits and fancy pictures which he is refusing every post is a surety of the fact. . .
What is Art?
Yeats is Art.

An artist who can laugh at himself and his profession this way will probably not be guilty of pomposity and will not be inclined to write much dull theorizing. He once told Thomas MacGreevy: "There's too much old chat about the Beautiful."[78]

It is a tribute to Yeats's seriousness about the nationalist aesthetic that he consented to go to Paris in January 1921 to speak on painting to the Irish Race Congress of the Fine Gaedheal party and then to allow publication of the talk. This lecture was printed in *New Ireland* on 18 and 25 February 1922 and, rewritten slightly, was published as number 8 in a series by "Cumann Leigheacht an Phobail" of the Dail Eireann as *Modern Aspects of Irish Art*. Its publisher, Dail Eireann, was the controversial Irish Parliament. The Sinn Fein Party members, after winning seventy-three seats in the parliamentary general election, had met; refused, as part of their traditional abstentionist tactics, to go to Westminster; held the first session of the Assembly of Ireland, or Dail Eireann, on 21 January 1919; ratified the establishment, in 1916, of the Republic of Ireland; and appealed to the "Free Nations of the world" to support Irish sovereignty. At its second meeting, in April, the Assembly constituted itself to provide "an alternative government in Ireland to which, rather than to the regime centered in Dublin Castle [the British Lord-Lieutenant for Ireland and his staff], Irishmen would naturally and instinctively turn."[79] Dominating many local government bodies and local arbitration courts, the Dail on one hand and the IRA on the other had some claim to being the legitimate government of Ireland; the Sinn Fein party captured roughly 500 of 800 seats outside of Ulster in the election of January 1920.

For two years before publication of Yeats's speech, this government, unproscribed for eight months and then "on the run," had been working underground while carrying on guerilla warfare against the British government in Ireland. "The Dail set up 'ministeries' paralleling those of the official government; it specialized in public declarations and manifestos aimed at the international constituency sympathetic to 'small nations,' and sent unsuccessful delegates to Versailles; it also declared a sweeping and wooly commitment to social and economic progressivism that was by no means approved by all the delegates."[80]

The worst phase of the guerilla war, which had commenced on the same day the Dail declared itself the legitmate government, had occupied the first six months of 1921. At the time his lecture was given, then, the "Anglo-Irish War" (often called simply "the Troubles") was in full rage. About 40,000 troops—7,000 demoralized Royal Irish Constabulary, their ranks swelled by the recruitment of the infamous Black and Tans (British ex-servicemen who continued to wear their khaki uniforms with black police caps and belts) and Auxiliaries, and the rest soldiers—were fighting 3,000 "working" members of the Irish Republican Army (IRA).[81] Skirmishes, reprisals, intimidation, hunger strikes, boycotts, fundraising in America by de Valera, and very good propaganda by intellectuals like Erskine Childers were features of this "war."

The Dail which published Yeats's speech was technically the second Dail, and was operating under the conditions of a truce declared in July 1921. The representatives of this Dail, not including de Valera, had signed the treaty that was "to split Ireland from top to bottom" in December of 1921. Under this treaty the "Irish Free State" was to become a "self-governing dominion of the British Commonwealth," not a "Republic." It was ratified in the Dail by a majority of seven votes, again not including that of de Valera, who declared against it early on. "Pragmatists lined up against irreconcilables and visionaries. . . . O'Higgins roughly defined the opposition to the new government as 20 per cent idealism, 20 per cent crime and 60 per cent 'sheer futility.' The nature of formal opposition, those soon to be called the 'Irregulars,' owed much to local conditions."[82]

The inside front cover of *Modern Aspects of Irish Art,* as the government monograph was called, has a message from de Valera as president of the Dail, in Gaelic with English translation. By giving this talk, and later allowing his talk to be published, Yeats allied himself publicly with the Republican forces. In March 1922, soon after Yeats's article was published, de Valera resigned as president and left the treaty-making Dail, forming his new party—"Cumann na Poblachta" (League of the Republic)—from among anti-Treaty delegates. In June, when the Republican anti-Treaty forces gathered in the Four Courts were attacked by the provisional government, who had just won a pro-treaty majority in the general election, the Civil War escalated. In

October, de Valera and the "Irregulars" from the IRA set up their own government.

It is against this background of war and ideological differences that *Modern Aspects of Irish Art* must be considered. By allowing publication of the pamphlet by this radical group, Jack Yeats took a different side than his brother, who became a senator in the Irish Free State created by the disputed treaty. By May 1923 the Irregulars had surrendered, and the formal Civil War was over, but the bitterness lingered on all over Ireland. The two brothers rarely saw each other after this time.

The official government version of Yeats's speech was published sometime before November of the turbulent year 1922. Erskine Childers, who probably convinced Yeats to give the talk, is listed as vice-president of this Cumann in Yeats's monograph; he was dead by November of that year, shot by the Free State which had jailed him for unauthorized possession of arms. Hilary Pyle records Yeats's reaction to Childers's death and the subsequent actions of Childers's family: "When he visited Mrs. Erskine Childers to commiserate with her about the death of her husband, and young Erskine Childers announced "The Republic goes on,'" Yeats was shocked at the child's use of the slogan at such a time, betraying in the family an unnatural obsession with political abstractions."[83]

Although Yeats did not like abstraction, political or aesthetic (Moore said of him that he took no interest in "anything except life" and his "deduction from life"),[84] he did form some theories. The social principles of the Republicans influenced Yeats's theories on art. The series of booklets in which *Modern Aspects of Irish Art* appeared was intended, de Valera said in his presidential recommendation of the series, "to expose current first principles and to bring exact knowledge . . . into every home in Ireland. A carefully thought out scheme of study is proposed."[85] The self-education of workingmen, such as the young Sean O'Casey, was part of the Republican scheme.

Yeats's first concern in the pamphlet is to de-mystify painting. He deplores the attitude that a painting is "a trick of juggling" and decries the separation of the artist from society. The true artist, he claims, "is a person who has developed observation and memory, which are common to all, though many by want of using this observation and memory have allowed them to become stiff and unworkable." The Republican reader studying the series, then, can attain to an understanding of art, if not to its creation: "I want to do away altogether with the idea that the enjoyment of pictures comes from pleasure in the understanding of a science. Pictures are a part of the life of us all, and the way to enjoy pictures and life is the same."[86]

A second intention was to decry elitism and coteries in art, appealing to feeling, a fairly universal attribute, as a criterion for good art: "[I]f the artist succeeds in making us feel that we are present, looking at the scene and feeling about it as he felt, then the picture is a success." False pictures, Yeats says, are painted "to show the artist's cleverness in some way" or because of his "pride in science" (3). Science implies education, an accomplishment Yeats himself lacked, as did his intended audience. Vorticism and Futurism are bad because they depend on science; true pictures do not depend on science. The true artist paints, Yeats says, "because he wishes to hold again for his own pleasure—and for always—a moment." So far we find a romantic aesthetic à la Coleridge and Keats. But, Yeats says, the artist also paints "because he is impelled—perhaps unconsciously, but nevertheless impelled—by his human affection to pass on the moment to his fellows, and to those that come after him." The idea that the artist needs to communicate the experience is found in the work of Ruskin and William Morris.[87] As Yeats expresses the idea, however, the operative word is affection, that desire to share a good with one's fellow man which, at its highest, impelled Republicans to work for the good of all.

A third concern, and not surprisingly in a die-hard Republican ambience, is cultural separatism, allied for these idealists to cultural purity; Yeats abjures the "jaded civilization and the slave civilization" which pull art away from nature (4). Several paragraphs of his monograph could have been written by AE, or Douglas Hyde, or other advocates of cultural nationalism and the de-Anglicizing of Ireland:

When painting takes its rightful place it will be in a free nation . . . And there is a country more ready than any other to lift painting into its rightful place, and that is Ireland, this land of ours. Because here we have not too many false traditions about painting to get rid of, and so we have an open mind, and the foolish civilization of the cities and the love of money for the sake of money has not yet stolen us away. (4)

These familiar ways of contrasting English culture—materialistic, exploitative, spent—with Irish culture—spiritual, nurturing, and fresh—persist in Yeats's fiction, particularly in *Sailing, Sailing, Swiftly* and *The Careless Flower*. These sentiments were sure to strike sympathetic chords in the Anglophobic die-hard Republicans for whom anything less than complete separation from England was like a profaning of the Holy Celtic Grail. Yeats goes on, in his advocacy of cultural separatism: "But we must look to ourselves for the springs of our art. We must not look to Paris or London for a pace-maker. London can only give us what she has learnt from Paris" (5).

A fourth concern is the rootedness which was a feature of Lady Gregory's and WB's manifesto, *Ideals in Ireland*, and was Jack's personal concern all his life, the necessity of a sense of place and past: "[T]he roots of every art must be in the country of the artist, and no man can have two countries; and this applies with greater force to the artist than to anyone else, for the true painter must be part of the land and of the life he paints" (4). Yeats defends the artist who develops this sense of place and past from the charge of provincialism by saying: "The painter who works in the land of which he is a part need not build a wall about himself. It will do him nothing but good to know and admire all the fine painters of the world. But he can never be any one of them—he can never be anyone but himself" (5–6). One can detect here the immodesty of the spear head he was soon to espouse.

Yeats's fifth point of nationalist aesthetics is a reiteration of the "peasant ideal," in words that could have come from Colum: "Ireland is nearer to nature than is a country overspread with cities. . . . In the country the veil between the artist and nature is more transparent. He feels he is part of everything that surrounds him" (6).

Finally, Yeats asserts a Republican ideal of egalitarianism: "Every child in every corner of Ireland should be encouraged in this natural desire to draw what they see, and not only every child, but every man and woman, for though some may be too old to re-secure, in its fullness, the natural power of making pictures of what they see, all can enjoy that power a little in some degree" (8). Even as *A Broadside* is both a personal and a nationalist document, so *Modern Aspects of Irish Art* is a personal as well as Republican aesthetic document. Yeats goes from asserting the need for art and for an artist to have a sense of place and past to asserting his personally revolutionary anti-conventional stance, describing those viewers who want an artist to stay always the same and to use conventions they can recognize without trouble: "But lazy people like the artist to be conventional because it saves them trouble. . . . The lazy half-alive ones are satisfied . . . but they have not felt the thrill and tramp of memories which they would have felt before a bold, free and true picture which had thrilled the artist who painted it" (10). The viewer must de-code the work of art, must engage the memory and enter actively into the aesthetic transaction. The three adjectives—bold, free, and true—derive from the nationalist aesthetic and were used, in turn, by art critics to describe Yeats's own paintings.

In his description of beauty, Yeats reviles a word which was much in the air in 1922 in Ireland, "compromise." He says beauty is "a just balance. But not a compromise; the artist compromises when he refuses to paint what he himself has seen, but paints what he thinks someone else would like him to have seen" (10–11). It was their refusal to compromise which drew Yeats to de Valera and the Republican side in the Civil War. His attraction to the hero and to uncompromising idealism made him more comfortable as the Outsider.

JBY, the original model for the artist/outsider in Yeats's myth, had died shortly before the speech was given. He had refused to compromise, to paint what the Academy wanted him to see and what the sitters wanted him to see. Though the family suffered for this decision of their father's, Yeats must, at some level, have respected JBY's dedication to artistic authenticity. No doubt JBY's death, as well as the Republican struggle, affected Yeats's aesthetic attitudes. The need to retain artistic authenticity becomes a prominent theme in the fiction and drama, reflecting the emphasis in *A Broadside* on the need for balance in the artist's relation to both muse and public. JBY, for his part, had respected his son because, as he told Lady Gregory, "Jack is an initiator."[88] At this time, when he was entering into a new phase of his artistic career, Yeats was striking out and initiating. Perhaps he was taking the difficult advice with which he ended *Modern Aspects of Irish Art,* "But be true to yourself . . . then you and Truth will be shaking hands." He tried to find new forms in painting, fiction and in drama through which he could be true to his vision.

The ending to "Ireland and Painting," the version of Yeats's talk that appeared in *New Ireland* in 1922, is explicitly nationalistic and visionary. In it Yeats expresses his personal ideal and predicts the future path of the most significant Irish art:

The artist must himself be free and his country must be free. . . .The world wants a new road in painting, and Ireland soon will lead the way along that new road. The painting of the future will be national in its growth, but international in its speech. . . . The old Irish painters of the eighteenth century and the early nineteenth century left traditions, but they were only partly Irish traditions. They were largely London traditions . . . but we will scrap all artistic traditions but the tradition of freedom.[89]

Some fifteen years later, Yeats contributed another, but less overt, aesthetic statement to a series in *The Listener* called "The Artist Speaks." In constructing a portrait of a fictive painter, "my friend," Yeats stressed the solitary nature of the artistic act in the spear head fashion:

By the time when the years had so accumulated that my friend thought he had reached his growth, he sat and let his mind wander over all he had done, all he had painted, all he had talked about painting and heard talked about it.

. . . But he knows now, if he has found on his forehead a "G" for Genius, and not a "J" for Journeyman, there must come a day when he walks up to his clean waiting canvas with his empty palette on his thumb. Without warning his attendant shades will squeeze out the colors for him, hand him his brushes, say nothing in his ear, and then push him into the pit where the fight is always to a finish, no time, no gong, and the sky the only roof.[90]

Yeats went on, after 1921, toward this state of solitary battle in painting, fiction, and drama: scrapping traditions, and allying himself with, if with anyone, the international Modernists among Irish writers, and only loosely with them. However, before coming to the time when the years had so accumulated that he thought he had reached his growth, Jack B. Yeats identified his own goals with those of his emerging nation. In 1921, the "Artist of Gaelic Ireland," as AE called him in 1901, had clearly achieved a sense of place and past.

3. Thematic Continuity in the Narratives of Jack B. Yeats

Mark . . . threw out before them . . . a tale of his own invention or gathering . . . a tale that if it had no meaning, significance or gluey adhesion, was be-dizened, be-devilled and be-jewelled with names and phrases from a stored memory. No, but from a sea of memory on which the dust bucket had often by him been emptied. With the same bucket he now was scooping back where still they floated isolated names and strung words which never had rhyme and reason together, but sometimes had the one and sometimes the other.[1]

While speaking of Mark Trimbo, one of the two protagonists of his last narrative, *The Careless Flower* (1947), Jack Yeats describes what may be his own method of telling his tales. No longer sustained by the sense of place and past he had experienced in 1921, he explored more explicitly, in his narratives of the 1930s and 40s, both the motif of artistic authenticity and new forms in which to embody the theme he developed from it. The culmination of his exploration of this motif, begun in 1908 in *A Broadside*, is found in this final narrative, where Yeats makes this statement, his most explicit statement on the narrative process.

Aware of his need to pursue the private vision, Yeats nevertheless thought that the authentic artist must remain in touch with the outside world; aware of the essential isolation of all human beings, he held that the artist must try to communicate his vision of the nature of the force that animates and orders the universe. His ethical and social ideals involved accepting the rhythms of this life force and, while acting as a "conduit" for it, attempting to communicate the nature of the experience of union with this force. He was particularly aware of the difficulties of communicating the private vision through language; a second important motif that runs through the narratives is the failure of language. Nevertheless, Yeats wrote seven major narratives, impelled, as he would say, by affection for his fellow men to delve into his memory and to try to communicate an experience through which he felt himself uniquely favored. He also, concurrently, attempted to communicate this vision through his paintings. The painterly attempts have received both more attention and more praise.

Yeats's reputation as a painter has undermined his reputation as a writer of significant narratives; James Mays very perceptively points out that "as Yeats's reputation as a painter grows so does the resistance to accepting him on other terms, the tendency to dismiss his writing as a distraction without paying it much attention."[2] Some critics who do find Yeats's writing significant, nevertheless advert to its "strung words" pejoratively. Roger McHugh, for example, said that "Reading *Sligo* or *Ah Well* or *And To You Also* is like listening to a rambling talker who doesn't give a rambling damn whether you listen or not."[3]

Others, like John Pilling, find the narrator's rambling significant: "The hallmark of Jack Yeats's prose is its apparent unconsideredness, its inconsequentiality; it is as if we have been made privy to the unmediated thoughts of an idiosyncratic personality blissfully unaware of our presence."[4] Still others, such as Marilyn Gaddis Rose, find the rambling ironic, in the manner of Sterne and Beckett: "The apparent authorial irresponsibility and arbitrariness that characterizes Sterne's style [is] that of Beckett and Yeats also . . . the authorial mastermind surely hopes that many readers will realize that the *persona* is more ironic than he realizes . . . [Yeats's personae] want to sound as if beset by a hyperscrupulous intention to say whatever comes into their heads."[5]

Yeats's narrative inconsequentiality is more apparent than real; his purpose in making his style appear "unconsidered" is to exalt the random and the chance, the acceptance of which he finds necessary to achieve both integrity of personality and that harmony with the universe he posits as the highest value. Motifs that develop into the theme of acceptance of randomness and chance appear in his early work, such as *A Broadside*. More clearly developed versions of this theme run through the fiction, rising out of his personal attitudes and his need to experience union and harmony.

Yeats was an artist who worked and re-worked the same thematic material. His literary universe is remarkably consistent. Motifs found in the fiction and drama appear in *A Broadside*. Similar metaphors for expressing similar truths are found in all his fictions; metaphors such as the traveller/outsider and circus ring appear frequently. Attitudes also persist throughout his literary work. Yeats's attitudes toward randomness and chance, death and life, social justice, the artist and his role, language and its limitations, and even toward change, are consistent. Tracing these themes, motifs, metaphors, and attitudes permits us to observe the progression in his narratives, the integrity of his literary universe, and the continuity in his work which previous commentary has not noted.

Yeats's description of Mark Trimbo's narrative method has special significance in this context. To understand Yeats's narratives is to realize that their author was attempting to scrap tradition, particularly English tradition; his use of the term "tale of his own invention" reflects this emphasis. Similarly, Mark's tales are "be-dizened" and "be-jewelled," with all the rhetorical implications of those terms, "with names and phrases from a stored memory" because memory was an important concept to Yeats. He was attempting consciously to reunite "isolated names and strung words" from an unconscious part of the self and place them in new combinations to express his private vision in literary forms both suitable and innovative. These attempts cause him to re-use material in a way that leads to a highly integral narrative corpus.

Readers looking for traditional novels may be disappointed in Yeats's fictions, but what appears to be the narratives' lack of "gluey adhesion" may also be attributed to the limitations of the aesthetic criteria readers apply to these works. Traditional Euro-centered concepts of legitimate narrative modes tend to exclude the nonlinear. However, traditions not imbued with the classical emphasis on "finishing" and "enclosing" tolerate more open-endedness in narrative. Katherine Gittes, examining Arabic narrative, for example, shows that it draws on a tradition favoring boundlessness and infinity, one associated, perhaps, with Arabic reading of numbers from right to left, grasping smallest numbers first and largest ones last.[6] The Greeks, who read numbers with the largest first, viewed them as contracting entities with limited progressions; their reading of numbers in this way had epistemological consequences. The Greeks took Babylonian computational mathematics and made of it a deductive reasoning system, one that influences Western European aesthetics, emphasizing the importance of the whole and the subordination to it of its parts. Seeking an underlying order in nature, the Greeks theorized about a universe that is "perfect, finite, and one." This basically mathematical ontological view has implications for aesthetics and literary criticism which go largely unexamined. Plato, for example, taught that a unit should always appear as a unit and not as a group of small pieces, while Aristotle maintained that tragedy should imitate a whole, complete action—with a beginning, middle, and end—and have a unity that can easily be comprehended. From these views comes the Western European attraction to linear narrative and to the theory of organic unity and its subsequent assumptions:

Literary works with episodic plots connected by loose transitions or not at all are the worst kind, for they lack continuity (*Poetics* 7–9). Aristotle carries on the Platonic belief that unity in art requires a well-proportioned and harmonious balance of parts. The model for this Greek concept of unity is geometric, for geometry deals with enclosed space; it stresses the whole, the complete, the finite and disregards the limitless and the infinite.

Like the Pythagoreans, who had connected the limited with good and unlimited with evil, Aristotle downplays the notion of infinity because he finds it imperfect and incomplete.[7]

To those critics brought up in the Aristotelian tradition of criticism, the linear form of narrative is a given. To see Aristotle's principles as based on geometry, and thus as tied to only one among many possible conceptions of the universe, is to see possibilities for nonlinear ways of organizing narrative. Yeats spoke to John Rothenstein, the art critic, of the artist's need to free himself from geometry, particularly from line: "I believe that the painter always begins by expressing himself by line—that is, by the most obvious means; then he becomes aware that line, once so necessary, is in fact hemming him in, and as soon as he feels strong enough he breaks out of its confines."[8]

Yeats's explorations in narrative form were also attempts to break out of the confines of progressive linear narrative modes, to shape his medium to the needs of his creative imagination. As his vision became more private and idiosyncratic, Yeats sought ways of expressing it which did not conform to the Aristotelian concepts of organic unity and which freed his work from the confines of linear narrative progression, although these modes had seemed adequate when he experienced more sense of community and commonality of tradition.

Rothenstein comments on Yeats's painterly "breaking out" after the Irish Civil War and perceptively attributes it to the needs of his new vision.

About the year 1922 Jack Yeats himself, like a rocket emitting a shower of multi-coloured sparks, burst suddenly out of the linear system which had served so well the racy, touching narrative painting of his early and middle years. This change was accompanied, or more probably occasioned, by a change in the focus of his poetic vision. The characteristic subjects of the earlier years are lucidly defined. . . . The later subjects are less specific, less firmly fixed in time and space, and they are suffused by a poetry . . . [his] abstractions . . . are in essence symbols . . . of his rich and various experience of Irish life since he was a boy . . . fiercely resistant . . . to the pressure of industrial urban civilization.[9]

The changes in his poetic vision affected Yeats's writing in the same ways that they influenced his painting: they required an expansion of the form. The subjects of his later fiction are also less lucidly defined, less specific and less firmly fixed in time and space than those of his earlier writing. Yeats's early fiction was conventional and formally linear, but his later fiction is much more like the "shower of multi-coloured sparks" characteristic of the post-1922 paintings. On the one hand, Yeats values limitlessness and boundlessness; on the other, the part and the individual unit. His fiction exhibits a preoccupation with large themes: identity and flux, life and death, randomness and order, and, also, a minutely observed and lovingly rendered detail of the natural landscape, personal appearance of characters, and sensory impressions. Yeats's fiction exhibits ways of viewing the world and of expressing his vision not characteristic of the classical tradition or the English novel tradition. Since he did not attend a university, he was not exposed, as most traditionally educated writers of English were, to classical education with its respect for the Greco-Roman heritage and characteristic ways of viewing the world. JBY said of his son's position outside the orbit of Greek culture: "Latin and Greek and learning never affected Jack, since by the mercy of God he never paid any attention to them."[10] His father also said, speaking of Jack's ability to transcend systems: "I think also he has received the education of a man of genius. His personality was given its full chance. It has at once the sense of expansion and the instinct for self-control. . . . He has the habits of a man who knows his own mind . . . and is responsible to himself."[11]

These are, perhaps, the habits of a spear head. Yeats's sense of expansion was intuitive, as was his instinct for self-control. His fiction simply follows a concept of organization different from that of most fiction of his time. The lack of critical attention his writing received indicates, perhaps, the unreadiness of critics to appreciate the ground-breaking nature of his narrative modes. In this context it may be pertinent to recall the difficulties experienced by another Irish writer, James Joyce, a decade or so earlier, in getting his revolutionary narratives published.

These narrative methods were deliberately adopted, and formed part of a new aesthetic. It has been said of Yeats's acquaintance[12] Brian O'Nolan (Flann O'Brien), "In pursuing the world of imagination and eschewing the realistic, mundane and moralistic tradition of English novelists, O'Nolan was returning to the Celtic models he admired and, at the same time, fitting very well into some of the main patterns of contemporary European writing."[13] The anecdotal and fantastic elements of earlier Irish fiction, especially of the seanchas, were being rediscovered and imitated by many Irish writers in English. Yeats, both as a nationalist and a self-proclaimed avoider of all conventions, would hardly be any more likely than O'Nolan to follow the conventions of a basically English literary tradition. Beckett, the most influential Irish writer whom Yeats knew well, was very consciously experimental.

Like Joyce's Stephen Dedalus, modern Irishmen tended to reject as alien a culture which was transmitted through England. Yeats's comments in *Modern Aspects of Irish Art* would certainly align him with that tendency: "But we must look to ourselves for the springs of our art. We must not look to Paris or London for a pace-maker. London can only give us what she has learnt from Paris" (5). In this same work he had said of Irish freedom from tradition: "There is a country more ready than any other to lift painting into its rightful place, and that is Ireland, this land of ours. Because here we have not too many false traditions . . . to get rid of" (4).

Yeats and other Modernist Irish writers in English avoided linear narrative modes, rejecting them as patriarchal, and preferring circular, matriarchal modes. The matriarchal tradition represents part of the Celtic, and even pre-Celtic, cultural heritage. One example of a dominant matriarchal motif in Celtic art is the *triskele*, a complex circular design motif which appears on works as early as the first century B.C.

The *triskele*, literally the "three-legged" pattern, consists of three elements that appear to move in the same direction about a single central point. There is no beginning and no end; the movement is continuous, yet the pattern is rounded and complete. This three-part symbol, energized yet coming to a quiet point of rest in the center, was tenaciously adhered to by generation after generation of Celtic artists. For the mystery implicit in the asymmetrical, apparently ever-moving triskele seems to have appealed enormously to the Irish imagination.[14]

Substitution for linear plot characterizes Yeats's fiction, if not, as some think, all of Irish fiction in the 1930s. Anthony Cronin's recent survey, *Irish Literature in the English Language*, asserts that "a devouring interest in ... monologue as a format," "stancelessness" and "disdain for plot" are characteristic of much of Irish fiction.[15] Disdain for plot involves conscious rejection of the realistic, highly plotted English novel of the nineteenth century with its emphasis on verisimilitude, characterization, and psychology.

Cronin's survey also finds in the subject matter of significant Irish literature written in English at this time an abandonment of the earlier "peasant ideal" which concentrated on certain subjects. Yeats had adhered to this ideal in *A Broadside,* but he abandoned it in the painting and writing of his mature style although his acceptance declined when he left the "orthodox" or "Irish-Ireland" subjects. Cronin's recent denunciation of the "phoney primitive" subjects in Irish literature, those Yeats abandoned after the Civil War, reads like a retrospective justification of Yeats's decision to abandon this subject matter in his narratives of the 1930s:

[T]he principal self-imposed obstacle to the production of work of genuine merit in Irish literature has been the concentration on certain kinds of alleged Irishness as subject matter. By a sad paradox the claim made for these subjects, at least implicitly, has often been that they belonged to the timeless or Irish-Irish aspects of the Irish experience. ... The prose writers have had more commercial inducement than the poets for their indulgence in the tawdry picturesque and the phoney primitive, but the poets with their fairground characters, travelling people, thimble-riggers and trick o' the loop men have not been guiltless either.[16]

Although Jack Yeats was not a poet, Cronin's list of characters sounds like the enumeration of his early subjects given by Anne Yeats in her introduction to *Broadside Characters*. Yeats's nationalism, and his willingness to paint and write of the "peasant ideal" subject matter in the "consciousness-raising" years of the Republican struggle did not interfere with his deeper intuitions to free his work of this objective, early nationalist reference and to allow the subjective to dominate. Yeats's disillusionment with extreme nationalism—epitomized for him by the enunciation of Republican slogans by Erskine Childers's son just after his father's execution by the Free State—freed him, in his writing as well as in his painting, to become, as his aesthetic espoused, the "pure conduit" for a private vision.

When Yeats went beyond Irish-Ireland subjects in his painting, going deep inside himself to universalize his work by commenting on the human condition rather than the Irish situation, he found new forms to express his mature vision. They were Irish forms, not because he was still consciously adhering to a narrowly nationalist aesthetic, but because he had become truly Irish; he had achieved a sense of place and past. Following his own precepts of *Modern Aspects*, he was attempting to be true to himself. After he consciously abandoned "Irish-Ireland" subjects, he imbued his work with the principles animating some of the best Irish writers of the 1930s and 1940s. If his "intensely personal, original stream of consciousness"[17] as A. Norman Jeffares describes it, his "quirky anarchic humour and philosophical questioning" can be allied with those of any group, it is with the work of the International Modernist Irish writers like James Joyce and Samuel Beckett, or Brian Coffey, Denis Devlin, and Thomas MacGreevy. Like them, Yeats goes beyond limiting nationalist ideals while remaining truly Irish in spirit. As T. G. Rosenthal, in his monograph, maintains: "Ireland was in his blood; his whole oeuvre is redolent of Ireland and, as is so often the case, his localness was part of his genius and his genius transformed . . . his localness into universality. . . . One could say that in the early work he was recording Ireland as he knew it, and in the later work he was using Ireland . . . to record the world.[18]

Yeats's narrative technique—his own method of throwing out before his listeners a tale of his own invention or gathering, "bedizened and be-jewelled" from "a stored memory"—like his painting technique, involved intuition and a dislike of convention. As regards intuition, he told his niece that he could not help her learn to paint because he himself did not know how he did it.[19] As regards convention, he said "An artist should avoid convention, even if the conventions are of his own invention."[20] Conventions, he thought, were only for "lazy, half-alive" viewers. When he turned his attention to prose technique, he exhibited an adherence to intuition, an avoidance of convention, a refusal to work within a world view passed on by an alien culture that also characterize his painting.

Not only Irish fiction writers rejected the realistic novel; so did later "new wave" French novelists. Alain Robbe-Grillet said in a symposium on "The New Novel" in 1971: "There are two fundamentally different positions for the writer facing the world. One kind of artist comes into a world that already exists and about which he will say something, the other comes into a world that does not yet exist and which he will create through his own language."[21] In his narratives, Yeats did not assume the position of the realistic novelist: that the world already exists and he will say something about it, but the other position: that he will create a world through his own language. John Pilling comments: "He follows the haphazard windings of the mind in the hope of catching those moments when the mind is bringing its reality into being. This is why there is always the sense of something unprecedented in Yeats's prose, as though the sentiment or the landscape or the character has just come into being at that very moment."[22]

Yeats's larger organization, in his portrayal of the world that has just come into being, seems loose, yet the imagery is concentrated. An analogy can be drawn between the loosening of macro-organization and the concentration of imagery in Yeats's painting and similar tendencies in his narrative structure. Writing about Yeats's painting, Rosenthal observes:

The paintings done between 1925 . . . and his death in 1957 present a remarkable resolution of the conflict between his rapidly loosening technique and the concentration of his imagery, in which ideas are sparked off and reverberate in the spectator's mind. . . . The later Yeats almost deceives one into thinking that one is looking at abstract expressionist work . . . so apparently unfigurative are the shapes. Yet beneath the riotous paint and the exuberant colours lurk strictly figurative paintings; like many a great work of art, a late Yeats requires more than a cursory study. Yeats's figures are often skeletal, like the sculpted ones of Giacometti, and again like Giacometti's, they turn out to be substantial, and the apparent homunculus is revealed for a Yeatsean giant. . . .[23]

In a similar fashion, if one gives more than cursory study to Yeats's narratives, and if one is willing to admit the validity of nonlinear narrative modes like the tale and the fabulation, one can find a skeletal frame to his fictions, as carefully crafted, in some cases, as a Giacometti. Yeats's narrative works, as Mays maintains, are prevented from being "merely whimsical, or self-indulgent and fantastical, by Yeats's clear awareness of what he is doing and why, of being at the end able to justify himself in what he has done."[24] Yeats's form is suited to his theme. The "instinct for self-control" has not deserted him even when his "sense of expansion" is given its full scope.

Previous critics have not noted the suitability of his form to his subject. Roger McHugh, who was sufficiently sympathetic to Yeats's work to edit a "centenary gathering," nevertheless found: "Jack Yeats's five other books follow the pattern of his first, *Sligo* (1930), which has no plot whatsoever but simply follows the stream of memory and its random associations. They are prose sketchbooks of memory."[25] The pejorative "simply" is reinforced by a comment on the next page: "I do not think he took himself very seriously as a literary craftsman." The idea that no serious literary craftsman would opt for any model other than the linear, structurally unified, narrative we find in the dominant mode of the English novel is implicit in McHugh's comment.

Marilyn Gaddis Rose, although she has written the only previous full-length book that extensively treats Yeats's literary work, does not truly take his writing seriously. Taking a cue from the art dealer Victor Waddington (as McHugh may have done) that Yeats himself did not take it seriously, she reports a conversation between painter and dealer in which Yeats is alleged to have said, "They should remember me as a painter." She comments, "His self-appraisal is at least partly justified." In her commentary, she assumes that he wrote "to serve his painting, in short, in an attempt to explain or to specify what the hieroglyphic drawing can only symbolize." She finds him "an unconscious innovator" and "a solitary man writing to see if he could."[26] Her conclusions from these premises are largely dismissive.

There is evidence that Yeats took his writing seriously and was a conscious innovator, while there is little evidence that he intended his prose fictions to be a gloss on his painting. The high value Yeats placed on the interaction of viewer (or reader) and work in producing the aesthetic experience would militate against any gloss and lead him to choose a nondirective point of view for his narratives. He desired the maximum involvement of his audience in both media. For this reason his narrative speaker, though often technically omniscient, rarely makes interpretive comments, just as Yeats himself rarely did. Speaking of Yeats's reactions to questions about his painting, Hilary Pyle mentions his characteristic refusal to interpret: "Yeats was reluctant to make any direct comment on his own painting."[27] Her judgment accords with James White's testimony to Yeats's decision to make all his art *sub rosa*. Yeats himself defined success in a painting in terms of the artist's ability to make us feel as he felt, without mediation: "If the artist succeeds in making us feel that we are present, looking at the scene and feeling about it as he felt, then the picture is a success."[28] Proceeding deductively from this choice of narrative point of view, we can conclude that he intended the telling of his tale to affect the reader directly. His high regard for the contribution of the audience to the aesthetic transaction would lead him not to "control" the narrative or "direct" the reader's interpretation. His artistry in both modes would consist in the selection of the details and in their arrangement in the way most likely to cause the reader to feel the emotion the artist felt in encountering the experience.

Since the associative principle, the concept of "half-memory," was important to him in both modes, he adopts changing narrative angles to permit inclusion of associative material in the fiction:

"Half-memory" for him meant a state where memory was stimulated and transcended by the imagination. He was freed from the past. The new state allowed memory to develop and fluctuate after it first gripped the mind, to distort the original experience. It gave license for the inclusion of extraneous forces, or for the addition of detail not necessarily relevant, but carried in by a fresh emotion at the moment of painting.[29]

The "extraneous forces" were important to him; if the part need not be subordinate to the whole, then the concept of the "extraneous" changes. Since the need to accept the randomness and chance of life is one of Yeats's primary themes, what is "carried in" by the fresh emotion at the time of writing, what comes by chance association from less conscious levels to his mind, will contribute to the desired effect on the reader, and is more important in his "whole" than linear narrative progression.

Consistency in narrative is, therefore, not an important criterion for Yeats. Shifts in the angle of vision are acceptable, perhaps even desirable. He dedicates *Sligo*, for example: "To / Venus / I Leave It To You Mam."[30] This changeable and remote goddess proves an apt dedicatee for Yeats's shifting narrative perspective. On page one the narrator is remote from the action, gazing from a rocky hilltop "like the Rocky Mountains." He is gazing not onto the prairies below the Rocky Mountains, which he nevertheless describes, but onto a lake with a regatta, which he does not describe. Here the concept of "half-memory" dictates the shift in perspective. The simile "like the Rocky Mountains" carries in a new wave of emotion at the moment of writing and gives license for the inclusion of the prairies he associates with these mountains. This new material enriches the original memory of the regatta on the lake by means of the submerged metaphor implied by the prairies.

Characteristically demanding a great deal of "involvement" from the reader, Yeats next shifts the narrative perspective from the heights, and shifts it in time as well as in space. The reader is indeed in Sligo, not in the present, but rather in "one time" when "long cars with unicorns of three horses, drove away North, East and West of it, and every now and then boys, going to School in good time in the morning, had their horse hearts cheered with the sight of an ordinary outside car with a tandem" (8–9). This passage repeats the mood of nostalgia of *A Broadside*.

The reader of *Sligo* is in Yeats's world of "half-memory" where vivid visual metaphors ("green woods creaming to one's feet") and other sensory images ("the mellow fire of whiskey") abound, "bejewelling . . . those names and phrases from a stored memory" Yeats spoke of in describing Mark Trimbo's narrative method. In this world, "Good Boys, going early to school, crossing the bridge, where the brown fresh water flows into the salt, Kush na Farrigeh, the foot of the sea, have other things happening before them. . . . Something to talk of. To try and make into a thrilling and romantic tale for the elders, who are as hard to amuse, as always" (9–10). This world is consciously and unconsciously summoned up: part the unsolicited memory, part the conscious world of the literary artist, one who makes "a thrilling and romantic tale" for someone else.

The perspectives keep shifting. The two things that happen before the boys, out of which they make "something to talk of " are "a pink-eyed albino with a rose red round in the middle of his white head reeling and weaving from the pathway, to the roadway, and back again: and two sturdy Citizens taking a sledge-hammer from the grip of a wild quayside man" (10). This world is like that of Synge, who, Yeats himself said, "loved wild sights." Both the sight of the quaysider (based on a memory of a real sight and suggestive of the violence barely contained in the dark-eyed men of the West) and the intensely visualized, carefully described vision of an albino horse (who with his "rose red round" is as symbolic as he is naturalistic) are given equal weight here. This is the Yeatsean *Sligo*: where the intensely private meets the public; where Gaelic meets English; where the fresh water flows into the salt; where "Ireland at its Westernmost and its finest" meets the universe of the mind—the "half-memory" world of the mature Yeats.

Less conscious elements, those brought in at the moment of writing, are as important as the consciously recalled elements based on memory:

The first motor to run regular trips to the river . . . Had a Time Table. But when the motor filled up it went; "is this the three or the four o'clock motor?" Who cares. The driver doesn't: a willowy girl leans over his shoulder. He is Sarsfield, the Black Thief of Sloan, the Boy Cuhullan, Steve Brodie "The man who took a chance." And when the driver takes his chances so do the people who meet him on the road. But if it wasn't for that girl he wouldn't kill a daisie. Who wants to kill daisies anyway! . . . "Beneath the daisies."
    Sound the Drum slowly
    Play the fife lowly.

From cradles—well not quite from cradles. But from daisy chains to graves They follow us; and give us our chance to wheeze at the big melancholy talk. With laughter we come, with laughter we go. Arms reversed. Muffled drums when I lie under the daisies. Drinks for the watchers . . . . Under the sod, under the cement, under the pulverising Star. . . . Perhaps someone will get up . . . and start a new star, "Hope." "The New Design" "The Adventurer" "The Stand Clear of Her when She Rolls."
    (10–11)

This long passage contains quintessential Yeats: characteristic heroes; characteristic attitudes toward death, chance, women, hope and time; and characteristic technique. In it the experimental exploration of dream states is not differentiated from true memory. Yeats blends the techniques of partial statement and suppression of expository links in an attempt to represent in language the complex associative processes of the mind, the processes he called "chain thinking." There must be some concessions to the reader—Yeats was aware of his audience— but, rhetorically speaking, the more one makes the reader do, the greater the reader's emotional involvement in the aesthetic transaction. By rendering as faithfully as possible his own fragmented experience, the artist enables the audience to participate in it. He creates a world through language.

In *Sligo* and *Ah Well*, Yeats was interested in capturing that state of consciousness which one critic, describing Nathalie Sarraute's fiction, has called "the first tender shoots of our mental life . . . not yet so conscious that it gets caught and stifled in the rough net of conventional language."[31] In Yeats's attempt to capture this mental life, the "motor," an object drawn from memory, is given equal weight with the subjective fantasy of its imagined driver. Further associations and generalizations from these associations are also given equal weight. All are rendered as immediately as possible. This type of anecdotal, subjective narrative mode reflects values other than those of the realistic English novelist. Yeats has a different artistic intent; and his form is dictated by his attempt to portray semi-conscious states and the associative paths of mental life.

Many writers of fiction have defied, or expanded, the convention of linear narrative progression to embody their themes. There are, for example, the two Irish-born writers to whom Yeats is often compared, Laurence Sterne and James Joyce. Although he did not express an opinion on Sterne, Yeats thought highly of Joyce. Speaking of the necessity for avoiding convention in producing true art, he used Joyce as an example of an artist whose prose style reflected the changes any real artist must necessarily make. He spoke of the Anna Livia Plurabelle episode in *Finnegans Wake* as an example of the changed style of Joyce. Joyce also compared his own work to Yeats's.[32]

Although the associative and dreamlike qualities of Yeats's late paintings have long been recognized, most critics have not paid attention to explorations in his fiction of association, dreams, and visions. His narrative modes, too, represent a consciously experimental and carefully crafted use of forms suitable to exploration of nonrational states. As Masefield was a strong influence on his early pirate drama and children's books, and Synge strongly influenced the aesthetics and the social attitudes of *A Broadside*, so Beckett influenced the late fiction and drama. The term "influence," when speaking of the effect of another artist's work on Yeats, should be taken to mean the effect of similarity of temperament and aims, mutual respect, and awareness of a friend's mind, not the result of conscious imitation of another's work as a model. Yeats certainly "knew his own mind," as his father put it, and did not try to write as other artists did, any more than he painted as others did.

For a long time his experimental methods in painting were not recognized as "serious"; his refusal to join movements, his independence, hindered his achievement of recognition. His refusal to join movements in writing, too, has contributed to his not being considered a "serious" writer. Part of the tendency to underestimate the seriousness of Yeats's authorial intent and his attention to technique is based on identification of his own intent with his narrator's comment in *Sligo* that he was writing "to jettison memories." ("Jettison" is surely a dismissive, if not pejorative, word.) A second factor is his light tone. "The reader must constantly discriminate between fun and foolishness . . . must constantly be alive to the subtlety in the simplicity."[33] Yeats's characteristic reserve also contributed to critical inattention or underestimation of his writing: "I have determinedly, and always, resisted the honest vanity of writing about how I write."[34] Yeats's self-deprecating tone or reserve are both understandable. A man whose older brother has won the Nobel Prize for literature must, if he writes at all, be modest in his published self-estimate of his work and must avoid seeming to invite invidious comparisons by taking himself too seriously, especially if that brother does not take his work seriously. Jack Yeats did tell an interviewer that he got "great pleasure, and honour" when a bibliography of his books appeared in *The Dublin Magazine*.[35] This statement is a more reliable indication of his feelings about his writing than the comment of his persona in *Sligo*.

After looking at what remains of his private library, one concludes that he was interested in serious writers. He owned the works of such writers as Ezra Pound, Wyndham Lewis, T.S. Eliot, William Carlos Williams, James Joyce, Wallace Stevens, and Marianne Moore. His own work was published in journals that contained the work of highly esteemed writers, so he must have been taken seriously as a writer by at least some of the editors of his time. Examining what his niece, Anne Yeats, has been able to store in her home in Dalkey from his personal library, one finds many "small magazines" and journals that were the repository of his own writing, of the best Irish writing of his time, and of important criticism, much of it published outside of Ireland. A list of works found in his library is given in the Appendix.

These journals and magazines, collected over some fifty years, indicate both Yeats's continuing interest in the work of other writers and his awareness of contemporary aesthetics. They attest to his serious interest in writing. That he was invited to contribute to some of them shows contemporary valuation of his writing. Sean O'Faolain, publishing in *The Bell* an excerpt from *Ah Well*, stated: "We print it because we believe that our readers will delight in it for its power to be, at one and the same time, familiar, strange, simple and lovely. . . . It belongs in this magazine, just as surely as a translation of an old shanachie's folk-tale would belong, being made up, like that, of the life we tread everyday beneath our feet."[36]

Although it is as difficult to speak of influence on his writing as on his painting, Yeats knew the importance of not working in isolation. Speaking on the danger that provincialism represents to a painter, he said: "It will do him nothing but good to know and admire all the fine painters of the world. But he can never be any one of them—he can never be anyone but himself."[37] Knowing fine writers of the world, he never attempted to be any of them. As O'Faolain points out:

[H]e is always himself. He resolutely follows his own nose. He never makes up books out of other books. His material and his methods are his own; his style and technique are his own. . . . He is also one of our most independent writers. What he writes, he writes: take it or leave it. . . . It is a chunk of life played over by a vivid imagination. He did it because he liked to do it . . . He is entirely free of the tyranny of audience.[38]

He had attained the ideal of the bareback rider.

An anonymous reviewer spoke of Yeats's work in 1941 as integral and autonomous.[39] The continuity of themes makes the work integral. The crafting of forms to express themes, at least in the narratives, makes the work autonomous. The following analysis of Yeats's individual narratives identifies themes that pervade his integral corpus, showing how they develop. It also suggests genres which are analogous to Yeats's "autonomous" narrative modes. This analysis also assumes that the reader has not read the narratives, since most of them are not easily available. In terms of progression of technique, it assumes, as O'Faolain does, that, "Yeats has gone on and on, developing the hint, drawing out finer and finer the light thread which connects the imagination with the original experience that excited it. However finely drawn out, the link is there. . . . Consideration, wisdom, experience have deepened and darkened it [Yeats's fancy] in the vat of the mature artist's imagination."[40]

Short Early Narratives

Jack Yeats's principal bibliographers, Hilary Pyle and Martha Caldwell, list among his works a number of short periodical pieces, some of which are narrative.[41] The earliest known narrative piece, called "A Cycle Drama," was published on 7 September 1895 in a periodical called *The Success*. An example of Yeats's puckish humor, the piece describes a fictional attempt to stage an amateur play. The tone, like that of *Jack on Jack*, is typically self-deprecating:

Of course my drama must be a melodrama, with a realistic cycle-track, a hero, a villain, and a puncture. My first thought was "Where should it be played?" My ambition started at Drury Lane, worked down to a suburban assembly room, and finally some kind friends offered to lend their back parlour, and I began to get my company together.

Many of Yeats's own plays were melodramas, and he was very concerned with their staging. The Yeats children often acted in plays, and this narrative piece may be partially autobiographical. It is short, about fifteen column inches, and carefully plotted and framed. The climax of the cycle drama was to be a race between the hero and the villain, with the heroine's favor as the prize. The first-person point of view of the writer-producer-actor who is on stage during the action sets up the sort of irony which was to characterize many of the later works:

At last the welcome pistol-shot rang out. A voice said, "Let 'em go." We heard two bicycles whizz down the slope; then came a horrible metallic crash and a bad word, and there wobbled in alone through the open door, a rider—the villain!—wearing a torn black jersey and a sanguinary nose. Such a thing had never happened before in the whole history of melodrama. Iniquity had won, hands down!

For the Christmas number of *Boy's Own Paper* of 1895, Yeats produced a much longer narrative, "The Great White Elk." Again the tale is carefully framed, but in this work the adventure of the hunt of the elk is recounted by an omniscient narrator: Yeats could write conventional linear narrative in several modes.

Nearly a decade elapsed before the publication of his next narrative. After having published three plays for miniature stage, all conventional melodramas, Yeats published, in 1904, the first of his illustrated "Books for Children," *The Bosun and the Bob-tailed*

Comet. An octavo volume with delightful drawings, it tells a simple adventure story for very young children, again using linear narrative.

In the following years, 1905 and 1906, Yeats published ten short, illustrated pieces in the *Manchester Guardian.* Masefield, who was probably the instigator of the series, offered to write articles to accompany the sketches, but then decided that Yeats should write them himself, since he would write "a lot better than I do, for you know the stuff and do it, while I only try to do it in a certain way."[42] The pieces all exhibit the wry humor and the keen eye for descriptive detail characteristic of the later narratives.

The first of these *Manchester Guardian* pieces, "On the Stones" (28 January 1905) describes the narrator's trip to a horse fair "up the Caledonian Road" with a chimney sweep friend who has "a strange knowledge of the town and a wide acquaintance among sportsmen." On the way to the fair, the bus driver tells a grotesque tale-within-a-tale, to the sweep, about "Curves," the "fattest conductor in London," who, while going to a barber's for a shave, tripped over the linoleum, fell, and devastated the shop. The interest in speech characteristic of Yeats's later fiction is demonstrated in this piece; Yeats's ear for dialect is as keen as his eye for the grotesque.

The descriptions in the various pieces are those of a graphic artist. The first three are set in working class London, and the rest are set in Manchester. Detailed visual descriptions of the huckster's wares at these fairs and markets are the prototypes of the "catalogues" in *Sligo.* The narrator of "On the Stones" sums up the scene as "a scene full of life and stir, warming to the heart." It was surely warming to Yeats's heart, as one of his highest epithets for art (recorded in 1906 in an unpublished letter to John Quinn) was that it had "some of the living ginger of life." The subjects described are those Yeats never tired of painting or writing about: skies, donkey races, boxing matches, other sporting events, theatre performances and fairs. He says of the fairground on the stones, "We reached the middle of the market, and I saw what I had never seen in London before—a sky that came down to the heads of the people without being stopped by brick and mortar." He also says, "there is no donkey that is not beautiful, for he has his splendid eye, his little hoofs, and the cleanest of legs." Tags from music hall songs, which pervade all of the later narratives, appear also as motifs in these pieces.

"Racing Donkeys" (26 August 1905) was published in tandem with Masefield's "Whippet Racing." Hilary Pyle says of Masefield's relation to Yeats at this time: "With Yeats he shared an enjoyment in a vigorous life . . . a delight in story telling . . . in these early days painter and poet were fresh in their unaffected spontaneity and their matter-of-fact joy in the picturesque whether it was verbal or visual. Masefield regarded himself primarily as a storyteller; and it was his love of stories that first impelled him to write."[43]

The sweep from "On the Stones" is again the narrator's companion in the second London piece, "Racing Donkeys." The two ride the bus again, this time far into the East End of London, but without hearing any interesting tales-within-tales. The crowd is carefully described, with details given of an eel-jelly seller and "a fine lass" who wore an "electric blue Newmarket down to her heels." There is narrative action, since "some donkey owners go a-racing on the old system of win, tie, or wrangle," and a fight breaks out when the backers of a disqualified donkey attack the Irish track owner. The Irishman triumphs, not surprisingly, given Yeats's attitude toward his countrymen.

The third London piece, "Shove Halfpenny," is fairly dramatic and tightly organized. After an exciting match, the halfpenny contest is won by the quiet challenger from "across the water" (north of the Thames), since the pub where the match is held is "on the Surrey side of London." There is some characterization of the colorful local man who is defending his title, but not enough to make his loss pathetic.

"The Melodrama Audience" is the first piece set in Manchester rather than London. It almost constitutes drama criticism, although it is cast in a narrative form. By illuminating what Yeats understood to be the primary characteristics of melodrama, the piece reveals much about what he was attempting in his own early dramas.

"A Canal Flat," the second Manchester piece, is reflective and descriptive, telling of a trip up the canal on a timber flat. On the leisurely voyage the narrator reflects on the need for names on ships, the various colors one should paint a canal flat, and states, "If it was not for these vile locks, I too should like to be a canal man." Typically, the humorous comment is self-deprecating, the wish being somewhat akin to wanting to be a chef, if it weren't for the heat of the kitchen.

"The Jumpers," the third Manchester piece, describes a sport now called low hurdles. There is little suspense and none of the emotional involvement in the race that marked the narration of the halfpenny contest. The tale of a small boy who fires a cap gun at a horse seems equally, if not more, important to the author than the contest referred to in the title, and it is narrated with more vigor.

Three of the next four Manchester pieces—"An Old Alehouse," "The Concert-House," "The Glove Contest," and "The Cattle Market"—are more reflective essays than narratives. The various customers of the alehouse and their debates furnish the material for the series of vignettes making up this first piece. "The Concert-House," like "The Melodrama Audience," is most interesting for its exploration of the reactions of the audience to the songs, particularly to the ballads. "The Cattle Market" is descriptive. "The Glove Contest," however, is a narrative. Since boxing fascinated Yeats (Masefield shared the fascination), the matches are narrated with skill, and conflicts are well delineated.

The last *Guardian* piece, "The Flat Iron" (1906), is significant for tracing Yeats's attitudes and techniques. An almost lyrical description of the joys of shopping in a Manchester open market (which got its name because it was shaped like a flat iron), this piece exhibits a nostalgia found often in the later narratives. The catalogues of incongruous items, the eye and ear for picturesque detail, and the touches of humor that characterize the larger works of fiction are all present. For example, the auctioneer says to the bidders: "Some of ye don't come to buy, s'elp me . . . ye come to *pinch*." The nostalgia for the leisurely, pre-industrial world resembles that in *A Broadside*. The reflective aspects of some of the shorter essays have developed in this final piece into nostalgic reflections on older, more humanly involving methods of shopping, contrasted to less personal modern modes:

And when you stop to buy you plunge immediately into the old primeval realities of commerce. Here you do not stand sourly while a pale-faced, short-tempered shopman whirls your purchase into a dexterously twisted screw of pale brown paper and sends your money trundling in a globe along naked wires. No, here before you make a purchase you can slap and thump a thing, and abuse and sneer at it, and the man behind the stall will slap and thump it too, and praise it; and at last you'll get the price down to near to what he will take and you will give. Then perhaps some old split-the-differ of the market rolls up and makes it a bargain between you.

The projected book of which these sketches were to form a part, *Sketches of Life in London and Manchester*, never appeared. Instead, Yeats worked with Synge on *Life in the West of Ireland*, a collaboration that was to have so much influence on his nationalist aesthetic, on his life, and on his later writing. The anti-industrial nostalgia and the longing for the simpler era which mark later works emerge here. Later these personal predilections were to be reinforced by the nationalist "peasant ideal" of Ireland. Descriptions of attractions across the road from the flat-iron market itself—the beloved merry-go-rounds or "whirly-horses," boxing booths or goal-kicking booths, and Maggie dolls, "strangely whiskered dolls, which fall over backwards like life itself if you hit them fair"—follow the descriptions of the market proper. The concessionaire in "The Flat Iron" reminds Yeats of the circus driver of Sligotown.

This piece is pivotal. It not only looks forward to *Sligo* and later works, but also marks the beginning of that turning away from English life which was to have such important repercussions for both Yeats's painting and his writing. We see in "The Flat Iron" the nostalgia he described in a letter to John Quinn, written at this time, for the joys of life one missed by living in "an alien country."[44] The ending of "The Flat Iron" is prophetic: "I . . . looked at the passengers on the merry-go-round, which had no dappled wooden horses, but cars in the shape of gondolas that not only went round and round but up and down with a sort of writhing motion. I did not mount the cars. I turned away from the Flat Iron and the revolving music and the smoking oil lamps." He also turned away soon from England, moving back to Ireland in 1910.

The next narrative, *A Little Fleet*, although its subject was Devon, was published late in 1910, after the move to Ireland. (Between these narratives, Yeats began, in 1908, *A Broadside*, with its blend of poetry and sketches.) In an unpublished letter in the collection of Anne Yeats, Masefield writes to Yeats of a ballad he did about this time in which Saxon ships were sunk by the Moby Dick, one of the toy ships of *A Little Fleet*, "As she slowly hove to carry the news that Ireland was now free." This reference may indicate that *A Little Fleet* as well as *A Broadside* contained a blend of political subtext with nostalgia. Certainly *A Little Fleet*, the second "book for children," echoes the nostalgia for a simpler, more humanly scaled world that ended "A Flat Iron." It may also reveal nostalgia for the "Cashlauna Shelmiddy" world of his early married years in Devon and adventures with the "pirate poet," Masefield.

Written in collaboration with Masefield, *A Little Fleet*, like *A Mainsail Haul*, is "richly illuminated, so fresh with the gaiety of youth."[45] The two artists had met in 1902, when Masefield was contributing to *A Broadsheet*, for which Yeats and Pamela Colman Smith were doing drawings, and had become close friends. *A Little Fleet*, like some ballads in the 1908–15 *A Broadside*, recalls Masefield's and Yeats's sailing toy ships on the Gara, a Devon river. This small volume is not pure narrative: "The owners think that any other little boys who live near a stream sufficiently deep to float ships drawing so little water might like to follow their example and build a fleet, therefore I am to tell you how each vessel was built, as well as the story of its voyage." (The intent of Elkin Mathews in publishing this book may have been to sell boat kits as the early plays had sold cardboard stage sets. The latter are still carried in London toy stores specializing in Victoriana.) The building and the voyages of the "Monte," a fore and aft schooner; the "Moby Dick," a paddle steam boat; the "Theodore," a fireship; the "Pasear," a topsail schooner; and the "New Corinthian," a brig, are vividly recounted. Masefield, "The Fleet Poet," provided verses with which to end each of the first three tales. All of these short pieces demonstrate Yeats's ability to write conventional narrative when that was his intention.

Sligo

The first long, published narrative, *Sligo*, did not appear for two decades. Between *A Little Fleet* and *Sligo* came the death of Yeats's father and the death of the Republic. Art critics have noted at this time the change to Yeats's "mature style" of painting; *Sligo* is the first example of the effects on his mature writing style of these changes in his personal and national life. *Sligo*'s relation to the earlier narratives is the same as that of the late painting to the earlier illustrations and watercolors; it is the serious attempt of an accomplished, reflective artist to express his vision of the world, incorporating his earlier material into a new synthesis. Art historians find in his late "expressionist" but not "abstract" paintings the themes and materials from the earlier paintings, transformed by his powerful vision. His later writings brood, as it were, over the same motifs noted in "The Flat Iron" and *A Broadside*. Yeats uses materials such as monologue and tales-within-tales in *Sligo,* and the eye and ear for the visually and orally picturesque, the self-deprecating humor of the earlier work are still present. But its narrative style is new, analogous to the freedom from line and the loosening of organization found in the late paintings, especially when this book is compared to the more tightly organized stories of the 1890s, to the children's books, and to the more reflective narratives and essays of the 1905–6 *Guardian* pieces.

Tonally, *Sligo* has much in common with the meditation begun in "The Flat Iron," an expression of profound nostalgia for a simpler, more idyllic time, a Sligo that may have existed only in Yeats's mind and in the minds of the nationalists who wrote about, painted, or fought for that ideal Celtic world they would like to have created, and which they believed had existed in the Golden Age of Ireland. Pyle spoke of Yeats's patriotism as "a dedication to perfect life, without blemish, where no man was subject to another."[46] *Sligo* reflects this vision.

How was one to sustain a vision like this in the face of the obvious political failures to create such a life in Ireland and elsewhere? How could one share a sustaining vision with one's country and the world, as an artist, in Yeats's terms, was "impelled" to do? How even remain an artist in the increasingly philistine world of Ireland?

In speaking of why the hearts of Irishmen grew "brutal," Peter Costello describes a predicament and attitudes which affected Yeats, particularly at the time of the writing of *Sligo*, a breach between the intellectuals and the men of action. Near the end of the Civil War, from the stage of the Abbey (which, ironically, had been lent without fee for a benefit for Republican dependents) an Irish military leader, General Mulcahy, issued a charge that characterizes the hostile attitude toward art of the troubled period through which Yeats had remained silent. Mulcahy charged that the military had been "deserted, at the present time and all through the fight put up in the country, by our poets and our literary people." After refuting the charge, and citing the writers who had contributed, Costello comments on this attitude of the "new regime" to the "literary elite": "The new leaders were not concerned, as Pearse and Connolly, Yeats and his friends all were, with a liberation of the spirit, the creation of a national culture, with new shapes of life. The failure of the revolution had begun back in 1918, when such unlikely and narrow men as Griffith and De Valera were ushered by the quirk of history and the enthusiasm of an excited people to the first positions of leadership."[47]

The ideal of life "where no man was subject to another" was defeated when the Labour Party stood aside from the General Election to let the people vote on the nationalist question. In a country with no strong social democratic tradition, the social vision of Jack Yeats and John Millington Synge had very little chance for survival. With de Valera's return to the Dail in 1927, the last of the die-hard Republicans drifted into the IRA. The small, agrarian property holders, who had just gotten land, and the commercial interests in the towns, those whom WB had earlier called "paudeens," had defeated the ideal. As WB said in "Ego Dominus Tuus": "What portion in the world can the artist have / Who has awakened from the common dream / But dissipation and despair?"

Jack kept himself from despair by going inward and backward. He projected and protected his ideal world by "assembling" memories from his earlier life. Inclined to be obsessed with unresolved issues from his childhood, he used them to produce art. He was doubly inclined to dwell on his memories in the face of the failure of the nationalist ideal. His friend Masefield said of Yeats's use of childhood memories: "Perhaps all that any artist ever does is to make significant in afterlife things that were delightful in childhood. Mr. Yeats is always making significant the delights of his days at Rosses Point."[48]

Sheehy, in a perceptive criticism of Yeats's paintings in this era, makes three statements about Yeats's work which are important to understanding *Sligo*: His detachment is operative:

. . . [His work] has a certain individualist detachment, as though seen by the eye of the spectator who is nearly but not quite at home.

He had been a significant nationalist artist:

It would be a mistake to think of Yeats as a militant nationalist; no artist could be that and remain an artist. But he certainly did collaborate in that renaissance of the spirit which culminated in the Rebellion and the Anglo-Irish war; and by so doing he liberated his art from the hitherto unrelieved provinciality of painting in Ireland.

He turned inward to a "Romantic individual vision":

. . . as though, when politics ousted patriotism, collaboration ceased and the artist was thrust back into himself and his own past. How often in his later manner does he not paint like a man lost in his own memories . . . I do not think his later work has anything like the same reaching-out towards the life around him as did some of the pictures painted in the early twenties. But then we might ask if the life today has anything to offer to the Romantic except the conviction of the inevitable solitude of the human spirit.[49]

Because of his "collaboration" in the nationalist enterprise, Yeats achieved his sense of place and past. He felt himself to be part of his community, up to 1922. *Modern Aspects of Irish Art* was delivered in 1921 to a real audience with whom Yeats was surely in sympathy.

Its delivery, for so reserved and private a man, indicates that Yeats had found himself and his people.[50] After the Anglo-Irish war ended, the Civil War tore Ireland apart, separating Yeats from his brother as well as from the nationalist majority. After the Republicans lost the Civil War and even the die-hard rebel de Valera gave up the dream, Yeats went on painting and writing about the Ireland of his mind. He did not emigrate; he did not stop writing or painting, although he no longer had any sense of a sympathetic audience. He wrote *Sligo.*

After 1922, his patriotism, still influencing his work, took a new form, the prophetic and visionary portrayal of a way of surviving the loss of an ideal. In view of the attacks by the Catholic majority on his brother, "the pagan Yeats," and of the Censorship Act of 1928, which banned the books of almost all the major Irish writers from their own country, it is surprising that he wrote at all.

He speaks in *Sligo* of his method of dealing with an unexpected rainstorm; he may actually be speaking of his own method of surviving in these hostile conditions. He says that the rain can be pleasant "if you give up the fight" against it. His great theme of the need for acceptance, for surrender to forces larger than the self, is stated in terms of surrender to nature:

But there can be great encouragement in rain once you meet it, as it were, in its own mood. . . . If you give up the fight, you are soon getting to wait for and enjoy the rhythmatic squelching of the water in and out of your shoes: savour it. Bathe the dryest side of your soul in it, and you will find the rain has lost its spiteful qualities and become a kind hand-taking comrade, and . . . about that time you are one with the clouds, the lakes, the falls and the full smiling rivers of a friendly land.
(117)

One survives by transcendence, by surrender to forces outside of the self, expressed for the Romantic through an experience of being "one with" the forces of nature. Achievement of plenitude seems to have been one of Yeats's needs, and the necessity for its pursuit becomes a pervasive theme of these narratives written in his sixties. Perhaps Yeats had reached the time he described in *The Listener* article called "A Painter's Life" as a time when the years have so accumulated that one thinks one has reached one's growth. Yeats's characters who grow learn to surrender to randomness or to chance and to give up their illusions of control. In *Sligo*, Yeats does not show characters surrendering to larger forces as clearly as he does in the more sustained narratives *Sailing, Sailing Swiftly* and *The Amaranthers*, but he conveys his own mature acceptance of randomness and reinforces it by his choice of a suitable form, the stream of consciousness. His relation to his audience changes, particularly in *Sligo*, from a rhetorical concern for the audience's needs to a more purely expressive mode, with the audience, overhearing, as it were, a soliloquy. Stream of consciousness is a form suitable to the expression of Yeats's major theme, the need to accept randomness and give up attempts at control; this theme is closely connected to the political and social situation of Ireland that prompted it.

An important new concern emerges in *Sligo*, one suited to Yeats's mood of solitude and to his awareness of the failure of communication. He speaks of the death of language: "This word business is nearly played out unless some new language blossoms to give a few new mouthfuls" (18). As early as 1913 he had felt that literature was a declining form. In that year, John Quinn wrote to him: "I do not agree with you that literature is nearly 'out.'"[51] For the ensuing decade and a half Yeats had communicated his vision primarily through painting, a wordless medium. His mistrust of language is part of a Modernist sense of what structuralists would later call the distance between signified and signifier. There is an entire area of experience that language as we know it seems inadequate to express. There seem to be sensations and perceptions prior to language for which we must find expression. That mental state of perception not easily expressed in language interested Yeats. In his work this state is conveyed through the type of "anti-form" that stream of consciousness represents. The adoption of an anti-form reflects both a Modernist trend toward the "growing disaffection with modern civilization" evidenced in "A Flat Iron," and Yeats's dissatisfaction with conditions in post–Civil-War Ireland:

The second trend [of modern literature] is founded on a distrust of language as a medium of expression and a distrust of form, which has impelled certain modern writers to cultivate chance and disorder as legitimate elements of the artistic process. . . . The suspicion of language reflects a more radical mistrust of reason, history and social organization. At bottom, the revolt is directed at those inseparable twins, Authority and Abstraction. For authority in social life and abstraction in language are corollaries; they are commandments issued to the flesh, coercing private experience into objective order. The two trends, we see, are aspects of the same quenchless feud.[52]

This "quenchless feud" with authority and abstraction was carried on his whole life by the senior John Butler Yeats, that argumentative bohemian. His letters are filled with warnings to his sons to avoid abstraction. For example: "I think if poets take to abstract thought . . . they lose their feeling for concrete thought. It is as though a man deserted his wife and children to give himself to philanthropy."[53] The tendency to revolt against authority and abstraction were encouraged by family influences; the political situation intensified the tendency; and the Modernist distrust of language and conventional forms confirmed Yeats's intuitions. Failure of language became a prevailing motif in *Sligo* and later fiction.

The narrator of *Sligo* explicitly denies the ability of language to express his vision. Writing is viewed as speech written down (an Irish tendency to equate literature with the oral) and speech is useless: "If this is going to be the last book written we cannot be very far away from the last thing "said." Speech is certainly on its last legs if it ever had legs. . . . What is it for anyway, information? We have sign posts. Communication of original ideas? They are not communicable, if they are original, through speech. . . . No, bury speech . . . and give little yells and yelps undecodeable over it" (42–43).

This unreliability of words, their uselessness for conveying an original idea or even a universally understood message, is a continuing concern to Yeats: "It is always a pleasure to me to come on slang that will not travel or change so on the voyage that it becomes something else altogether. . . . Slang is like slippers, worn to fit the first users only" (114). If speech is slippery and useless, and writing is merely speech written down, why write? The self-deprecating humorous answer: "At the same time I write this Book because I want a couple of million (pounds) quickly, and as it may be the last Book written in the world it should have a very large sale" (40).

The new reasons for mistrust of history and social organization provided by the failure of the nationalist ideal reinforced his father's injunction to distrust abstraction; thus, Yeats was particularly ready to adopt this modern mode, this anti-form. His own anti-form, his reaction in *Sligo* against linear progression in narrative, while similar to his "breaking out" from line in his painting, was not simply idiosyncratic but part of that larger movement of "formal disruptions of the relation between language and reality . . . toward disintegration and reintegration"[54] which characterizes the major literary works of the Modernist period and of which Yeats was aware. The narrator of *Sligo* says that he is interested in how other writers achieve their effects: "What is this trick or lucky stroke that some few writers have? I have read three books by an old writer of sensational stories, and in each he has but one moment of move- ment, described so well that while he makes the picture before you, the chosen words which make it are ringing in your head." (19–20). The interest in both description and the sound of lan- guage which characterized the *Broadside* poems and the early *Guardian* pieces is still in evidence in this narrator's comments.

An interest in language as sound rather than as a medium of communication is well suited to Yeats's romantic imagination. The modern romantic artist's awareness of the inability of the medium to express his vision is "the beginning of silence, a literature with- out words, or to be more precise, a literature which disdains all but the most primitive and magical use of language."[55] (In their manifesto, Beckett and MacGreevy called this type of language "mantic.") One can see from *A Broadside* that the incantory use of words fascinated Yeats. His own ideal of writing was probably based on the ability to make words "ring" in the readers' heads as well as to "make the picture" before them. In *Sligo* there are fre- quent references to literature that has been read aloud. (JBY read aloud frequently to his children, judging from the testimony of Willie, Lollie, and Lily; Jack probably heard some of his readings.) There are also references in *Sligo* to recitations remembered as sound patterns.

Yeats's interest in the "thing written down" as a version of "the thing said" is typical of the Irish writers' interest in writing as recorded speech which has been noted, for example, in the case of Beckett: "And through the cold black print sounds what was rare in French fiction of 1946—the vivid rhythm of a speaking voice."[56] This influence of the primarily oral Gaelic literature on the literature written by Irishmen in other languages was transmitted primarily through the "Shanachie," the professional storyteller, who was still active in the Sligo of Yeats's day, and to whom O'Faolain compared him.[57] This influence may also account for Yeats's love for the interpolated tale, one of his characteristic narrative devices.

As prevalent in *Sligo* as they had been in the early *Guardian* pieces, these interpolated tales are often told in the remembered words of others. The narrator meets, for example, "The Man-Without-a-Shirt," who tells him tales in exchange for drinks (37–39). This tale-teller appears in *Ah Well*, demonstrating the way in which the characters Yeats created became, in his later works, "his own inseparable companions, with whom he could discuss and on whom he could rely."[58] (This tendency of characters to come alive is similar to the tendencies of characters in the later works of Flann O'Brien.)

The most thematically significant interpolated tale in *Sligo* is Johnnie Ropes's story of "the great people from whom I come." This fourteen-page story covers the migrations of the Ropes family through several continents, islands, and centuries. There is irony in this story and also reinforcement for the theme that it is futile to attempt to assert control over events and wise to accept things as they happen. The tale, an oral genealogy or history, can be read as a parody of attempts to impose pattern on events. The ideal in *Sligo* is, as Mays maintains, "an ideal of openness to things as they are, a willingness to participate in the life of the present and not to evade it through its possible causes and consequences."[59]

The tale of the Ropes family migrations also employs a significant motif, the Outsider. The Ropeses are outsiders, like Yeats himself and like the tinkers, pirates, clowns and other members of his "repertory company." The Ropeses "move on" when they run out of "something new to say." For generations they had a stock company; then they invented tennis and played that across several continents. Scorning agriculture and other settled ways, they prefer living on their wits. They prefigure the response to their situations of other artists in Yeats's work. Their nonviolent, happy, carefree existence also foreshadows that of several primitive groups James Gilfoyle encounters in *The Amaranthers*. Their rural existence takes place in a kind of utopia, the only locale left in which Yeats's values are able to survive, at least according to the nostalgic view exhibited in "The Flat Iron." Yeats creates utopias as a significant device.

The way Yeats ends the Ropes story foreshadows the ending of *Sailing, Sailing Swiftly*, a tale that also enunciates the ideal found in *Sligo*. The Ropeses met "a whole lot of dunfaced people looking out for the slit on the Sea where the Sun went down. Ropes' people were disgusted. It was so like the first old stories they used to hear that they decided to rest on their paddles and bide their time" (59). Yeats favors circular endings.

Ropes's tale is the only extended interpolated narrative in *Sligo*, but short tales are interpolated into comments on drama, journalism, horses, vanished smells, races, lion tamers, ships' stewards, trains, boxing, gambling, standing on quays, "uplifters," raconteurs, and a host of other subjects. Sometimes narrative material is reused: a story of barrow racing (44) is taken word for word from an early *Guardian* piece, "Donkey Racing," and the story of the "Shove Halfpenny" match is adapted from the *Guardian* piece and shortened.

The apparent randomness in *Sligo* is deliberate. The form reflects the theme. Mays describes Yeats's ideal as "openness to things as they are." To reflect this theme suitably, "continuity indeed is explicitly rejected, the chains of linked thinking are deliberately broken . . . and the relation of parts to one another and to the whole, or, rather the contrived absence of logical relation," both reveals Yeats's world and reflects it. There is no linear progression: "In any ordinary sense one gets no further than if one had participated in any of the non-events described."[60] Lack of linear progression and the absence of logical relation do not mean that Yeats was a talker who did not give a "rambling damn whether you listen or not," as McHugh contended. There is thematic unity in *Sligo*, and Yeats does care that a few will listen. His ideal of a select audience reflected his sense of isolation within his society, and his sense that experience, where communicable at all, can be communicated to only a few.

In addition to the book's nostalgic tone, to its familiar outsider/ traveler motif, to the theme of the necessity for openness to experience, and to the inadequacy of language motif, several new concerns are introduced in *Sligo*. A concern for the persistence and right use of memory and a concern for breaking the chain appear first in this work. The first "memory game" played in *Sligo* (98– 101) is confined to inanimate objects, and "so that they may be forgotten again" no player may write down his list of objects (98). This game is related to an earlier comment on the persistence of memory and difficulty of forgetting selectively: "About this memory business. Buy or steal your memories instead of stuffing yourself with your own. Other people's memories are easier got rid of: . . . it is very difficult to break up your thoughts and keep them apart. We are nearly all chain Thinkers" (28).

A similar game is played elsewhere in the book, a game of remembering scents, "recalled from memory's still room." The list of remembered scents is two pages long (120–22) and is accompanied by another comment on the strength of associative memory: "Any one smell suddenly brought before one's nose is able to call up the others, so that you can tick them off " (121). The narrator also issues a warning about the discipline required for remembering accurately: "But to play this game truly you must learn to read your nose purely and only. To say that black gloves smell of testaments and last Wills and pickled walnuts is only allowing the eyes to deceive the nose" (122). The "right use" of memory permits association, but not symbolic transformation. Additionally, Yeats's concept of memory permits selective forgetting when there is sufficient motivation; we do not want to be reminded of "too great a wad" of our youth. "Give us the high bright spots that flickered fast and let us forget the hours and days that dragged" (131). We break painful chains or look only at the best sections.

The speaker's description of one of these bright spots, the fair at Carricknagat, which stirred both Yeats's creative imagination and his nationalism, is typical of the use of "half-memory" in *Sligo*.

From the rock of Carricknagat you can see the sea: you can see the weather rolling about the sky and the Ox Mountains rolling to the west, and you can see the roads to Sligo and to Ballina, and you can see the rivers and the falls. At least I believe you can see all these things, and I wouldn't mind seeing them at this moment.
    (111)

This description comes from the mind's eye, not the body's eye. Yeats is not interested in being the kind of artist he deprecated in *Modern Aspects*: "the man who painted a five-dollar bill on a side-walk of New York so correctly that the passers-by were actually trying to pick it up." What he wants to give us is "the memory of a moment which once was as it appeared to the artist,"[61] or as he would have liked it to appear. If you can't see the sea and mountains and the roads to Sligo and to Ballina all from one spot, you should be able to. Whatever association brings with the actual memory belongs with it. The Ireland of the mind is as important as the Ireland of the body's eye. Sheehy, again commenting on Yeats's painting of this time, makes a statement that can be applied to *Sligo*: "It is an Impressionism of the mind rather than of the eye, an attempt, which frequently succeeds, to paint 'the light that never was on sea or land.'"[62] Sligo does often represent a world that never was, the ideal of Synge and Yeats, a world where no man was subject to another, the world he described in *Modern Aspects* as that in which a man "can stand upright on his feet and run and spring into the air."[63]

This world belonged, as Yeats noted, to the artist. The artist is one who can use memory, who, in his trance-like state, when the sensory impression of the present moment touches a nerve which brings back the past, can superimpose the two in a universal vision that he then communicates to the participating spectator or reader.

Generally, the viewer or reader cannot do this for himself. It is this visionary world that Mays, too, thinks Yeats is attempting to describe:

> Gradually it becomes clear that what Sligo and pursuits like boxing and racing represent for Yeats is a life in which a man can stand upright on his feet and run and spring into the air. Aspects of life in London and Devonshire do not exclude this, naturally, but Yeats celebrates Sligo above all other places because it emblematizes a state in which he can be without impediment true to himself. . . . A difficulty is that this is an elusive ideal not merely to state but also to embody.[64]

Critical misunderstanding of *Sligo*, and its consequent dismissal as whimsical or idiosyncratic, comes from the difficulty of embodying this ideal and from a failure to see a connection between the book's theme and its form, as well as from a failure to understand that its randomness is more apparent than real. The details selected for inclusion in *Sligo* all reinforce Yeats's concept of the ideal world of the Sligo of his mind. Yeats does not present them randomly; his narrator does not call our attention to their arrangement, since he does not wish to direct our reactions, but there is an arrangement. As rain stood for uncontrollable forces in an earlier passage, shop windows may stand for products of artful arrangement. When the narrator is speaking of shop windows, Yeats may be speaking of his own understated method in this text of arranging details: "All shop windows smile out at you in return for notice, and all are artful. A green glass bottle with a half a dozen of peggy's legs in it, three apples, and a large matchbox in a very small shop in a narrow street in a country town are all in their places from conscious instinct" (123). If the artist no longer arranges his narrative to please or make the connections for an audience, with a feeling of security about its needs and his sympathy with them, he nevertheless satisfies his own instinct for order. As his father said, Yeats's instinct for self-control regulated his sense of expansion. The reader, or viewer, if he chooses, makes the artist's shop window smile for him by his "notice." He participates in the artist's original instinct for order and takes pleasure in it.

Yeats's apparent randomness, his refusal to highlight connections obviously and thereby lessen the reader's pleasure in participation in the aesthetic transaction, has been taken for ineptitude. "The mistake of the academic purist lies in his assumption that what is obscure must be accidental."[65] The appropriateness of *Sligo's* ending to its theme is not obvious, but it is artfully arranged. The narrator speaks of his experience of reading, in the reminiscences of an American journalist, a reference to "the Irish and their determined bent for freedom." The journalist quoted the old song: "As well forbid the grasses from growing as they grow"; Yeats's narrator adds, "and so do I." This ending is not only an echo of the ending of "On The Stones," but also a fitting expression of the kind of world *Sligo* represented for Yeats, and an indication of the proper, natural, response to such a world. The ideal dweller in Yeats's literary universe accepts the natural order and does not interfere with natural processes.

Sailing, Sailing Swiftly

Sailing, Sailing Swiftly, the second of Jack Yeats's long prose works, is a more focused narrative than is *Sligo*, but it embodies the same primary theme—the necessity for acceptance of the rhythms of life. Hilary Pyle describes *Sailing* by stressing this theme:

[W]ith this inborn willingness to accept life no event can prove completely disastrous. The philosophy is projected from the first. . . . Each moment . . . is lived and accepted to the full, whether joyous or tragic. His frequent references to death or disappointment have no tinge of bitterness. Such sad occurrences are inseparably chained to life and joy. Death is complementary to Life.[66]

Sailing is closely allied in form to the literary tale, a non-realistic genre which employs a series of events rather than a plot or causal sequence. Pyle says: "The events described cover the years from 1868 up to the 1920s, and leave an impression that the tale has not ended yet."[67] In an analysis discriminating the tale from a novel or a romance, Mary McCarthy mentions a number of characteristics, many of which are common to the type of tale Yeats was writing in *Sligo*:

1. The tale deals with the marvelous, and often with the mythic, with journeys and with death.
2. The tale often relies on coincidence, or an event unlikely or even unusual on the face of it.
3. The teller of the tale doles out incidents, piling them one upon another using the "And then . . . And then" pattern.
4. Each incident of the tale has equal weight, without the increasing pressure of building toward one or more climaxes that is typical of the novel.
5. The tale can only be stopped; it does not end.
6. The tale has a flat tone.[68]

Sailing is an integral part of Yeats's literary universe, using motifs, devices, and style characteristic of the earlier work. It is the most mythic of the fictions, describing miraculous journeys like the sea voyages which form such a large part of Celtic mythology and are preserved in epics and ballads even to the nineteenth century. The interest in the sound of words noted in *A Broadside* and *Sligo* is characteristic of *Sailing*. In describing characters and scenes, the narrator exhibits both the eye and the ear for the picturesque detail characteristic of the *Guardian* pieces. In describing the first pair of travellers in this tale, for example, the narrator notes unusual speech characteristics and facial features: "He had several things he always said. He never said 'all my eye,' but always 'all my eye and Betty Martin.' He had dyed side whiskers sticking out like door knobs from each cheek, and contrary to the usual fashion in dyeing in those days, they were coloured a rich russet, and not a jetty black."[69] Yeats's tale-teller characteristically describes each character he introduces in such external physical detail, through the eye of the graphic artist sensitive to individualizing traits; the second traveller, for example, had an "old-fashioned leonine" face. However, Yeats rarely attempts internal characterization, perhaps because of his belief in the essential isolation of individuals, and the consequent difficulty of truly knowing what another thinks or feels. Unlike a novel, Yeats's mythic tale is not concerned with psychological verity and character development.

The same interest in ballads that motivated Yeats to edit *A Broadside* is evident in *Sailing*. The strongest unifying device in the narrative is a ballad:

> On the deck of Patrick Lynch's boat I sat in woeful plight,
> Through my sighing all the weary day, and weeping all the night.
> Were it not that full of sorrow from my people forth I go,
> By the blessed sun! 'tis royally I'd sing thy praise, Mayo!
> 'Tis my grief that Patrick Loughlin is not Earl of Irrul still,
> And that Brian Duff no longer rules as Lord upon the hill:
> And that Colonel Hugh MacGrady should be lying dead and low,
> And I sailing, sailing swiftly from the County of Mayo.
> (3)

The first stanza of this poem was published with his own drawing as "Patrick Lynch's Boat" in a 1907 *Queen's College Belfast Fête Supplement*; Yeats kept a copy among his private papers. The ballad's reappearance here, twenty-five years later, also shows how Yeats reused and transformed old material.

The primary importance of this ballad reference, however, is not its re-use but its thematic and formal unifying function; the last line is used as the book's title and echoed at climactic points in the tale. It functions as one of those repeated bits of detail with which Yeats brought his earlier short narratives full circle. The line's meaning is also transformed, in a way characteristic of the universalizing tendency of his mature style. As the song of the political exile, full of nostalgia for better days and grief at the defeat of his race and the necessity of flight, the ballad could have appeared in *A Broadside*. But as the line is treated in *Sailing*, it also has universal significance: we are all exiles in the world, sailing swiftly from home and security, from birth to death.

The primary theme of this tale is the importance of acceptance and of immersing oneself in the rhythms of life. As a myth, *Sailing* is concerned with life and death; its form, like that of *Sligo*, is appropriate to its theme. In the tale, as Yeats writes it, events appear isolated and of equal weight, with no apparent causal connection between them. As in a myth, the deaths in *Sailing* often appear to be random, caused by unforeseeable accidents. Yeats believed that to properly appreciate life we must accept this randomness, must resist the temptation to believe that we can control forces larger than ourselves. In this tale, the theme is more successfully embodied than it had been in *Sligo*, since a unified narrative illustrates it. *Sailing* is unified first by the allusions to the ballad and second by the controlling metaphor of the sea journey introduced in the repeated ballad refrain; the "sea" represents the larger life in which we all participate.

The journey motif dominates this tale. At its opening, two characters who have met at a horse fair are in a railway carriage; their journey is only one of many significant journeys in this narrative. They, like the protagonists in many of Yeats's narratives and dramas, are frequent travellers. The significant journey alluded to in the ballad begins in Mayo, a place of significance in Yeats's imagination.

In this narrative, county Mayo represents, as did county Sligo in the earlier narrative, the ideal world: the world where no man is subject to another, where a man can stand upright on his feet and run and spring into the air. Ireland is, as it was in *Modern Aspects*, the land of the artist where a man can be natural and be true to himself, because he has fewer cities and false traditions to come between himself and nature. Ireland is, as it was in *A Broadside*, the land of the fierce dark men of the West and the land of gaiety and youth.

The familiar nationalist contrast between English decadence and Irish natural virtue is set forth in further descriptions of the protagonists, two Irish and English "types" respectively named Thady O'Malley and Jasper Newbigging. The consequent English fascination with Irishmen as representatives of the life-force is also immediately set up. When the Irishman (who bears the same surname as Grace O'Malley, the pirate queen known in *A Broadside* as Grannuaile) opens his eyes:

They delighted his companion opposite, for the eyes were to him the footlights to the drama that, to him, was built into the Irishman. . . .

Both the men were in the early forties, but the Englishman thought himself an elderly man, and that was why he enjoyed gazing at Thady O'Malley, who represented to him what a man in the early forties might look like, if he was very lucky, and if he had Irish sparks for eyes, and a disposition so gaily virile that only, it appeared, for a moment as the sun sank low, could anything like melancholy touch you if you were such a one.
(4–5)

After establishing that this Irishman was not atypical, at least of an earlier era—"John Thadeus O'Malley, in his own Mayo, did not pass for any wonder for mercuriality. But perhaps all the sons of Mayo had gay hearts then"—the narrator puts forth a reason for this English attitude toward Irishmen: "[O]r perhaps it was that anyone who knew him in England spoke of him as Thady, which suggested the Broth of a Boy" (5). As the Black Power movement in the 1960s affirmed, to use a diminutive, to think of another man as a "boy," is a dismissive social transaction.

The complications set up by this type of transaction between two cultures are multiple. The person dismissed is deprived of a ruling role in society, society as it is dominated by the conditions and concerns necessary for civilization. These may be characterized as "Apollonian" concerns. The dismissed one then becomes, in the eye of the dismisser, a "Dionysian" force, essentially anarchic. As Freud tells us in *Civilization and Its Discontents*, society is based on a repression of individual gratification. The representative of the dominant culture, dominant because of his success in repression and his preoccupation with Apollonian concerns, nevertheless envies the liveliness and naturalness of the dominated one, at the same time that he recognizes the appropriateness of the other's failure to "get ahead." In the terms of the Irish-English situation, the relation is connected to the nationalist preoccupation with the outsider, which for Yeats was a primary motif. Brian O'Doherty, in an essay written for the Yeats centenary collection, analyzes the transaction:

[T]his legend of the Irishman as romantic outsider is an English formulation. It is born of these lethal reciprocities we now understand better than we did— the bourgeois society exiles its subversive longing in the subject race which it then indulges between abrupt and savage repression. In this sense the romantic Irishman represents the Englishman's dream. . . .

So the only way the stereotype could be dignified was by making heroes of those of no fixed abode (still an address of honour in small Irish courts) those vagrants in motion as much across the country's imaginative as [its] physical landscape. Jack Yeats (and Synge—the two bear a comparison . . .) infuses the alien stereotype with national pride. . . . The way in which he did it is typical of the paradoxical transactions between master and servant . . . he made it . . . heroic. In a transcendent gesture he flung back that image to the master—who is now revealed as cloddish, dull and venal.[70]

This outsider, as Yeats portrays him, functions cheerfully on the fringes of civilization, inviting both manipulation and envy. Mark Trimbo in *The Careless Flower* is such an Irishman, and Thady is such an Irishman in *Sailing*. Jasper reacts to him in a predictable way. Behind Thady are all the outsiders Yeats featured in *A Broadside* and the Ropeses in *Sligo*; he prefigures the heroes or antiheroes of the later narratives. Both familial and nationalist influences are at work here. One must remember in this context the very graphic way in which these societal conflicts, even within Irish society, were presented to the young Yeats in the Pollexfen envy/disapproval of his artist father, John Butler Yeats, with his social status and brilliance but inability to "get ahead." JBY, a prototypical Irish landlord who extolled "natural" values to his sons, was equally scathing in his disdain for Pollexfen commercial values which he saw as a product of Irish capitulation to English industrial and commercial ways.

The use of the outsider motif, the relation between the English and Irish, and the attitude toward Irishmen given in *Sailing* are characteristic of Yeats. The relation set up here between Thady and Jasper (who are not named until they have been set up as types and carefully described) foreshadows the relation between Thady's son Larry and Edward Tarleton in the next generation; it is important to the theme as well as to the narrative. Yeats continues his description of their relation:

[F]or he [Jasper] was always at his ease, physically, at any rate, with his Irish friend. In the queer little world of the spirit which had little spirit fingers which sometimes pinched the little sinews round his heart, he was not quite so much at his ease. But anyway, Thady was the Broth of such a Boy as he himself might have been, had another star passed over him than the one which had appropriated him.
   (5)

Jasper's ethnic stories turned on "the solid sense of the Englishmen, the carefulness of the Scot, and the wit, courage, and general valiance of the Irish" (6). Thady is Jasper's alter-ego and hero who seems to him to belong to some other world: "So wildly did he combine in his speech and actions, intelligence, fatalistic courage, and careless good nature, which was symbolized by a full laughing mouth of teeth, which turned, in one shining moment, into a trap that bit to the bone, and spat out the piece" (7). This description of an Irishman recalls the Ernest Rhys poem "In the Train: Portrait of a Navvy" from the October 1908 *Broadside*, with its description of "the cave-man's jaw to make you fear / The half-burnt feast that should employ / Those teeth of iron and ivory / Cracking a bone like biscuit there." Jasper loved Thady not simply because he prevented him from being swindled out of 450 pounds, but because of his primitive qualities, and because he "could handle other men." Jasper "entwined his friendship about the shaft of the pillar, that was to him the character of Thady" (8).

   Jasper finds his friend a wife, in an adventure that has mythic overtones, and the newly married couple, Thady and Annette, leave on the book's second significant journey, their wedding trip to London. The sailing metaphor is continued: "They sailed about, the handsome pair" (36). They take journeys by water and by horse, with Thady's brogue thrilling exiled waiters and pleasing Annette, to whom he sings "Sailing, Sailing Swiftly." A typical Yeats traveller, Thady never grows tired of the road (39), and, after returning from his wedding journey, he travels west, accompanied by Jasper, to prepare a home for his bride. This symbolic journey of the two friends is brought to a ritual end at Chester, where their first train journey together began, by their accidental death; a run-away engine cuts out of the train the carriage in which they sit (42).

Chance and randomness are present in a Yeatsean universe, but they are not the only forces. There is also Providence. Randomness in the form of a runaway engine may have ended the trip, but Providence ["It was written on some scroll"] determines that the pregnant Annette should be on the platform when the bodies are returned. Providence, in the form of "The Captain" who was present at her mythic meeting with Thady, then intervenes to save her from death: "She was away and off her balance, falling, falling, between two coaches and under the wheels, but the Captain's thin elasticity had whirled him round to the other side of her . . ." (44). (Note the repeated participle "falling" to echo the keynote's repeated participle "sailing.") Thady's providentially preserved child is ready for his mythic prenatal journey, which begins in the second section of the tale.

The Yeats form of tale requires a listing of events in orderly series; the teller doles out the incidents, piling them one upon another according to the pattern "And then . . . And then," giving equal weight to each. In the second section, Yeats gives us more of these equally emphasized events and journeys. Annette travels "across the water" to Ireland. She too sings the theme ballad, or two significant lines of it: "Through my sighing all the weary day, and weeping all the night, And I sailing, sailing swiftly" (51), as she goes on her own journey to, not from, Mayo.

The mythic resonances of Annette's journey continue. In Mayo she is instructed by Thady's two uncles, who bear an occupational similarity to Yeats's own Middleton and Pollexfen uncles. Patrick, representing Christian Ireland, blesses the new life she carries: "The blessing of God on Thady's son" (55). Daniel, whose name implies the prophet of an older civilization, instructs her in the ancient pagan wisdom which, according to the nationalist aesthetic, had taken refuge in the West. He tells her to listen to the ancient voice of the curlew, who may be "the very curlew himself" that sang "when first Diarmait and Grania walked these roads" (57). Both of these lessons are learned, significantly, beside the sea, and are presumably intended as prenatal instruction for Thady's heir. As the ancient Celtic society was matriarchal, with inheritance through the mother, it is appropriate that Annette (Mrs. Dunaven-O'Malley) return to the source of her own heritage before the birth of her child. After having heard the ancient curlew's "querulous, imperative cry," intuitively wise Annette says: "There is no answer" (57). (Although most women in Yeats's literary universe are intuitively wise, male protagonists, like James Gilfoyle in *The Amaranthers*, come to this wisdom only at the end of their quest.) Annette is brought home from the sea "by a round," that matriarchal circular movement beloved of the Celts and favored by Yeats. At the uncles' home she is further instructed by a solicitor who, like Yeats himself, loves life and loves the sound of words, who would "rumble to himself, rolling, sounding phrases" (58). An American visitor sings two songs about the relentless march of the seasons. Americans are often intuitively wise in Yeats's universe; in *A Broadside*, they are characterized as being in touch with nature. Those Irishmen who emigrated to America represented, in the nationalist myth, the best of Irish wisdom, gone one stage farther west than the coast where many of the true Gaels were banished. Having been fully instructed in Yeats's primary theme—the necessity for harmony with nature and its God, for acceptance of (not resistance to) the rhythms of the universe—Annette sails back to England to give birth to her child. This sailing ends section two of the tale.

In section three a birth and more deaths occur, all part of the rhythms of life. Thady's son is born and then his guardian uncles die within the year. The birth and deaths interlock, illustrating what Pyle calls Yeats's "conception of a continuous existence of successively changing people where life and death interlock."[71]

The fatherless Larry has a series of male mentors to function as Thady's uncles functioned for him in the previous generation. These mentors serve as vehicles for introducing other familiar themes. The first mentor is his mother's former employer, Mr. Oldbain, a watercolor and landscape artist by avocation, whose own son dies in the Orient (where, incidentally, "the ingenuous west still hoped to grab wealth out of the sky, which sky belonged to a time before pity" [67]—Yeats saw the West, or its entrepreneurial branch at least, as not having learned to accept the rhythms of the universe). Oldbain is a good mentor, "one of those rare discoverers who let others discover as they will" (70). Perhaps he is based on Grandfather Pollexfen, who, according to JBY, gave Jack the education fit for a genius by letting him expand naturally. Larry discovers with Oldbain that an artist must respect the limitations of the medium for expressing artistic vision, another favorite theme of Yeats, one related to the mistrust of language: "Neither Oldbain nor his pupil, if pupil he could be called, painted within measurable distances of their imagination. So their streaky wipes and nervous dabs of colour were always following will-o'-the-wisps of tiny shining splendour" (70).

Under Oldbain's tutelage, Larry learns lessons related to the primary theme: he learns to swim (to survive in the flow of life forces) and to ride horses (animals associated with the sea god). These gains in knowledge are related to the primary theme, the importance of remaining in sympathy with natural forces. In this most mythic of Yeats's narratives, Oldbain (whose name may derive from the French for bath—"bain") has some traces of the Celtic sea god, Mannanaan Mac Lir; his daughters, for example, are prodigious swimmers. They swim every day, and once they swam so far "that they might have been away to Heligoland after the sea captain who dwelt there. He that had the tusk and knew all about the Sun O King, the Great Sun, round and round in a fiery ring" (73). The sun king, Lugh, and the circle Yeats conflates with his name are other important elements in Celtic mythology and associate "Oldbain" with favorable natural forces, as one might expect of an artist in Yeats's literary universe.

Larry's next mentor, Tarleton, illustrates the primary theme negatively; he is not in tune with natural forces. Although Mays sees Tarleton as one of the inheritors of Thady's spirit of joy,[72] he can be seen as life-denying in that he does not make the commitment to living fully that Thady represents. Unlike Thady, who also at first protests busyness when Jasper suggests marriage but then changes his mind, Tarleton continues to be "too busy" when called to marriage and reproduction, and he is not at home in the elements. One generation closer than his predecessor Jasper to the all-consuming dedication to Pollexfen values Yeats saw as coming to dominate the world, Tarleton prevents Larry both from union with his "fated" love and from succeeding as an artist. When introduced, Tarleton seems to represent the good side of English urbanity—he lives in "St. Paul's Churchyard, London," and speaks with "sweet dignity"— but his urbanity is not, finally, a positive quality, since he is not at home in nature. When he is invited to swim, for example, instead of springing off the board, as Larry does, he is timid: "[T]ender-of-toes, creeping along, with a hand always ready to catch an upstanding rock." He climbs down a ladder and swims from that to the manmade iron support of the diving plank: "It was all done with scrambling strokes from his arms, and a kind of digging run with his legs, and when he reached the iron upright he had to hang on for a full minute to regain his control of the *machinery of the sea propulsion* [emphasis mine] before he launched away on the return journey" (84). Having made "the last fearful voyage," the representative of a mechanistic industrial society requires help from his protégé to get back up the ladder.

Like the decadent culture he represents, Tarleton, an Apollonian not Dionysian force, is afraid of life. He exhibits negative attitudes to women. Like Jasper, he avoided marriage, although "there were two women already who thought themselves rather ensconced in his life" (89). He is as afraid of Annette as of the sea, and feels safe only where no commitment is called for, visiting the O'Malleys only when Annette will not be alone. Yeats disapproved of this life-denying attitude toward women; espousing it prevents Larry from achieving happiness. He misses the love of his life by being too cautious. At a crucial juncture in the relation, Larry and the young woman are journeying by water from London to the nearest approximation of country—to Richmond Park and Greenwich— when they meet "Uncle Ned" Tarleton. Perhaps, having an Anglicized mother and being less lively and less in tune with the vital force than his fully Irish father, Larry would not have been courageous and good natured enough to have seized his opportunity in any event, but Tarleton's intervention is not helpful. The vivacious woman goes off to America with a more adventurous and life-affirming craftsman. Knowing Yeats's positive feelings about

America, the land of opportunity, we can assume her move was the proper one. Tarleton illustrates, again negatively, the secondary theme carried over from *A Broadside*: the need to retain artistic authenticity and balance. He, like the culture he represents, is not authentic. While he dresses elegantly, his coat is made of a feigned Irish frieze, "O'Foolem." There are indications other than his coat that Tarleton's culture may be a veneer. He presumes to tell the Oldbain sisters, natural swimmers of heroic stature, how all the greatest water feats were done, yet he can barely swim. His knowledge of literature is also superficial: "Oldbain talked of the books he had read, and Tarleton, where his own knowledge was slight, filled in the space with an: 'Ah, Dickens for the engravings. Ah, Scott for the Highland fling'" (88). His hypocrisy and artificiality make him a less desirable mentor than Oldbain, and prove damaging to Larry, personally and artistically.

Tarleton's mentorship introduces a theme from *Modern Aspects*, the difficulty an artist will experience trying to maintain authenticity while living in a city. Yeats also thought artists should stay out of cities: "But the artist [working in the city] will be bothered with many pitfalls, he is too often tempted to see things in the form that others have seen them and not with his own fresh eye" (7). He might have theorized, if he were familiar with these terms, that the artist would lose his Dionysian/Yeatsean orientation and take on an Apollonian/Pollexfen preference for civilizing repressions. The rural-urban controversy goes back to the nationalist "peasant ideal" and runs through Yeats's drama and fiction. The contrast of Pollexfen and Yeatsean values also enters into the tale of Larry's generation. Tarleton, with his Apollonian/Pollexfen values, knows how to "get ahead" and teaches Larry. He gets Larry rooms in London and a job designing furniture, encouraging Larry to imitate other works of art, in this case carvings of marine horses. Yeats believed that an artist should know the work of other artists and should work hard to learn his technique but, like his father before him, had harsh words, in *Modern Aspects*, for those who merely imitate others or do what is conventional and expected.

Part of what Yeats thought the artist must do to keep the "conduit'" to natural impulse open was to avoid convention in composition: "An artist should avoid convention, even if the conventions are of his own invention. But lazy people like the artist to be conventional because it saves trouble" (10). If one imitates models one is adopting the conventions. But Yeats's most explicit statement against what Tarleton is advising is his condemnation of compromise: "Beauty is truth and a just balance. But not a compromise; the artist compromises when he refuses to paint what he himself has seen, but paints what he thinks someone else would like him to have seen" (10–11). Partly as a result of Tarleton's influence, Larry compromises artistically; he stays in the city, a place where it is difficult for an artist to become authentic, and designs furniture which is "what someone else would like him to have seen." By doing so, by JBY's standards which his son seems to have internalized, Larry forfeits the title "artist" and becomes a "craftsman." He also makes a great deal of money, a sure sign for JBY that he is not authentic.

In the portion of the tale describing Larry's adventures, as in his father's, there are mythic journeys and providential encounters. At one point he is sent on a journey west, where he meets an enigmatic figure, who may represent biblical wisdom, "a small doubled-up old man [who] was lighting his pipe, strong but sweet, like the honey in the lion's carcass" (121). This old man wishes Larry luck, and Larry replies with the title of a later Yeats narrative, "And to you also" (122). By the type of coincidence acceptable in a tale, this old man was "The Captain" who had been present when Larry's parents met and who had saved his life by saving his pregnant mother from falling under the train. This coincidence is, in a way characteristic of the tale, an unlikely one.

The tale continues in section five with the "flatness of tone" also characteristic. The tale-teller flatly tells the incidents of Larry's rise. A good Apollonian, he gets a rise in salary, invests wisely, and ultimately marries, if not the boss's daughter, his niece. Larry's rise continues, and so does the piling up of events in the tale. Both he and Tarleton become prosperous enough to move to the suburbs. "And some time passed along, or slithered along—the policeman in the rubber boots" (138). His wife's uncle dies; he has two children: birth and death. The war forces the furniture factory to make munitions; and money rolls in: "The war went on. The war was over" (143).

Ultimately, in line with the primary theme of the tale, Larry's loss of his connection with nature, coupled with another unlikely coincidence, causes his death. Successful in Apollonian concerns, having sold out his artistic talent, Larry has lost contact with Dionysian forces and can no longer swim: "perhaps a little over-tired and weighted with an overcoat," symbol of his prosperity by an extension of the clothing symbolism of this tale. He has to be held up "limp and unhelping," after a fall into the sea (155). He can no longer survive in the natural arena Oldbain had helped him to be at home in. As he is carried on a stretcher to a nearby hotel, a bystander sings about a sailing trip:

> And when I sailed away,
> Not a blessed one was there to say,
> "Good-bye, old son, good-bye."
> And when I sailed away,
> Hell's blast the one was there to say,
> "Good-bye, old son, good-bye."
> (157)

In continuation of the tale's flat tone, the narrator says of the singing bystander: "He wouldn't have sung if he'd known the contents of the stretcher, or perhaps he would have, who knows" (157). Death is a part of life and must be accepted. To those who are in harmony with the universe, a desirable state in Yeats's opinion, death is not an extraordinary event, but a phase of the cycle. The narrator, predictably, does not direct the reader's response by pointing out the connection between the song and the theme of sailing, sailing swiftly. The reader is left to complete the aesthetic transaction. "Now you tell me what it means," Yeats often said to a viewer of one of his paintings, after telling him a story about it.

Although the death of this protagonist might be the end of a novelistic sequence of events, it is not the end of this series. Continuing the mythic overtones of this tale, Tarleton, returning from

Larry's funeral, experiences an apparent death and resurrection. He is rescued by a blacksmith-turned-car-mechanic, who still has the forger's ritual knowledge, though his fire is an acetylene torch. After drinking an elixir the blacksmith offers, Tarleton rises and utters a thematic pronouncement:

> To-day . . . you have done great work; you have plucked me as a brand from the burning, . . . one down t'other come up . . . Your elixir could lick creation; what is it but creation itself? You see before you a Man who feels . . . that he is the Phoenix, not Phoenix A., B. or C., but the first Phoenix. The stock Phoenix. The Phoenix from which all Phoenix came . . . But from my heart I thank you. Now, farewell.
>
>   (166–7)

By drinking the elixir, part of the force that creates, Tarleton renews his life. The phoenix rises. Life goes on. The brand plucked from the burning is a metaphor Yeats uses again in *The Charmed Life* for a miraculous rescue from almost certain death.

The book ends with a coincidence involving the next generation of O'Malleys. Returned to the home of "The Squire," Tarleton notices that his host is reading a book called *By Celia's Arbour*. He comments "That's a strange thing. Poor Larry's left a daughter called Celia" (170). Another generation goes on. This last instance of randomness ends the chain of events in the tale. One novel would have ended with Larry's death, culminating one thematic thrust as Larry sailed swiftly to his death, with not a one to say good-bye. A novel with a different thematic thrust would have ended with Tarleton rising like the phoenix from his apparent death, representing the triumph of society over the failed artist. The tale, however, as Yeats used it does not employ a linear progression toward one or more climaxes as does the novel; his tale is endless and leaves the impression that the series is not ended.

The close of the tale is not artless, however. As he often did in the short narratives, Yeats comes full circle. He ends as he began, with one member of a male pair watching the other sleep. This time instead of Jasper watching Thady sleep in a railway carriage, the Squire watches Tarleton. The Squire introduced at the end, as is often the case with Yeats, appears in a later narrative, *And To You Also*. As a further element of closure in *Sailing,* the Squire "closes his book" and the last thing Yeats shows on the page is a sketch of a closed book beneath a reading lamp. This device of metafiction calls the reader's attention to the process of reading fiction, as characters in Yeats's metatheatre call to the viewer's attention the process of watching a play.

Critical reaction to *Sailing, Sailing Swiftly* has been meager and has noted neither the tale's mythic overtones nor its cyclic structure. These evidences of careful craftsmanship are important aspects of Yeats's literary universe. The book is also important as a clear illustration of Yeats's primary theme, the necessity for acceptance of the rhythms of the universe, and of his secondary themes: the aesthetic counsel that the artist must maintain his authenticity and the social counsel that man must not get too far from nature.

The Amaranthers

The thematic continuity of Jack Yeats's longer narratives is strong in the narratives of the 1930s: *Sligo* (1930), *Sailing, Sailing Swiftly* (1933), *The Amaranthers* (1936), and *The Charmed Life* (1938). The actions of the last three fictions involve a quest for an ideal way of life and those of the last two involve, additionally, a quest for balance between an imaginatively projected world and the real world. In all these narratives Yeats is trying to balance the Pollexfen against the Yeatsean way of life projected for him by his father. His disillusion with the failure of the nationalist ideal made him cautious about the possibility of realizing any ideal. Yet he believed that the artist must sustain his ideal world, if only in his mind; must try to express it; and must not "sell out" to the Pollexfen "get ahead" values. The artist must function in both the Antaean and Narcissistic worlds, like the two clowns tumbling in the *Broadside* drawing, one giving support to the other.

Although he continues and develops the themes of *Sailing* (and of *Sligo* as well) in *The Amaranthers*, in the latter, Yeats uses a more complex narrative structure. The relatively straightforward mythic tale of *Sailing* is developed in *Amaranthers* into what might be called a "fabulation."[73] Yeats is aware that reality cannot be recorded, that language and experience are discrete phenomena, and that language often fails to express experience, yet he wants to offer models showing the consequences of human action. Yeats was a writer of the Modernist temper for whom realism in fiction no longer offered an adequate mode. Although Yeats would not have known the term, an understanding of the term fabulation illuminates *The Amaranthers*.

Several characteristics of the fabulation are useful in elucidating this work, two formal and one thematic. Formally, *Amaranthers* exhibits the aesthetic dimension of fiction characteristic of the romance genre in general and of the fabulation in particular. The fabulator delights, for example, in creating a tale within a tale, in designing a fiction, in a way the novelist does not. Robert Scholes says of the form he calls fabulation: "With its wheels within wheels, rhythms and counter-points, this shape is partly to be admired for its own sake. A sense of pleasure in form is one characteristic of fabulation ... which will serve in part to distinguish the art of the fabulator from the work of the novelist or the satirist. Of all narrative forms, fabulation puts the highest premium on art. . . ."[74] In this fiction, Yeats creates a complex aesthetic design with two narrative strands; the first focuses on the "Amaranthers" and their "escape" to the island of the fugitives, and the second focuses on James Gilfoyle and his quest for unification of two worlds. These two narrative strands are brought together at the end of the work, when James rescues the Amaranthers, physically and spiritually. This form of double interlocking narrative shows both Yeats's delight in design and his growing confidence in his writing technique.

A second formal characteristic of the "fabulation" which applies to *Amaranthers* is its complex relation to known reality; while its world is often radically discontinuous from the one we know, the laws of its universe are not totally unfamiliar. Yeats's graphic art also remained within the bounds of the representational (as opposed to the abstract), no matter how expressionistic it became. While the utopias in this narrative are more complex than those of *Sligo*—the island of the fugitives, the jungle cities, and the Great Man's sound stage are among the utopias found in *Amaranthers*—few are completely outside the possibility of known reality. Mays describes its island utopia: "an offshore island paradise, a Hybrazil compounded of elements of a Mayo village, a Hollywood film-lot, tropical South America, the Caribbean and the South Seas, and Coney Islands on either side of the Atlantic"[75]—a unique blend, like the blends in his visionary paintings, but one in which each element is grounded in the known world. In keeping with his own tenets, Yeats does not abandon the known world in favor of the presentation of the visionary. He had been exploring the optimal relation of the visionary and the known since editing *A Broadside*.

Thematically, *Amaranthers* exhibits a third characteristic of the fabulation. Fabulators accept their "inability to reach all the way to the real, but aim at telling such truths as fiction may legitimately tell in ways which are appropriately fictional."[76] Yeats was trying to tell a truth about the existential situation in *Amaranthers*. Through James's quest and the Amaranthers' escape, Yeats was trying to embody in "appropriately fictional" ways both his primary theme, that acceptance of "unarrangeable reality" (to borrow WB's term for *The Charmed Life*), of chance and randomness, is necessary for survival, and his secondary theme, that the artist must maintain authenticity and balance.

It is clear that Yeats is exploring both themes in *Amaranthers*. Mays sees, at the center of the island to which the Amaranthers flee, the utopia of the imaginative artist:

[T]he fugitive Amaranthers play with their model boats and trains and the whole populace meets for a theatrical event—"beings from happy dreamland" (*Am* 102). It is a world of imagination in which time and space and getting and spending are left behind; set apart and protected by quicksands and tides, it makes up "a tranquil picture more tranquil than the reality" (*Am* 40).[77]

A utopian world, the Amaranthers' island also serves as an indirect social criticism of the unreal, doomed island of the Anglo-Irish Ascendancy in the 1920s. Although its book jacket calls *Amaranthers* a "satirical fantasy about an island which is sometimes recognisable as Ireland seen through the laughing yet sympathetic eyes of Mr.

Yeats," it is neither a satire nor an allegory in the strict sense. Yeats offers, through his fictional model of reality in *Amaranthers*, a solution to the problems of the Anglo-Irish that he himself adopted: accept the end of the Ascendancy world, recognize the social conditions that made its end necessary, and survive by acceptance of the outside situation and by imaginative self-nurturing through the inward vision. As the narrator had advocated in *Sligo* that one quit struggling against the rain, so, through the fabulation *Amaranthers*, Yeats advocates acceptance of natural and social forces. However, like the two tumblers of *A Broadside* who support each other, one must keep a balance between both worlds, the outer and the inner.

The world of *Amaranthers* is like the Sligo of Yeats's mind, a world where imaginative beings are free to run and spring into the air. Its most visionary aspects—the Amaranthers' club and James's railway car—illustrate one of Yeats's secondary themes, that the artist must nurture and be true to his private vision, while maintaining an awareness of what is going on outside. The interpretive crux of this fabulation, the voyage by water undertaken by James and his guide "O" (whose name was shortened from it original form "Ohoh") is more directly related to Yeats's primary theme: the need for acceptance of forces outside of one's control. The river in *Amaranthers* is a metaphor for life, as was the river in *Sailing*, but James's experience of it has a double focus, making it more complex than the metaphor in the earlier work:

A river was like life—it would never do anyone any harm. That was what James thought in his philosophic days. . . . Now he looked back at "O" very busy with his steering-oar; busy all the time even when the bow-man had given no warning cry, and when all was serene on the dimpling surface so brown and comely. As he looked, James observed with his wisest eye that the steersman was steering for the sake of steering, and he tried to make this fact fit into his deep old thought of the Harmless River of Life. But the old thoughts had lost their savour, and James was well content watching for a second macaw to fly across the river.[78]

Unlike Thady or Larry, the protagonists in *Sailing* who float along, apparently without self-analysis, James becomes reflective in the course of the narrative and then transcends abstract thought to become wise. Unlike the characters in a tale, James learns and then behaves differently, providing a model for the consequences of human action. As soon as chance had provided the means of sustaining economic life and, by eliminating the necessity of preoccupation with earning a living, had enabled him to enter the speculative life, James had become a "philosopher." (Yeats's socialist emphasis on the primacy of providing for economic needs persists.) Poorly educated, but interested in abstract thought, James had set up idiosyncratic systems: "From philosophy to explanations of the universe. Number Seven, four horses with two passengers and one man driving. Symbolism! Splendid!" (130). Vaguely aware that nature might offer an answer to his questions, he takes a walking tour, thinking that "on this tour some new idea for a key to unlock the sideboard tantalus of Whither and Why-so would be won. But nothing came his way except the smell of fresh grown hedges, and many-flavoured beers, and an affectionate respect for the air he breathed" (134). Gaining experience and tolerance are preferable in Yeats's literary universe to finding abstract answers to the questions "Whither and Why-so." Smells and tastes and all sensory experience give rise to joy and an affectionate tolerance for whatever life brings. The desirability of this abandoning of abstract thought and transcendence of "systems" is part of Yeats's primary theme.

James does not at first know where to look for joy, although his instincts are good. An exiled Irishman in England, as Yeats himself was for many years, James longs for O'Connell Street Bridge, where he experienced his first transcendent moment. James goes back to the bridge and has an experience similar to one described in *Sligo*. In romantic fashion, he experiences union with the universal forces through nature. In Yeats's narratives the enlightening aspect of nature is often a river. The use of this metaphor recalls Yeats's saying, related by his father, that he wished he had spent even more time looking over the bridge in Sligo town into the river:

> He stood and looked up the river, the same sun time
> as when he first stood there, and he felt
> there, fanned out within the reach of a long arm,
> stood all the round towers, the green hills, the monuments,

> the little lakes, the little colleens by the lakes, the sea bays,
> the sea islands, the lake islands, the fiddles, the dancing floors,
> the shamrocks of the field, the leaping salmon in the rivers.
> A warm sea of fancies loved, lapped so close
> that he could dabble the fingers of the hands of his long arms
> in the little waves breaking among the infant sedges.
> (134–35)

This catalogue represents all that Yeats loved about Ireland; his ideal world is the Mayo of *Sailing*, or the Sligo of his mind. This world is discontinuous from the world as we know it. The elements are recognizable, but, as in *Sligo*, the blend is not literally possible.

James does not immediately seek the world within, the "heaving place of his own heart," his own private vision; he "wavered." Like Larry, who imitated models and saw what others wished him to see, James turns outward at first and seeks fulfillment in the dreams of others by going into a cinema. James learns, as Larry did not, to seek artistic authenticity in the private, incommunicable vision, which is different for each man. However, he must learn the lesson of Yeats's primary theme—to give up "thought," and belief in controlling systems and to accept immersion in the larger forces of the universe— before he can learn the second lesson—to preserve and be true to his own vision, while maintaining balance.

At this point in the narrative James is still preoccupied with getting and spending. He has a plan "that would settle his carnal world for ever," "the universal lay-out" (135). Halfway through the book (Yeats's craftsmanship is careful), James is sentenced to a quest of discovery and expiation connected with the fabulation's primary and secondary themes. Because of his timidity in embracing life and his failure to be true to his own vision, he must go on journeys. Finally, he has an epiphany on the river (described above), gives up his "deep old thought," accepts his lack of control, responds to the natural forces, and finds joy in acceptance of harmony perceived through nature. As soon as he surrenders the illusion of control, and recognizes the folly of "steering for the sake of steering," he is ready for the second quest. He learns to balance between the two worlds, and recognizes the necessity for preserving the imaginative life and seeking within himself the authentic, unique vision.

Like Larry in *Sailing,* James has several mentors on his voyages, and encounters some men who give negative examples. Unlike Larry, however, he is able to tell the good examples from the bad ones. One of the good mentors is his landlady's husband, "a man able to put happenings in their place and use them" who helps James learn to do the same. Accepting what happens is part of the ideal, opposed to steering for the sake of steering. One must accept the inability to control "happenings" in this world; one must not, however, entirely cease to act or become incapable of acting. To give up steering is not to give up acting.

A negative example in the narrative is a given by a steward on one of James's voyages who is given a cigar holder, "a horse's head with a magnificent crest and mane." James observes that the steward is unable to act to obtain this cigar holder: "He longed for this holder, but if he had lived to retire on a thousand a year, a house, and a motor-car, he would not have bought it for himself, he knew that" (138). James had been similarly unable to act on his own instinct, so this is an important lesson for him. As do most of the Irish men in Yeats's work, James has suffered a kind of Joycean paralysis.

On the same voyage, a second negative example influences him to give up philosophy. He had already partially retired from philosophy "on that shock day when his income came to an end" (140). (Yeats knew, as JBY did not, that you must have a secure income to afford philosophy.) Learning to give up systems and abstract thought is part of the prior learning necessary to James's acceptance of natural forces. James is confirmed in his decision to give up philosophy by recognizing the foolishness of a scheme based on an abstract speculation on ethics. The "philosopher" explains an almost Swiftean scheme for making people happy. (Yeats, like Jonathan Swift, had little faith in abstract systems.) Like a projector in Laputa, this empirical philosopher will measure "perfectly happy" men, average the measurements, and, having built molds of a semi-elastic material, will set up "Happy Clinics." In these clinics people will be placed in the molds until they become models of happiness and then released to radiate their happiness, producing a world of happy men. (Unlike *Sligo*, where comments occur anywhere in the book, following the logic of association, and are addressed directly to the reader, philosophical speculations in *Amaranthers* are restricted to suitable situations in the narrative, are put in the mouths of suitable characters, and are set up for James's instruction. The fabulation is an aesthetically designed form.)

A second good mentor influences James to accept the essentially private nature of human experience; having given up philosophy, he learns to give up reliance on human intellectual companionship, as well, and to accept the reality of solitude. He is advised by a true mentor that all men are essentially isolated, a Modernist attitude prevalent in Yeats's work. The solitude experienced is not an anguished one. If Yeats is Modernist, and even existential, in his sense of man's isolation, the knowledge does not cause him pain. His narratives, as Pilling notes, are "full of people suddenly encountering one another, exchanging anecdotes and parting again" (as James and his mentors will part), "but the fact that relationships do not endure is not something that reduces Yeats to helpless anguish, since he knows that man is a resourceful animal and that the next person will have a story to tell."[79]

The next stage in James's voyage of discovery takes place when he is forced to internalize the knowledge that he is isolated from other men. The people in a village he travels to seek solitude and isolation. The inhabitants of this utopia refuse to pay taxes, so that no tax-funded roads will be built into their village. The isolated refuges from urban industrialism are few, and Yeats, with his hatred of industrial society, approves of maintaining them. After a sojourn in this village, where he learns personally the difficulties of communicating with another, James, ever the traveller, takes the trip by water which marks his acceptance of isolation and lack of control and then experiences the "epiphany" which is the crux of the fabulation.

His quest continues, and James is assisted by his last mentor, Pensamiento, who reinforces for the reader the perception that human experience is incommunicable. This man had "outlooks and values which were different from his companions, which was very natural for he had had an experience which no man among his friends had ever been through" (185). This wise man had once fallen off a horse and, having accepted the limits of human control, had, like James, been granted a mystic experience. The description of his experience reinforces Yeats's primary theme. Pensamiento, too, learned on his journey to accept union with nature, to "feel completely steady, undefiant as the rocks which broke up the little brown waves which quivered about them. He had a part with earth, air, and water, busy on holidays of their own invention" (187).

Having learned his own crucial lesson, James is prepared for the formal end of his quest. Helped by Pensamiento to get to the railroad, he journeys to the town where he has an interview with the President of the Railroad. After a stockbroker tells him the railroad scrip he has been carrying on his quest for fortune is worthless, James has a mock death. He is revived by an elixir, as an elixir administered in *Sailing* had restored Tarleton. This drink also resembles the "Romance" fixed in the Amaranthers' bar, and is called a "Western Railroad Engine" (211). Thus revived, James receives from the President, in exchange for his now worthless stock certificates, and as "his share of that railroad," the President's cream-colored private coach named *"I fear neither Friend nor Foe"* (213). Again, with the overlapping common to this design, James also finds an unexpected end to the quest begun on O'Connell Street Bridge, the quest for a way of supporting himself. Having accepted the worthlessness of the scrip and given up his "plan" for getting and spending, he is rewarded, ironically, by gaining his end. At every railroad stop his "big cream-coloured house, his mount of luxury" (216), is charismatic. By encouraging the railroad people along its way to bring James gifts at every stop, it becomes "the coach that fed itself" (218), the economic utopia, also desired by characters in *The Old Sea Road* and *Rattle*: "He felt as if his tale was told. The happy ending in luxurious surroundings had come. . . . He was singing

> I wheel my wheelbarrow
> Through streets broad and narrow
>   singing

Cockles and Mussels
Alive, alive, 'O.'"
  (218)

The Dublin song neatly ties up this part of James's quest. "His life was rolling about in pleasant places with no politics as far as he could see . . . nothing unpleasant had come too close" (218). (Politics equals unpleasantness.)

This fabulation has many aesthetic resonances and depends, as do later narratives, on imagery to bridge its discontinuity. The cream-colored horse James rides, for example, is related imagistically to the cream-colored railway carriage which still later carries him on his last important voyage. Samuel Beckett says there is only image, no allegory and no symbol: "The discontinuity . . . [proceeds] from the same respect for the mobility and autonomy of the imagined world (a world of the same order if not so intense as the "ideal real" of Proust . . .) The cream horse that carries Gilfoyle and the cream coach that carries Gilfoyle are related not by rule of three, as two values to a third, but directly, as stages of an image."[80]

Like the horse/coach image that had linked sections of James's quest, light and dark imagery, so natural to a painter, functions in this design both to reinforce the first theme and introduce another. This alternation of light and dark is to function similarly in Yeats's last fabulation, *The Careless Flower*. While James is on the coach that feeds itself, he is safe from poverty. Like Yeats himself, James sees poverty around him, however, and is particularly disturbed by the sight of a boy eating the paste from the back of a posted bill. He comes to accept this alternation between poverty and plenty as part of the rhythm of life, perhaps the way Yeats himself came to accept the failure of his socialist ideals. "So he thought, 'first a sombre town and then a gay one.' But that was hardly true . . . streets side by side in one town were sombre and gay. Perhaps it was just the sun's law, shadow, or shine. . . . The long summer of light, the long dark winter" (225). This imagery occurs again to link to the earlier ones the third utopia—the film lot where "flickering glory" represents speeded up alternation between the accepted shadow and shine. Both the secondary theme, the quest for authenticity and balance, and the narrative line leading James to the Amaranthers' island begin when his cream-colored coach reaches "the Mountain Hollywood," the film lot. Since he has free transportation—the President of the Railroad had also given him haulage of the coach—James is recruited by the Film Magnate first to seek the stagestruck who will pay to be in the "Great Man's" films and then to transport them to the lot and back.

The book's world becomes more radically discontinuous when, en route to find more would-be actors, James joins a party going to save some islanders, stranded by a hurricane, among whom are the Amaranthers. In the car ahead of him he sees a back he thinks he recognizes and has a vision of his old friends and mentors, analogous to the summary illustration at the end of the first volume of *A Broadside*. The controlling metaphor is theatrical, and James, being partially in control, "stages" his fancy. He thinks he sees "The Judge":

James looking at the admired back imagined that perhaps he was on the verge of a nest of old friends, and he suddenly saw in their midst, holding hands down by the footlights, the Grand Finale of the Pantomime. Alec the steward, Mr. Bowlen [the Philosopher] and Captain Anstruther [who told him about human isolation] . . . And while you are imagining why stint yourself, forgetting the changing of the guard of the years, James called up besides, his landlady's first husband, responsible for his passage over the ocean. Standing in the circle, was Sailor John. The brother of Ayleen [James's wife]. He who lifted him from the kerb trade . . . There was the ballad-singer on the bridge . . .
    (254)

Yeats draws neatly together the important narrative elements of one quest. The narrative comes to a point of rest in the circular movement he preferred to a linear narrative. An "endless tale" might have stopped here, with this "curtain call" resembling the *Broadside* drawing in which all the characters from Volume I stand in a circle watching the artist who called them into being. But the fabulation is more complex than the tale. It attempts to provide a model for the known world through the radically discontinuous world and is an "ethically controlled" form. The need for sustaining balance yet being true to an authentic imaginative life, Yeats's secondary theme in *Amaranthers*, is not yet satisfactorily dealt with. While the first theme, that of the necessity of surrendering control and accepting the power of the forces that guide the universe, had been illustrated by this point in the narrative, the second, the need for sustaining the private self by nurturing the creative imagination, had not. As the two narrative strands were drawn together in James's arriving at the island of the Amaranthers, so the two themes are united by the conclusion, and Yeats's social criticism is reinforced.

Several illusions relating to the secondary theme, both James's and the Amaranthers', are destroyed together. One must not confuse the inner imaginative life and outer ordinary life, the Narcissistic and the Antaean worlds. The man in the car ahead of James turns round, revealing that he is not the Judge: "James' staging of his fancy was over. He was caught in his own cobwebs" (254–55). When James gets across the causeway to the island, the "Hope On" hotel has collapsed, and the skyscraper which housed the Amaranthers' illusory world is cracking. Like the Anglo-Irish in Yeats's *Broadside* drawing of the end of the world, the Amaranthers, caught up in their world of pleasure and their toys of power, tried to live in the world of illusion, recreating it on a smaller island (Ireland) when forced off the mainland (Great Britain). When their structure fell, "the five men were standing in the roadway, looking in a shaken way towards the people grouped about the fall of Lilliput" (267). Swift is invoked in the reference to the impossibility of living in a self-limited, self-referential Narcissistic world.

Recognizing the connection between the end of their illusions and the ending of his own staged fancy, James is freed to act. He wakes "out of a gloomy reverie," follows the Amaranthers, and takes their party "across the water," off the island where they have tried to preserve an isolated, privileged world. He is going to take them out of time and space to an "Anno Domini defying" life, across a "curious frontier" up in the heights onto "The Lot." He will take them in the cream-colored coach, out of time, sailing past a landscape which will look "just as each of you likes it to look" (272).

(The motifs of human solitude and the impossibility of sharing a vision persist.) Here, he tells them, "you will begin to think, and then you will stop thinking . . . and begin to fancy, and then you will stop fancying and begin to imagine" (272). After acceptance of the end of the Ascendancy world, one sustains the self by nurturing the creative imagination.

The almost prophetic tone of this passage is reinforced by its biblical language: "And what James foretold came to pass" (273). Then follows a veritable apotheosis, with the presence of imagination and the desire to go beyond the known life as criteria for entry to the higher world. In apotheosis, James and the five Amaranthers go "Up, up, up" to the town of the Great Man where skies are "ether clear, or speckled, just as you like" (273).

The fabulation ends with these words. Yeats's model of reality distorts slightly, but illustrates his second theme. The ideal world, which is truly within, can be attained only in art, out of time; it must not be confused with "opposite everyday values," as Mays points out in speaking of the ideal: "its true sources are within. One arrives, at the end, at the beginning, uncovering a truth known all along—'Anno Domini defying,' 'out of time.'" (*Am* 269, 71)[81]

The themes of the fabulation are complex, and its form is suitably complex. Like the stream of consciousness mode in *Sligo*, or the tale in *Sailing*, the mode of *Amaranthers*, which we now call the fabulation, makes an excellent vehicle for Yeats's social criticism and his themes. Like other fabulations, *Amaranthers* presents models of reality. Yeats knows the limits of both the Narcissistic and Antean worlds, and the need for balance between them. As the *Broadside* tumblers depended on each other, so do the Yeats and the Pollexfen worlds.

Samuel Beckett recognized the interdependence of the two narrative strands and their relation to the themes embodied in this narrative and its form when he reviewed *The Amaranthers* as "An Imaginative Work": "Of the two themes, in whose coalescence the book ends, the Amaranthers and James Gilfoyle, the first is invaded by the play in the "Hope On," then dropped for a hundred pages, and the second broken into three by the episodes of Ohoh and Pensamiento. An imaginative adventure does not enjoy the same corsets as a reportage."[82]

The Charmed Life

The thematic continuity in Yeats's narratives extends to *The Charmed Life* (hereafter *Life*), published in 1938. *Life* treats many of the same themes as *Amaranthers*, *Sailing*, and *Sligo*. Its first five pages introduce both Yeats's primary theme—the need to accept the rhythms of life and immerse oneself in forces larger than the self—and his second theme—the need to balance the demands of the imaginative and practical worlds while maintaining artistic authenticity. Yeats did not simply reiterate the same themes. In embodying theme one in *Life*, he gives a new dimension to the forces larger than the self. He inserts into his treatment of the second theme two new considerations for determining artistic authenticity: the nature of the authentic self and the perception of the self as divided. The divided self motif is reflected in the narrative form by the use of paired protagonists.

Yeats's primary theme—the necessity to accept all aspects of life, including death and apparent randomness—is both more clearly stated and further developed in *Life* than in the earlier works. Larry O'Malley of *Sailing* died no longer able to unite himself with the flow of life, and James Gilfoyle of *The Amaranthers* only learned to submerge the self in larger forces at the end of his quest, but both Bowsie and Mr. No Matter of *Life* flow with life's rhythms and accept the random throughout the course of the narrative. As early as page four, No Matter speaks of "a large mysterious parcel in a bran pie. It might be Miss Frederick's old boots. But it might'nt [sic], it might be a crown of glory on a red cushion."[83] The implication is that one should accept the unknown parcel or one might miss glory. This veiled hint is followed by a more explicit statement when No Matter says: "Then we, you and I, must take what comes. And here comes Chance leading a horse by a hay rope . . ." (6). Both Pensamiento and James Gilfoyle met such a horse in *Amaranthers* and rode it to good things. Here, the horse will not be seized, but breaks away, leaving the man who had led him in despair. The man who has lost his horse tries to hang himself with the hay rope, signing to Mr. No Matter to help, but No Matter, who had earlier described himself as "Eternity's fool," is not ready to help another into eternity. If the bran pie parcel doesn't have a crown of glory in it, one must accept it anyway. If the horse gets away, one must accept the loss. Like Beckett's fools of eternity, one must go on. Suicide is a "poor" solution. After the man leading it has disappeared, the horse comes back. No Matter's response was the correct one.

Both of the book's paired protagonists know not only how to accept what life brings, but also how to keep the balance between abstraction and intuition, between the external and private worlds. "No Matter never indulged any Schoolmaster within in his hard thinking. . . ." He could catch trains or buses when he needed to, but "that was all the hard thinking of the teeth-setting brow-bending kind he ever used. The rest of his thoughts were communings with his inner ear" (2). He realizes the dangers of preoccupation with these communings and advises the reader not to close his eyes and become "languid" in the presence of the "ineffable," but to snap them open again, "sharp, and look about you, and see something funny" (5). The companion/antagonist of No Matter, Bowsie, who indulges in fancy, nevertheless knows, too, when he must bring himself back to reality: "But Bowsie knows he may bring his fancy with him right up to the moment when he sits down on the stool behind his table, but, when he turns his face towards the horizons of the land, that are about him, he knows that his plan cannot strut there. It will not mix" (110).

John Pilling comments perceptively on the tendency of characters in this book to control their imaginative flights, saying that characters catching themselves distorting reality administer to themselves "a cold shower of truth that is savagely sad."[84] The theme of the necessity to keep the balance between two worlds is pursued here as in *Amaranthers* or in the illustrations of *A Broadside*. As the structures of *Sligo, Sailing,* and *Amaranthers* served to reinforce and link their prevailing themes, so the "fore and aft" movement of this fabulation's structure reinforces the theme of the need for balance between two worlds, as well as the theme of accepting the ebb and flow of life's rhythms.

In *Life*, to attain the good, one must surrender the illusion of control and preserve balance while seeking the private, authentic, self and its imaginative vision. These two themes are familiar from earlier narratives. In *Life*, however, attainment of the good is described in more orthodox Christian terms than in the earlier narratives. In *Amaranthers*, for example, although there is biblical language preceding the apotheosis, the nature of the journey up the mountain is clearly secular, and has more to do with preserving authenticity than with uniting oneself to forces larger than the self. Two characters in *Life*, Tim and Bowsie, are both "saved," not from loss of vision or from inauthentic visions, but from what appears to be certain drowning. Tim, who was saved in infancy by human intervention, lives "the charmed life" of the book's title. Over and over, he reads a fictional account of a hero saved from destruction by unknown forces. A new question is raised: Why was the hero saved? The answer is given, as in *Sailing*, in terms of Providence, using the same metaphor of snatching the burning brand used to describe Tarleton's return to life in *Sailing* after he drank the elixir administered by the blacksmith/mechanic:

Can it be that the tide has reached its flow? A ray of hope, like a gleam of sunshine, through a rift in the stormy sky, darts into the man's mind. He cherishes the idea that the worst has come, and watches with breathless interest the motion of the waves. Ah! his chin is uncovered, and presently the water only washes his shoulders. Saved once more as a brand from the fire! And wherefore? To do good in his day and generation, or to work iniquity and clothe himself with crime as with a garment?
(53)

This passage not only echoes Tarleton's rescue, it also foreshadows Bowsie's rescue; he, too, is left behind by an ebbing tide. The biblical allusion sets up a Christian ethical framework for the use of life preserved. Bowsie perceives himself as saved by superhuman means, by "supporting unseen hands. He looks at his own, white and hairy, against the door-posts, and thinks that the hands which held him, and helped him to safety, in the flood were not like these" (180). Next morning, thinking of his experience, Bowsie uses language like the language of Tim's reading: "Bowsie, his head bowed on his breast, will be most immeasurably thankful that his life is his own for a little longer, that he may do good deeds, and think good thoughts, and make his friends better, and proud of him . . . eyes shining with the glamour of the brand-plucked" (185).

Up to this time Bowsie has not been a socially responsible man. His salvation, like that of the Amaranthers in that narrative, involves a conversion as well as physical rescue. Early in the book, his companion attributes to him a song about "the darling of the Gods" (11) and even earlier he is described as an "artful blackbird" (8). The blackbird in medieval Irish literature is a Dionysian force. As a blackbird, Bowsie is presumably outside the bounds of duty, convention, and other Apollonian concerns. His alter ego, whose name "No Matter" identifies him as the spiritual force in the spirit/matter dichotomy of Christianity, says of him:

I know you thus far, Bowsie. You glory in your mitching freedom from ever getting within a distance of all these named duties. If you had a little Jew's harp now against your teeth, and could play it, you would send forth a farewell to duty. But it is well you haven't the harp, for the solo would complete your sense of freedom in one performance, whereas now, as long as you live, you will always freshly hug another duty not performed. (119)

"As long as you live" are the operative words. After Bowsie's brush with death by water, his attitudes change. Before his salvation experience, he was a Dionysian drifter, but after it he becomes concerned with Apollonian values. He leaves the seaside resort where he and No Matter have journeyed and returns to Dublin to take a job. Whereas his previous plans had all avoided duty, he now embraces it. What Providence sends must be accepted. However, he has some reservations about giving up his old life, and some ambivalence about his new self.

He thinks that this is the most ridiculous moment in his life, since he grew to manhood, and became, in the world's eyes, the master of his own fate.

He thinks it is ridiculous that he should leave this pleasant place of sun, and sea, and air . . . Is it a life for a man with a heart in his breast? Is it a life? I don't know what to make of it. I suppose when I'm older I'll get used to it.

(227)

The sense of a divided self and of shifting personal identity are developed in this narrative. The doubling of characters common in Yeats's prose narratives, plays, and paintings represents an objectifying of the perceived halves of the personality somewhat akin to WB's sense of self and anti-self. The division of self is stressed in *Life*. Not only is Bowsie aware of being half of a pair ("There was one man from whom No Matter never vanished, that was his worn old friend, Bowsie" [2]); he is also aware of a divided self:

Bowsie is very much above himself, but he is also timid within himself, as he raises this monster, which he believes he may become, which he believes, he hopes, to become. He is afraid that some uneasy plank i[n] his bridge, the bridge that takes him from his old self to his new, may tip over, and bring down the whole concern into the depths.

(217)

Yeats may be exemplifying his own sense of a divided self in creating these two characters. No Matter, the narrator of much of this fiction, may represent Yeats's dominant sense of self, since his first speech employs a metaphor of self-identification which Yeats employed in his own epitaph: travelling without a ticket. No Matter says: "Through or over, I go in without a ticket, except a complimentary one. I give myself that one" (3). Yeats said: "I have travelled all my life without a ticket . . . when we are asked about it in the end, we who travel without tickets, we can say . . . even though we went without tickets, we never were commuters." Bowsie may be Yeats's second self. He also has traits identified with Yeats: he is "comfortable," he wears a long overcoat, he has attentive eyes, and he is a quiet listener. Terence de Vere White, who knew Yeats when he wrote *The Charmed Life* said of him: "I recall the attentiveness of the eye, the total absence of condescension. . . . His presence was ageless and classless, not as if he was unaware of such differences, but as if he was above them. . . . His overcoat came to his heels and had large sleeves. . . . He looked, in fact, very like a figure in his early drawings of country characters."[85]

Several persons who knew Yeats asserted that he was a "comfortable" person who put others at their ease. Speaking of Yeats as a child, de Vere White adds: "He was always, we are told, cheerful and self-reliant, the sort of boy who gets on very well with the busy because he is companionable, observant, and does not get in the way."[86] Bowsie exhibits these characteristics throughout *Life*. In the same essay de Vere White also gives us the final and most telling similarity between Bowsie and Yeats. Speaking of Yeats's habits, he says: "Jack was not of a didactic turn. He was up and doing rather than talking; he listened . . . but made no attempt to discuss."[87] Of Bowsie, Yeats says: "Bowsie had not cast himself for a speaking part while on earth; he listened well to all he heard" (2).

Several critics have noted the importance of Yeats's pairing of characters: Marilyn Gaddis Rose has made much of their similarity to Beckett's pairs in her essay "Solitary Companions in Beckett and Jack B. Yeats." Pilling says of the paired relationship in this work: "Bowsie and No Matter are firm friends. . . . They go their own way even when ostensibly together . . . and join up again without feeling the need to communicate their separate experiences. . . . But they belong together. . . . Bowsie . . . is on the symbolic level No Matter's *alter ego*. . . . Bowsie and No Matter are in fact complementary figures, No Matter nervous and oppressed and contemplative, Bowsie powerful and strong and active."[88] Jack Yeats had employed pairs of men in *Sailing*, but their relationships, mentor to pupil, or Irishman to Englishman, were quite different from the Bowsie/No Matter alter-ego pairing. This form of paired personalities characterizes the later fiction, and is present in graphic work from the drawings of *A Broadside* to the symbolic late paintings.

WB, who used a similar pairing of contemplative and active men for his own dialectic, explained this book in terms of his brother's characteristic attitudes, saying that it contained his brother's mind even more than *Sligo*: " . . . my brother's extreme book, *The Charmed Life*. He does not care that few will read it, still fewer recognize its genius; it is his book, his 'Faust,' his pursuit of all that through its unpredictable, unarrangeable reality least resembles knowledge. His style fits his purpose for every sentence has its own taste, tint and smell."[89]

The movement of *Life* follows this pursuit of "unpredictable, unarrangeable reality." While Bowsie and No Matter savor each event, not as part of a sum, and respond to the unexpected and unarrangeable, there is, nevertheless, a distinct arrangement to Yeats's strategy of narration of their pursuit which emphasizes his two main themes.

The narrative motion in *Life* is similar to Yeats's description of time: " . . . Time, little time, Big Time is just fore and aft" (10). The narrative motion, similar to time's own rhythm, reinforces important aspects of Yeats's themes. The design of this fabulation focuses attention on the larger rhythms of life, the rhythms in which the individual must immerse himself, and on the movement between two worlds which is necessary to preserve balance. This "fore and aft" movement dominates the book. The forward motion—the journey to the Pride Hotel—occupies 149 pages, about half of the book.

The symbolic aspects of this forward journey—a metaphor for the quest for an ideal world as are the journeys in *Amaranthers*—are stressed. Near the end of their journey the companions are "jaded"; they "plod on"; they are "breasting the storm of fatigue." No Matter encourages Bowsie to keep the rhythm: "Now, stride more handsomely, up, up, up. Three ups. Three efforts. Now down into a sloping stroll, to bring the battering hearts to quietness, and we are in the Pride's mouth. Successful wanderers from no prosaic shore" (149).

Their journey is a movement toward death as well as a journey in the real Ireland. The walls of the "Pride" (Hotels have almost Dickensian names in Yeats's narratives as does the "Hope On" hotel of the *Amaranthers.)* remind No Matter of a coffin: "I have never got any but a mournful feeling from looking on pitch-pine walls. . . . Iron tabernacles lined with it long ago, kept many a soul from its true heaven, a while. Too long, is the purgatory of sloughing old skins" (149).

The landlord's speech patterns, as well as the journey motions, reflect life's rhythms: "[E]very conversation of the landlord's of more than a quarter of an hour's duration, is paired by the rising, and falling, of this man's life, from the cradle until this moment. The speed, the rise, and fall, is a running water to the news of to-day which he is telling us" (151).

The smaller sections of this fabulation also employ the fore and aft motion in space and time. Like the three "ups" or three efforts, the 150 pages of journey have three subsections of fifty pages each which are quite carefully planned. The first fifty-page section serves to set up the motifs and characters. The two companions arrive at the town from which they commence their journey. They take a short evening walk out—fore—and return to the hotel—aft. They see the "Woman at the Window" and her tale is told. This tale goes back in time sixteen years to the rescue of Tim who, like Bowsie, was washed away in a flood but had a "charmed life."

A backward and forward motion in time, of interrelated characters, is set up. First the narrative goes back in time to the story of the building of the Pride, a place of importance where "travellers' tales" are told. Carefully planned, these interpolated tales are important to the motifs of the larger narrative: the rhythms of life, divided and shifting identity, and human isolation motifs. For example, the human isolation motif is demonstrated in a wonderful ten-page subsection where the would-be landlord attempts to tell his "travellers' tales" to the "ballad-singing carpenters" who are building his hotel. They constantly interrupt him with snatches of ballads. It is a virtuoso performance in counterpoint.

Precisely on page 51 (so carefully crafted is this fabulation) Bowsie and No Matter begin the first day's journey. This second section (pages 51–100) has its own motif and also has a "fore and aft" motion in its internal and external structures. Viewed externally, it picks up motifs and characters from section one and prepares for section three. Within the limits of the fifty pages there is fore-and-aft motion as well; the characters move forward one town in space, one day in time, but also go backward in time and space through two interpolated tales. Additionally, these two interpolated tales introduce the motif of loss, which unifies the subsection. The first tale is of a ballad singer who lost his child, and the second is of a man who lost his love. The paired protagonists lose each other twice on this journey. Since even close companions cannot always be in harmony, the essential human isolation motif is reinforced. Precisely halfway through the section, at page 75, No Matter proposes they take two roads: "Each of us will commune with our own nonsensical souls, which at these times will not be said nay to." On page 100 they are reunited, the end of the section falling just where it should.

The third section of fifty pages is also divided into two subsections. In its first twenty-five pages the companions are divided more radically than they had been on their separate walks, by a failure of sympathy arising after they pass "the Bush of Argumentation." Reunited by page 125, they have an experience that reinforces the dominant theme: they seize what chance brings them, an opportunity to bet on a horse their landlord has dreamed about. Anxious at first about the sum they bet, they soon decide that "the sum was the right sum for the event. The event opens to the moment. The height of the sun which opens the daisy, is neither more, nor less, but sufficient. Two daisies, we" (124). The daisy imagery from *Sligo* is repeated here and its overtones of "lilies of the field" reinforce the Christian context of *Life's* theme.

On the third travelling day, when they are joined by another walker, the subject of human isolation is again accentuated: "He has only a blow-away interest in us, and why should he have more. We are unable to see the grain of the material of his memories. . . . We neither get the pictures of his old mind in the detail, or in the broad swing" (140–41). The interpolated tale of this day acts as a foreshadowing, telling of a boy who is brought back to life, as Bowsie was to be. These tales link the narrative form to the theme. Pilling observes: "[T]he interpolated narratives are much more under control in *The Charmed Life* than in other works of his."[90]

Not only the interpolated narratives are under control. A very tight structure underlies this narrative. In the second half of the book, the events set in motion are brought together skillfully, showing the love of design characteristic of fabulation. Miss Julia Starrett, rescuer of Tim in an early interpolated tale, now needs rescue from a storm. Tim's chivalrous attempt to bring Miss Julia a package she has requested results in Bowsie's fall into the river and his subsequent need of rescue. A stranger, the would-be rescuer of Bowsie, is open to randomness as a Yeatsean hero should be, and is as willing as Miss Julia had been to risk his life for another: "If, instead of a river of water, it had been a river of fire, that gaunt man was for it . . . he ran, for all which came his way" (174). In spite of his effort, he fails to rescue Bowsie. This unification of the narrative lines involving Tim, Miss Julia, and Bowsie occurs on page 175, a strategic page which begins an account of Bowsie's mythic and visionary experience.

The "fore and aft" motion between two worlds is very pronounced in the next subsection of twenty-five pages. Bowsie and No Matter are widely physically separated now, and the narrative goes "fore and aft" from one to the other. Each is thinking of the other, but they are unable to communicate. After the rescue attempt in which he participates, No Matter goes back to the hotel mourning the supposedly dead Bowsie. Bowsie, meanwhile, is saved by the "unseen hands" (180) and gets to a cabin. However, its owner, Silvanus, who with his wood god's name represents some healing natural force, is crippled and cannot take him back to the hotel in the dark.

The treatment of the motif of human isolation, introduced in *Amaranthers* through Pensamiento, is reiterated the next morning when Silvanus predicts that Bowsie will never be able to share his experience of transformation in the sea, since no one will understand it, as Pensamiento could not share his experience of his adventures riding the mythical horse:

You were in it [the sea], rolled in it, lost in it, found in it, and the tide left you, so you are a son of the sea. The Good God has rinsed you in it. . . .

The man who has never been handled fully by the tide of the sea is always in fear, not so much of his body, but of his spirit. . . . But a man such as yourself knows that the spirit of the sea will never touch your spirit— your spirit lives above the waters. . . . you will always have your secret

understanding. The other bathers . . . will not know anything about it, nor could they understand if you tried to tell them. If they looked in your face, as lovers look in each other's faces, they would see there your sea companionship. But nobody not a lover is able to see another's face like that. They make a mask and look at it.
(188–89)

In addition to the fact that others do not look at us as lovers look, but look at a mask, communication is difficult because language is an unreliable medium, language and thought are separate entities: "And Bowsie answers slowly; he's thinking as he speaks, which is unusual with him. His thinking, and his speech, with him are separate, both arranged carefully, as tableaux, on different stages. His thoughts lie about a dry dock, repairing, while his speech is afloat" (190).

Bowsie's immediate reaction to Sylvanus's profound observations and to his knowledge of Bowsie's own character is acceptance. Having surrendered to the potentially destructive forces of nature and then been saved by a force above nature, Bowsie desires to prolong the experience of transcendence. He desires to feel himself surrounded by the sustaining forces which are larger than the self, manifested through nature: "I have no desire myself to know myself any better than I do, at this moment. But to watch the sun come pouring through your little easterly window . . . and to know that all outside this house is belted, and circled above, and around, with the dazzle of the sky" (190). The Yeatsean universe gives this comfort to the sensitized, or sensitive, being.

However, one cannot remain in the visionary world forever, as Yeatsean heroes know. The fabulation moves on, and its motion brings Bowsie back to the ordinary world of the hotel. At page 200 Miss Starrett's coffin is taken out of the hotel, fore, just as Bowsie is brought back by Silvanus, aft. One is unexpectedly dead, and the other is unexpectedly alive.

The interpolated tales and discussions of the next subsection contain explicit statements of the themes. A man called Small Voice tells of sudden death, first of his employer and then of a funeral guest. When Bowsie joins the walkers Small Voice says: "We were discussing the bagatelle of life—how the balls go rolling around, getting in each others ways, until in a moment, they come to rest, and those in the holes, look as if it was the only place for them" (215). Bowsie, who has just received a telegram offering him a job, finds that saying apposite to his own situation, since he will now stop rolling around: "Ending up in a hole" (215). Chance becomes design, in a reinforcement of the primary theme, as Bowsie goes off, leaving No Matter behind.

The "fore and aft" motion is again dominant in the last two sections, in which No Matter's principal walking companion is the Judge, after Bowsie has gone off to his job in Dublin; the motion again reinforces the theme. "We are all sitting down except the Judge who keeps on his feet, and moves slowly up and down, fore and aft, aft and fore" (264). In this section, the Judge "keeps disappearing into the darkness, and coming back again" (269) going between two worlds as No Matter had when first introduced. His motion and the fore and aft nature of the dialogues that make up the "symposium" reinforce through narrative structure the primary and secondary themes. In the previous discussion, while they were all waiting on the hotel verandah for Miss Starrett's recovery or death, the Judge and others had gone between two worlds, had kept coming in and out of the dark. Lights had been struck and quenched; light had entered the dark room when the door was opened.

Even death is seen as a movement between two worlds; the Judge says:

But I have the experience, constantly now, as I grow old, of viewing the moment of disappearance. I view the living. I wink my eyes and I view the place where they moved in life. I pass a man at the same time, in the street, near my lodgings, every day. . . . But one day I don't see him; he's dead. Stept away back out of this place. . . . One time that would have made me uncomfortable and mopy [sic]. Not now, I just take my walk in future where I meet younger-looking passers-by.
(242)

He continues his meditation on death, employing the metaphor of the crowded dance floor for the in-and-out movements to and from the "World of Spirits": "[A] girl or a young man would pass from the light into night for a moment, in the dance, and then come into the light again. Well, that is the way the dead die on me" (245). To step back out of this place or to step out of the light are not fearful things; the other world is very close as in *And To You Also.*

The form of these sections, where the forward journey and its themes are recapitulated and where the characters meditate on Bowsie's journey to death and back, reflects the same alternation of light and dark imagery as *Amaranthers* and *The Careless Flower.* Hilary Pyle has compared the flow of the book to a Sibelius symphony.[91] In its carefully delineated sections and its repetition of and development of themes, the motion can be seen as symphonic.

In the narrative's coda, to extend Pyle's symphony metaphor, many of Yeats's themes are recapitulated, and a motif to be taken up in *Ah Well* and *And To You Also* is introduced. The seven "symposium" members speak of "those who have gone on before" as lingering between two worlds, listening to conversations of the living; the seven walkers in the park speculate at length on this lingering state in *And To You Also*; and the possibility of departed spirits remaining nearby is also taken up in *Ah Well.* A discussion of sea chanties brings in the motif of the necessity for seeking artistic authenticity (268). The failure of language motif is also reiterated; language is deemed inadequate "even for giving information, or for pure statement" (270), and its separation from reality, or even thought, is stressed: "[W]hat we say, and what we think, are two different things" (278).

The ending, as one might expect, comes full circle. Conversation being at cross purposes, No Matter starts a new naming of characters, as his own naming had opened the book. (His name was of no consequence—no matter—this in an Ascendancy world where names mattered a great deal.) This process of naming is part of the last consideration of a motif in *Life*, that of shifts in identity, and of the reconsideration of a motif from *Sligo*, mistrust of language. Names change; individuality is inconsequential, of no matter. Speakers plagiarize each others' thoughts. The first group of seven speakers (which parallels the group speaking the "coda") while walking in the first town entered on the journey, speak of, and then exemplify, this truth:

And now we fall into another stage. Three in front, and four in the rear. Those in front discuss the old times. Those behind the times yet to come. Neither use their own imagination. But each one who speaks, speaks from the lips of his friend next him—mentions events with a shape that he knows his friend believed they took upon them. . . . Everyone notices that he is being plagiarized, and is flattered. . . .

(88)

The reuse of words and ideas by several speakers is not ineptitude; it is a deliberate technique. Speech codes are not specific to Yeats's characters because the speeches are not intended, as they might be in a novel, to characterize the speakers; the internal development of characters is not part of Yeats's concern. Moreover, repetition is deliberately used to stress the unimportance of individuality, relative to union with life's rhythms, and to stress the unreliability of language. Speech in *Life*, as in *Sligo*, does not convey experience: "But the gentle fall of the rose-burning turf . . . makes a small noise, and I think I can see, feel, and scent, the noise. But now it's gone. The word 'rose' remains only with me, a description and translation, a man's attempt. Now it has gone" (191).

Speech does not convey identity. The seven speakers in the extended colloquies of *Life* are not always identifiable to the reader. The colloquies are meant to emphasize the motifs of shifting identity and individual inconsequence, the failure of language to convey meaning, and the inability of humans to communicate. Every character in *Life* experiences difficulty in making language an index of feelings.[92] Language failure is one of the important motifs in all of Yeats's narratives and is related to the theme that the artist must look inward. Since no one can truly communicate a vision to another, each must look within, although the artist, at least, must try to express private truth as clearly as possible.

This narrative raises some important questions: the nature of salvation, the nature of death, the nature of identity. The opening of the next narrative, *Ah Well*, continues the meditation on these questions The thematic continuity, apparent in the narratives written in the 1930s—*Sligo, Sailing, Amaranthers* and *The Charmed Life*—persists into the three narratives of the next decade.

Ah Well

Published in 1942, this short narrative continues the thematic continuity of Yeats's work by developing several motifs related to death, an important motif explored in *A Charmed Life*: the motif of aging and the motif of suicide. Each of these motifs is, in turn, related to the primary theme of the need for acceptance of life's rhythms, since death is a part of life. Yeats develops his secondary theme, the need for preserving artistic authenticity and balance, in *Ah Well*, in association with several motifs: the motif of narcissism, the inward focus necessary to preserve artistic authenticity, and the motif of language failure, the difficulty of communicating one's vision.

There are echoes from earlier narratives. As he does in *Sligo*, Yeats has his narrator speak of the selectiveness of memory: "I myself would live short spells again. There are ten dawns I would see again—if I was able."[93] From *The Charmed Life* comes an echo of shifting identity and its relation to names: "I was introduced to each man by a wave of the hand and a name, which you never heard me called. It was the first time I heard it and I forgot it again before the day was over" (49). Identity is not tied to names, (a truth a name-conscious society such as Yeats's would have a hard time accepting) as "No Matter's" name indicated in *The Charmed Life*. The primary theme (the necessity of giving up the illusion of control and accepting life's rhythms) is treated at length in the colloquies of this narrative, as it had been in the discussions in *The Charmed Life*.

There are formal as well as thematic resemblances to earlier works. Songs are interspersed in the narratives as in *Sligo* and *Amaranthers*. After drinking of an elixir, for example, a character with a generic name—The Absolute—sings a seven-page "Song of the Wave." (Wave imagery is dominant in several of the dramas.) The song turns full circle on itself, in the narrative motion Yeats employed as early as the *Guardian* pieces.

Although in the book's subtitle Yeats himself calls it a Romance, the mode chosen for *Ah Well* is best described as a subgenre of romance, fabulation. Like other fabulations, *Ah Well* has both an ethical and an aesthetic dimension; through the creation of a radically discontinuous world, here signalled by the use of fairytale language, Yeats attempts to present models of reality showing the consequences of human action. His manner of presentation is similar to the one he used in the *Amaranthers*, setting forth an ideal and then giving an exemplum demonstrating one man's quest for the ideal. The fabulation's mythic resonances, including the use of the journey motif, hark back to *Sailing*; there is also in *Ah Well* the hint of a ritual sacrifice, a mythic resonance explored earlier in the play *Rattle*. The narrative ending is characteristically crafted in the *triskele*, closing circle, pattern.

Yeats introduces his themes in a way suitable to an ethically controlled work. The book opens with a meditation on death, that reality "we had better accept." In this treatment of the theme the narrator asks: "'Death where is Thy Sting?' We can all say that with cheerful courage every now and then. But who can say it always . . .?" (3). In the four years since 1938, when Yeats published *The Charmed Life*, death had become a very present reality, both personally and cosmically. He had lost two siblings: Willie died in January 1939; Lollie died in January 1940. Before WB's body could be brought home from Europe for the September private burial at Drumcliffe that Jack had arranged, World War II broke out. Yet, as the work's title suggests, the seventy-one-year-old writer's response was an acceptance of the reality, "Ah Well," followed by transcendence through the power of imagination, suggested by the subtitle, "A Romance in Perpetuity." Within the first paragraphs, three aspects of the secondary theme are touched on: that one must pursue one's own vision; that the artist must keep the balance between two worlds, the Narcissistic and the Antaean; and that one must accept the limitations of language.

These themes are exemplified in the fabulation. The narrator speaks, in a tone which suggests a radically discontinuous world is being established, to a "grand shining fellow," one of those who "play out their games" in a "fair land." A fabulation, by definition, "tends away from direct representation of the surface of reality but returns toward actual human life by way of ethically controlled fantasy."[94]

In *Ah Well* Yeats is presenting an ethically controlled fantasy about death. One of his purposes in this work may be to inculcate in the reader a proper attitude toward death. The first aspect of death Yeats considers is one which he also considered in *The Charmed Life*, that the dead remain close to the living. The shining fellow tells the narrator, later called "Jack," that "those others," those who have passed to another state, spend their years, "in having good thoughts about you and yours." (The duty of the living to have "good thoughts" for one of "those others" is the subject of Yeats's last play, *In Sand*.) Exploration of the closeness of the dead to the living is a subject difficult to deal with in realistic fiction, but suitable to fabulation. In *And To You Also* Yeats continues to explore the state of those lingering between two worlds.

The protagonist of *Ah Well*, "Dusty Brown," forms a proper attitude toward death. He thinks he is about to die while attempting to rescue a drowning child (like Julia Starrett in *The Charmed Life*) and (like Bowsie in the same work) he experiences a new conception of death while he is in the water. He realizes the possible attraction of death, (a truth No Matter in that work had begun to grasp just before his separation from Bowsie). The drowning child is laughing and not fearful, attracted to the river by its rhythms: "It wasn't that he was such a brave child or a foolhardy child, but in the river so strong with the sleep of death, it was the rolling and groaning and snoring of the river water which called him in to play . . . a tussle and a maul, and perhaps, a long sleep in the centre of the field of play" (39). Like Bowsie, Dusty comes out of the ritual death a changed man.

Halfway through the first section, while leaning and looking in the river (as Yeats himself was fond of doing) Dusty meets a man who gives him still another view of death: "There's nothing in the death. They have us humbugged. Sure half the people in this town are dead. . . . Or, with more of them, it is that they had a chance to live and they threw it from them" (41). This motif of death-in-life as fear of life dominates *Harlequin's Positions*, an important, socially critical play. In *Ah Well*, as everywhere in the Yeatsean literary universe, one cannot be afraid and hold back from an enterprise because of the risk of death. Like Grandpapa Pollexfen, one must jump into the river for good cause, immerse oneself in the rhythms of the larger life, and accept what comes. One should not, however, jump deliberately to end one's life; suicide is not a proper acceptance of life's pattern.

Like death and the attraction to death, aging is part of life's rhythms and must be accepted. As they begin a descent on the ritual journey that forms much of *Ah Well's* action, seven men and the narrator hear:

> On boys on.
> Such old boys! A Boy's a boy
> As long as he says he's a boy.
> His boyhood rests with him.
> (71)

Boyhood, however, is more a psychological than a physical state, in this sense. As part of a game, the eight "boys" construct a tale by putting words on pieces of bark and drawing them out of a hat; chance dictates all, even art. The true nature of boyhood, the capacity of some men to grow psychically younger as they grow physically older, is an important motif. This emphasis on youth is noteworthy and related to the myth of "Tir na nOg" [the Land of the Young]. "Whatever its historical causes, this perversion in time—everyone was born old and grew younger—seems inseparable from the Irish experience. At birth the weight of history was added to original sin, so growing old held the youthful promise of ditching both (Tir na nOg was a revealing invention)."[95]

A strong contrast is created in this fabulation between the child's attraction to death and the old man's attraction to life. Near the end of the narrative the speaker realizes that true boyishness, the proper response to aging, consists in using the wisdom life brings to see its goodness and not in worrying about the future or mourning what has passed and cannot be recovered.

I thought: I am glad I'm no longer a foolish giddy-pated fat red-faced boy, desiring to be for ever throwing stones, to make a little splash in water, or a little splatter in mud. And I was at that moment a little old brown man and an hour before I would have been insulted, and wounded, to be called "a little old man." I thought to myself: It can't be so bad to be old, if you have no aches. Have I any? Not a one. But I may have plenty another day. But what about another day? "Beautiful lake" I said . . . "it is an insult to you that I should not be happy gazing on you so severe and anxious to give away happiness with the air above you."

(77)

True wisdom brings happiness in union with nature and acceptance of life. Despair and suicide are crimes against life, struggling against its stream. The protagonist learns this lesson through the fabulation's action. One must neither fear death nor seek it, but accept it when it comes, as one accepts aging, death's approach, and all the rhythms of life.

Other themes—that an artist must keep balance, pursue the private vision, and attempt to express it fully in language—are treated more explicitly here than in any other narrative. In the opening of *Ah Well*, the private world of the artist is described using the metaphor, "the way of space":

[T]here is a way of space, so we may call it, where there are no things. When we see a waterfall rushing up into the sky to lick a star, we don't want to say: What sort of a thing is that? We just want to cut a little slit and let "thing" drop out of our vocabulary. If we drop a word which we don't care much about every little while we might find ourselves understanding the boys who disintegrate space so as to make a little nest . . . in which to live and take the polish off their ideas.

(3)

This "nest" is the creative imagination, where the artist deals in images, like the boys who disintegrate space. Like the Amaranthers' visionary world, this one exists outside the limits of objective reality. In this "nest," one can visualize the world subjectively, ignoring what reason and the senses reveal; waterfalls can rush up to lick stars. One can avoid words, things, and ideas, so as to deal in images. The artist can transform the world and present it to those less gifted.

The idea was not original with Yeats. Freud in his *Introductory Lectures on Psychoanalysis* speaks of the true artist's ability ("the mysterious power of shaping") to transform the wishful constructions of his life of fantasy to yield pleasure beyond that experienced by the ordinary man. The artist is consoled by his fantasy and, by transforming it and then sharing it with others, consoles them by allowing them access to their own subjectivity in a way that their repressions do not ordinarily permit.[96] According to the critic John Berger, Yeats's success in this transformational process, the leaving behind of the customary way of seeing the known world, partially accounts for his greatness: "He transforms everything within his imagination. And if I had to give a single reason why I believe he is a great painter I would cite the consistency of this power of his to transform."[97]

In the value he placed on the private vision, the intuitive and nonlinguistic aspects of the creative process described in the "way of space" passage, Yeats was closely allied to a younger generation of significant Irish artists. "Poetry is Vertical," a critical manifesto that Beckett and the poet Thomas MacGreevy signed in 1931, was concerned with the sources of poetry, with the need for the artist to turn inward to nourish his artistic life: "We proclaim the autonomy of the poetic vision, the hegemony of the inner life over the outer life."[98] Published in Eugene Jolas's *transition*, this manifesto was issued shortly after MacGreevy had introduced Beckett to Yeats.

The meeting led to a friendship between the two artists which may have contributed to the prevalence of similar aesthetic preoccupations in their work. MacGreevy wrote to Yeats about Beckett's reaction to the meeting: "He was completely staggered by the pictures and though he has met many people through me he dismissed them all in his letter with the remark 'and to think I owe meeting Jack Yeats *and* Joyce to you!' "[99] Yeats and Beckett became good friends, despite the thirty-five year difference in their ages, and "discussed their writing on long walks together whenever Beckett was in Dublin."[100] They were so close that when Yeats's wife Cottie died in 1947, Beckett and MacGreevy were the two friends Yeats invited back to his apartment after the funeral.[101] As late as Christmas 1956, Yeats's last Christmas, he received a card from Beckett saying, "This plain card to bring you, from my heart here, warmest greetings, warmest wishes for Christmas and for all the days of 1957. Ever your affectionate friend, Samuel Beckett."[102]

The two artists had not only similarities of background on which to base their friendship, but also aesthetic ones. Like Synge, the close friend of Yeats's youth, Beckett was also a Southern Irish Protestant and therefore subject to the same feelings of alienation and the same search for artistic identity. Both artists were concerned with the failure of language as an expressive mode and with the need for the artist to be true to his own private vision. Beckett mentions the similarity between Yeats's vision and his own; in a 1934 essay, published a few years after they met, Beckett cites T. S. Eliot and Yeats as examples of artists who are aware, as he himself is, of "[T]he new thing that has happened, or the old thing that has happened again, namely the breakdown of the object . . . the rupture of the lines of communication. The artist who is aware of this may state the space that intervenes between him and the world of objects. . . . A picture by Mr. Jack Yeats, Mr. Eliot's 'Wasteland,' are notable statements of this kind."[103] The suggestions given in "Poetry is Vertical" for crossing this "space" between artist and object are similar to ones Yeats makes in *Ah Well*. Arp, Beckett, MacGreevy, and the others who signed the manifesto said that language for an artist should be "mantic," a word which suggests divination or contact with other worlds. They were willing to invent a new hermetic language to describe experiences with worlds beyond the known. In speaking of "the way of space," "where there are no things," a world where, in artistic terms, subject dominates object, Yeats suggests that the artist must alter language, letting even the word "thing" drop out of his vocabulary, divorcing language from objects. Writers must get rid of overvalued language progressively, getting rid of words "we don't care much about," "letting them float away like paper money of an inflated coinage" (3).

The sources of true art are within; art is narcissistic not mimetic. "It's the Narcissus business that matters," not holding "the mirror up to nature": "You can't see anything in a mirror that isn't in your-self. You can make up pictures, by muscular contractions, like an English Public School accent on an Irish schoolboy. But they are painted with the grey and pink, and blue, matter of your own brain. The mirror is another cup of tea altogether" (9). For this reason, the artist must pursue the private vision.

Although the usual themes predominate in this fabulation, not all the subjects treated are related to Yeats's primary or secondary themes. Yeats makes a political/social commentary in *Ah Well*, as he did in *A Broadside*, in *Sailing* and *Amaranthers*, and in the dramas of the 1930s. Again, as in *Sligo* and *Amaranthers*, he makes his commentary through a utopia: "It was a sinless place, a kind of a fool's paradise" (22). Contact with nature—gained principally here, as in *Sligo, Amaranthers*, and *The Charmed Life*, by gazing into the river—improves human nature: "Every evening, rain or shine, you would see two or three persons leaning over the rail. . . . No man within an hour of coming from that river ever beat his child, even in gesture" (18). This communion with the river represents a particularly appealing form of self-improvement. John Butler Yeats tells us that his son found great educational value in this pastime. "Here is something which Jack once told me and which I think throws some light on . . . Jack's idea of self-education. There is a river meandering through the town of Sligo spanned by two bridges. Beneath one of these bridges is a deep pool. . . . Jack told me that he has spent many hours leaning over that bridge looking into the pool and he regrets that he did not spend many more hours in that apparently unprofitable pastime."[104]

The utopia of *Ah Well* reflects socio-political, as well as personal, ideals. The social ideal Yeats shared with Synge—a world where no person would be subject to another, and all would be ennobled by contact with nature—comes alive in this E-shaped town "no one ruled," not even the mayor. "It ruled itself. He ruled himself, with the varied tone of the river" (18). The town was in tune with nature, its inhabitants accepted life's rhythms, represented by the river. Craftsmen predominated in this pre-industrial world; Willam Morris would have loved it. Among the good tradesmen in the town were men who could make barrels, and bootmakers, and carpenters and joiners; there was even an anchor smith (22–23). There was a Fair Green, and two theatres performed historical and heroic plays, melodramas, and amusing plays. Sometimes, not surprisingly in a Yeats utopia, a circus came to town.

The town was not pre-Lapsarian, however. People were not always happy, but "they knew always, awake or asleep, walking or sitting, leaning or springing up, that there was a happiness" (28). There was evil; they had "Hell and hate and evil desire. . . . They neighed after the things they saw in the shop windows just when they didn't have any money" (29).

On the level of social criticism, this narrative shares values with Yeats's drama. The town had many of the qualities of Ireland in the thirties; people were often hard up and the economy was "ramshackle." They had seen better times, like the Anglo-Irish: "One time some people had had some capital. But it would be hard to tell in the time I'm speaking of who had any now. They were owers. They loved owing" (29). The town also exhibits much of the paralysis of Joyce's Dublin: "But all the time I was there, there were no births, and no deaths . . . there was a kind of stagnation . . ." (31). This last-named trait of Ireland had been the target of Yeats's social criticism plays of the 1930s.

Unlike the dramas, *Ah Well* exhibits the degree of radical discontinuity from the world we know that characterizes a fabulation; for example, the inhabitants of the town had an elixir (like the drink "Romance" in *Amaranthers*) which "was all things to all men and for all women too" (37). This "elixir" suggests a metaphor for the life of the imagination, as does "Romance" in *Amaranthers*, or "the spring of the careless flower" in the narrative of that name. The initial exposition of the theme equals the subjectivity of *Sligo*, using the logic of association, giving an example of how "the boys who disintegrate space" operate, dealing in images. While he is in the utopia the speaker learns to give up thought and deal in images: "But as soon as I got up there [to a good thinking place] I found I wasn't thinking, that is, thinking out, planning my ideas, laying one idea against another, one fashion of thought against another" (36).

"Dusty Brown," the teller of the exemplum or interpolated tale designed to illuminate Yeats's principal theme, is introduced in a way that prepares us for a fabulation. He is, like Bowsie, created for "company," so that "Jack," the original narrator, has someone to speak to. Quite clearly, he is a nonrealistic character, like the "grand shining fellow." He is a clay man brought to life, "my unshatterable friend of clay. He is a dusty brown." He is next described as "the small man come away from his setting" the man "just seen" when

> Once on a day
> When days were good
> In a day of long ago
> When an old brown man
> On a small brown horse
> Rode up a whingey hill
> And stood against a sinking sun—
> That sun is sinking still.
>   (5)

This fairytale opening matches in tone the interpolated tale's events.

In addition to its delight in design and discontinuity from the known world, *Ah Well* exhibits other characteristics of the fabulation: unusual encounters, the journey motif, the ritual sacrifice; it also has the characteristic Yeats *triskele* ending. Dusty Brown, like other Yeats characters, encounters men and women who give him cryptic messages and then disappear. Yeats's works are, in Pilling's words "full of people suddenly encountering one another, exchanging anecdotes and parting again" and the people the protagonists encounter are "usually of obscure provenance and almost always materializing out of nothing and disappearing for ever, their story done."[105] The appearances, and encounters too, are radically discontinuous from the world as we know it. In a country where for centuries everyone who was anyone—priest, poet, teacher, hero— was "on the run," the outsider, stranger or traveller might well be someone of eminence on an important mission. The proper response to a stranger was to accept unquestioningly a task or an invitation.

One of these materializing strangers, introducing the journey motif with its mythic resonances, invites Dusty to ride on a small horse up a hill, perhaps, following the language of the narrative's opening, a "whingey " hill. Dusty is invited to go on a ritual journey with the principal men of the town, to view it properly, from the heights. O'Doherty, speaking of Yeats's paintings, has noted in them the importance of the journey motif and its mythic resonances. Speaking of the Irish myth of "promise and regret," or "before it starts" and "when it's over," he says that most of Yeats's paintings belong to these two groups: on the one hand—youth, dawn, encounters; on the other—age, evening, departures, with travelling common to both. He finds that the titles of Yeats's paintings make up "an idiosyncratic, poetic litany—of wayfarings and journeyings"; travel "is laden with symbolic meanings . . . focussed by twin ideas—of the Quest and the Expulsion."[106]

The elements of the Yeatsean journey are by now familiar. The travellers, as in *Sailing* and *Amaranthers*, drink a ritual drink, here explicitly linked to imagination: "[L]ift it to your lips and let imagination gurgle down the rich garlands of the ne'er do betters" (48). This elixir for the journey is Romance or Imagination. Similarities to *The Charmed Life* are notable. A single companion appears and then six others: "From left and right, East and West, appeared two small groups. Three horsemen each. Solid men" (49). There were seven speakers in each of the three colloquies in *The Charmed Life*. These travellers also assume new names for the journey, as they had for the colloquies in the earlier narrative.

After the journey to the top of the hill, there is an attempt at ritual suicide which brings about an epiphany. There had been earlier foreshadowings that the journey was to end in a ritual sacrifice in which the small brown man would be expected to participate. Now the travellers all sit in a line and speak of boyhood—their strength, humor, and imagination in boyhood. They speak of the imperceptibility of the aging process and debate the merits of being young again. Then, without warning, a nameless speaker takes the hand of two others in the line and starts the downhill run "toward the low brambles at the cliff top" (84) for a communal suicide plunge.

The small brown man, who had previously decided old age wasn't so bad, sits down from his position at the exact center; by leaning back with all his weight and dragging his heels while keeping his hands linked to those in the linked line, he stops the whole line of runners just short of the brambles. This plunge attempt resembles the one No Matter had contemplated making with the Judge and Bowsie in *The Charmed Life.*

As they return to the town, the brown man has an epiphany involving linked half circles: "We mounted and our horses stepped gently along the piece of level road, placing the curve of the crescents of their shoe marks facing West, above the crescent of the morning which had faced East. I looked down by my horse's gentle side, and in the soft ground I saw, that symbol of my life [,] a crescent on a crescent reversed and interlaced" (85). This tracery, representing both beginning and ending, is an appropriate symbol for Yeats's concept of life. The brown man has an experience of being outside of time: "We were in a state neither dawn, nor evening, nor midday, nor night," and of being carried by the larger forces of the universe: "like straw bottles floating on a sea" (85). This powerful vision carries the message of essential optimism, an answer to the opening question, who can say always with cheerful courage "Death, where is Thy Sting?" A seventy-year-old man who has experienced the death of two siblings and seen a Fascist nightmare sweeping across Europe, all in the same year, presents for the reader a triumph over the temptation to despair. Immediately after using the straw bottles image, the protagonist says, in biblically resonant language which changes the universal force from randomness to Providence: "I declare to my God, I never in all my days in that town, saw the fountain pouring its strength up into the air so strongly" (85–86). Dusty Brown's epiphany of the interconnectedness of life's aspects is accompanied by the imagery of the powerful flowing water. In Yeats's utopia, contemplation of water, the source of life, improves humanity. Not only the sleep of death but also the strength of the life force is to be seen in water.

The metafiction ends with a new journey, by horse, when a mysterious stranger offers Dusty a ride out of town to where another stranger leads another horse, by a straw halter, of course, and bids him ride up, into a new town. "And so the whole story, in a way which is by now customary, rounds upon itself."[107] The final comment from the small old man, Dusty Brown, is similar to the endings of other narratives in calling attention to its own fictionality. "I mounted the brown [horse] and rode up the hill and that's my story, sir" (88).

And To You Also

Thematic continuity is maintained in *And To You Also*, published in 1944 (hereafter *Also*). Yeats treats in this narrative all of his principal themes: the need to accept life's rhythms; the need to attend to the inner vision while maintaining contact with the outside world; and the need to accept essential human isolation while continuing to make an effort to communicate.

The form of *Also* is not easy to categorize. Most of the first section of the book is, like *Sligo*, almost pure stream of consciousness. In this work however, Yeats uses his narrator more skillfully to provide clues to what he is attempting to do; he is "jettisoning memories" again. At the same time he is trying, using "half-memory," to record the process of creation, without altering beyond recognition his authentic vision; his recording tool, language, is a failed medium of communication. Sensing the difficulty of the task of writing while still absorbed in the vision, his narrator expresses the wish for a scribe: "How nice it would be to have a private egotist within . . . who would write under a nom de plume while we dozed. Even if we heard the nom de plume through our cloudy ears we would forget it, be lucky, and have no responsibility."[108] *Also* represents an exploration of those semi-voluntary, semi-conscious states in which Yeats's projected selves enter into a colloquy.

These states came increasingly to fascinate Yeats. His writing as well as his painting became increasingly visionary. Family influences partly account for his pursuit of the visionary. WB dabbled in the occult for most of his adult life, interested in ways of inducing trances for evoking visions and releasing creative energies. WB told

John O'Leary that the mystical life was at the center of all he did, thought, and wrote. Jack's favorite sister, Lily, was a "seer," and her dreams were often discussed at breakfast in the Yeats household. JBY, who opposed WB's mysticism, acknowledged that Lily "had an unusual kind of foresight, seeing visions that proved remarkably prophetic." She usually experienced these visions while awake or in the "half-waking state just before or after sleeping."[109] Lily, who did not court these visions but treated them rather matter of factly, was the member of the family to whom Jack was closest from his earliest years; it is natural therefore that he would be interested in nonsolicited visionary states, particularly half-waking ones, those his narrator describes as "dozing."

He himself seems to have needed a trance-like state for release of creative energies. He told his niece Anne that he did not know how he painted, that subjects came to him. (The sculptress in Athol Fugard's *Road to Mecca* describes this process as having "pictures" come into her head; she cannot begin work until the picture is clear.) Anne Yeats remembers that interruptions during Yeats's always-solitary painting sessions seemed to put him off for the whole day. He may have written under the same visionary influences Fugard's sculptress describes, and *Also* seems to be a more thorough exploration of the visionary creative process, more of the excavatory type than the exploration in *Sligo*. Perhaps Yeats's friendship with Beckett and MacGreevy, who were both interested in the "vertical" creative process, had made him increasingly interested, in the decade between these two books, in exploring his own creative states.

Like Lily's visions, Yeats's moments of transcendence are not sought or forced. His narrator says in *Also*, after speculating on the convenience of having a private scribe to keep memory states undisturbed, "But, whether we will it or not, there is no farewell to those moments in our memories when only one sense drinks alone at the clear well" (96–97), when our memories of past sensory impressions are "split away to nothing" and the sensations of the moment hold us. He was aware that memory held him in "a closely gripping hand, that can never be loosed" (97). These moments when a strong sensory impression in the present both evokes and overwhelms the memory of a past impression are Yeats's equivalent of the Romantic poets' mystic moments or the Proustian experience. They form the basis of his art, both visual and verbal. These moments and the associations they bring are the subject matter of *Also*, and are closely related to the artistic authenticity theme explored in other narratives.

The first of the evocative sensory experiences explored in *Also* is related to the same subject that dominated *Ah Well*: death. Not unexpectedly for a child whose immediately elder brother died when he was two and whose baby sister (born on his fourth birthday) died before he was five, Yeats had strong early memories of funerals. It is also not unusual that a seventy-two-year-old man whose eldest brother and immediately elder sister had recently died (a year apart almost to the day) would have these early sibling deaths close to his consciousness and superimposed on by recent similar experiences. The first moment of memory recorded in this fiction involves a sensation of cold, "a cold church not as cold as death, another coldness. But our body is cold from bone to bone" (97). The next image is of the condensing breath of the mourners rising in the church, their shoulders shaking from crying, and of their "grim," "sorrowful" faces.

Consideration of the need to accept death leads to the consideration of the need to accept essential human isolation; death is only one of the momentous experiences we face alone. The sense of isolation the narrator experiences as some mourners move behind the others to file past the coffin, and look at the names and the messages on the cards, causes him to conclude: "We have no friends, and all are our friends" (97). All try to console us; no one really does. Like "Jack" in *Ah Well* or like the speaker in Beckett's *Company,* the narrator invents a listener, or another speaker, in order not to be alone. However, he knows that the true human state is isolation and that communication is impossible: "I would like to talk to myself now a sad talking about old friends that were only friends because we both imagined we had a friend" (98). The self he talks to is viewed as another, separate from the first self. First he considers summoning Bowsie, the listener of the paired protagonists in *The Charmed Life,* but this choice proves slightly unsatisfactory: "If Bowsie were here I doubt if I could talk to him right out openly. But I created Bowsie to listen to me, and he began to talk to himself, and even his back never looked like listening" (98). The speaker summons instead another creation from an earlier book to listen to him now, the "Man-Without-a-Shirt" from *Sligo*: "[Y]ou used to listen to me and looked as if you did . . ." (99). He says farewell to this listener also and concludes, "I must just amuse myself." Communication is rarely possible.

The relation of artist to audience motif is explored, again in ways that foreshadow Beckett's *Company*. The need for a listener is reiterated as is the need for another speaking voice: "I would have been tired of myself and of waiting. Then would be the time when I would wish for Bowsie and the light guitar of his trickling thoughts" (107). The narrator fancies a new, "a listening Bowsie . . . imagine him by me listening to what an early bird reviewer, of an early worm work of mine, said I 'was pleased to call' my 'thoughts' " (107–8). The second listener is again recalled, the Man-Without-a-Shirt; he must be convinced, however, by a man with the gift of the gab that he has a gift of joy in listening. The audience must be trained. The need for a listener is intimately related to the artist's need for an audience and to his proper relation to that audience. This problem of maintaining artistic authenticity and balance had occupied Yeats extensively in *A Broadside*, and in *Also* he is still ambivalent about the relation. Having mentally summoned up the listeners for whom he has acknowledged a need, the Man-Without-a-Shirt and Bowsie, the narrator now reminds himself that he must, like the bareback rider in *A Broadside*, focus on the experience and not on the audience: "I talk to amuse myself and only on the off chance after the event will I give a thought to amusing the shadow of Bowsie" (121).

The subject of the proper relation of the artist to audience was particularly apposite in *Also*. By the time it was published, two of Yeats's plays, *Harlequin's Positions* and *La La Noo*, had been performed at the Abbey, but *In Sand* had recently been turned down.

Reviewers had found *La La Noo* baffling, and in this narrative Yeats transforms his own experience by representing a playwright called up on the stage to find only one spectator in the theatre: " . . . all the others, men, women and nut-headed daughters, gone home." The author thanks the spectator for staying to express appreciation and says: "I am indeed deeply moved. It's not by the numbers of appreciable skulls we are rolled to splendour, but by the intensity of the appreciation of one skull." And the audience says "And I thank you for your play, and for nowhere in it, or since, telling me what it is all about" (127). The author must not interfere in the aesthetic transaction or comment. In a letter to his director written at about this time, Yeats used a similar vocabulary to describe his dismissal of the difficulties of his audience: "I do believe that any audience whose skulls weren't filled with crumpled cellophane alone, [who] were well shepherded into a not-too-big theatre, would get entertainment out of any of my plays. . . ."[110] The subject of the proper relation to the audience must often have been on his mind. The narrator goes on to say in *Also*: "Sometimes it comes on me that it would be better . . . if in whirling my thoughts out of my skull, and down on to the cold paper, I should not think of any listener. Bowsie I sacked. And the Man-Without-a-Shirt, I don't know whether he's here listening with his ear open or not. I should perhaps think of no one unless, unless, ah yes . . . the GOOD BOY" (127).

The Good Boy represents the ideal audience, "One of the all rights . . . One of the picked" (128). He would be the participating viewer and listener, one who would be persuaded that he had the gift of joy in listening and would thank the playwright for not telling him what the play was about. As Yeats had maintained since *Modern Aspects*, the audience-artist transaction must be a two-way street. Once the artist explains, or "panders" to the needs of an audience whose skulls are filled with crumpled cellophane, true art is no longer possible.

There is no objection, however, to giving hints as to what you propose to say, "just as the grand old giants of the printed World of Fiction used to head their chapters" (130). In the most Sterne-like of all the sections, the narrator gives us "a short chapter heading all ready for a Chapter, which I never wrote," followed by "a list of suggestions for the contents of a chapter which I will not write. But I will not waste the last [sic, "list"] so here it comes, and as you have been standing up to breast the gravelly storm as far as this without a breather, I'll call it

> Chapter Two,
> and here goes:"
> (131–32)

The two themes (the need to accept death and human isolation and the need to keep a proper relation between artist and audience) having been introduced, the four-page list of suggestions for a chapter he will not write (132–35) serves to introduce the colloquy narrative. The list contains such familiar items from the Yeats repertoire as Marionettes, The Lambeth School of Arms, Shapes the bus conductor, New York, Circus, Ballads, Watteau, Bret Harte, Slang, Cow Boys, Pirates, Bookplates, Scents, Writers like Kipling, Dime Novels, The Fancy, Press Cutting Books, First Nights, Old Plays, New Orleans, Old Sketch Books, Old Legends of Ireland, Rebellion, Revolution, Islands, Farewell to Hollywood, Comrades, Boat Races, Poetry on Death, Boxers, Old Inns, California, Hospitality, Friendship, Humanity, and The Shabby Genteel. The list ends "And a very nice Chapter Too!" (135). The speaker then portrays himself as throwing his notes over his shoulder and turning to the Good Boy, his third created listener and ideal audience, in the setting for the main colloquy. The setting recalls both the mind (blue and grey were the colors of the brain and therefore of visions) and St. Stephen's Green: "I notice that we are strolling gently in a blue, grey, and green pleasure ground, woody, in the middle of a city. High houses all round the edges" (135).

As in *Amaranthers*, *The Charmed Life* and *Ah Well*, the main discussion of the themes has seven participants. Two other groups of talkers and listeners join the narrator and the Good Boy, pacing in time to their talk. A new couple ("an old blade, gay but droopy" and "a stately young woman still in the mind of the Eighteenth Century") joins the Baron (the Man-Without-a-Shirt) and Bowsie, becoming the fifth and sixth speakers. They are described as moving in ways that recall the fore and aft motion of *Ah Well*: "[M]oving this way and that, but always parallel to myself and the Good Boy. From time to time they all talk a little, sometimes to each other, and sometimes to themselves" (136). In keeping with Yeats's attitude toward human isolation and toward the consequent incapacity of language to communicate, they may as well talk to themselves as to others. In keeping with Yeats's attitude toward identity, characters are not identified when they speak; only occasionally, in keeping with the idea that individuals are all part of the greater life, does a speech identifiably come from one of the seven speakers. The colloquy proper has a two-line introduction.

> From then on we all talked
>   in and out of turn.
>   (136)

The last speaker, lurking among the trees, proves to be the park keeper, who locks them in St. Stephen's Green for the night. This expository portion of the book occupies about one-third of the total; the main colloquy, replacing the exemplum in this fabulation, occupies two-thirds.

There are recognizable elements from other narratives in this colloquy. The new couple is described as "pacing in time to our thoughts," and the rest of the colloquy portrays parallel movement and paced speech, like the "fore and aft" movement of the long colloquy in *The Charmed Life*. The real subject (like that of WB's *Memoirs*) is "Reverie," "memory under the sweet sway of intuition," or "the sinuous ways of memory,"[111] the subject of *Sligo*.

Fifteen years of experience writing plays and fiction, however, have enabled Yeats to make *Also* more aesthetically pleasing than the earlier work. The alternation of speakers in the later work (although all of them are still recognizably projections of the one mind operating in the half-light of reverie, half-memory, or the trance of creative imagination) makes the flow of the narrative smoother than the movement in *Sligo*. The jerkiness of transitions that made *Sligo* appear to one critic "a book less to be read through than to be dipped into"[112] has been eliminated. The dialogue is far more skillful, and interactions between speakers more interesting. For example, while one speaker of the original pair—who has been characterized as speaking "like a book with a bright green cover and golden clasps and mottled edges" (137)—is singing a song, an "ignorant creature obtruding his noisome corrosive ideas on the fair bosom of the night" interrupts. The interrupter is told, "You talk out of turn and too much," and is bid to remain silent by still another speaker. The original speaker then complains that his thoughts have been dissipated "like old square-rigged wooden fighting ships in a gale in a picture by a marine painter in his cups" (138). Other original similes and metaphors are mixed with sardonically uttered clichés in a fashion that strikes a reader like Vivian Mercier as witty and a reader like Marilyn Gaddis Rose as whimsical. Either way, the language is livelier than the monologue of *Sligo.*

Some of the subjects discussed in the main colloquy of *Also* are familiar ones, going back to *Sligo* and beyond. Human isolation is the colloquy's first and most common motif. The Good Boy is frightened because he sometimes thinks "there's only you and me in the world, and then I think there's only me. Then I get frightened." He then asserts that he owes it to those who named him not to be frightened, so he tries to "catch hold" of himself: "So I clean my boots, I get a shine on them, and out I go" (140–41). His response to frightening solitude is typical of Yeats. The young boy who at age two was "so cheerful and comic that everyone liked him"[113] grew up, expected, and expecting, to "catch hold of himself." Grandpapa's favorite, Jack was the original "Good Boy." The shining child shown in many of Yeats's late paintings, sometimes slightly grown up, is the Good Boy of *Also.* He represents another projection of Yeats's personality, an addition to Bowsie and Mr. No Matter of *Life,* and to Jack and Dusty Brown of *Ah Well.*

A second projection of the Yeats personality in *Also,* the Man-Without-a-Shirt, discusses the inability of frightened, isolated humans to communicate, to bridge the gap each feels, when he says that he never speaks directly to the other speakers, nor they to him. He speculates that he and the Good Boy speak the same language, but is warned by the latter that if he wishes to be happy he must remember that no one else ever speaks the same language he does. Reluctantly the Man-Without-a-Shirt agrees and says that he has always known it "since I left the years of discretion behind me and left all to the the advice of a licked finger held in the air" (146). Truth in Yeats's literary universe is not learned by discretion, or by systems of rational thought, but by accepting what comes, uniting oneself with natural forces such as the wind that informs a licked finger held in the air. The paradox of growing psychically younger as one grows physically older, explored in *Ah Well*, is also implied in this remark.

The limitations of friendship to bridge the gap of isolation are noted: "I always think back to myself, the decrepit old egotist. . . . I have friends . . . I like them well, as well as I am able to like any one. And they like me as well as they can like any of their friends" (162–63). But, isolation is still unconquerable. For this man whose father described his capacity for affection as an "unsunned well," the isolation of his childhood was never completely overcome. He was lonelier, more distant than most, the child of a nonresponsive mother and an absent father.

Nostalgia increases a sense of isolation by adding a temporal dimension. The blade, speaking of an unsuccessful attempt to get a response from a fellow human, says poignantly: "Ah! The days of yore . . . we shall never see those days again, they are gone. I count myself hardly past my prime, but most everything I value has left me standing still, or perhaps it is that those who used to value me have not been able to pass on the faint and fragile interest they took in me, and such as me, to their sons and daughters" (148). The blade's response to his predicament, however, is accepting—like the response of The Good Boy, or any other wise character in the Yeatsean universe: "But why repine?"

There is a break in the discussion at this point. The seventh speaker, "a man in the shadows," who seemed at first a visitor from the spirit world, proves to be the keeper who must lock the park gates for the night. He bids the characters a "fond" farewell and they each reply, one speaker in Gaelic and the last with a variation of the title: "And you also" (158). Five of the peripatetic speakers, who had been using the same fore and aft motion noted in *The Charmed Life*, now sit down and talk, by agreement, about isolation.

The actress (the first female speaker in the predominantly male world of Yeats's fiction) speaks first and tells of an early experience of isolation when her first love, an actor who played Willie Reilly opposite her, committed suicide after the performance. The Man-Without-a-Shirt (alternately, here and elsewhere, called The Baron) speaks of an experience of noncommunication with one of the strangers who come and go in Yeats's narratives, this one a house-breaker who came twice in the same night. All human contacts seem abortive, reiterating the theme of human isolation.

The Good Boy now takes over as principal speaker and discusses a new aspect of the theme, the means for overcoming isolation: love. As *Ah Well* had been concerned with the proper response to death, *Also* is concerned with the proper response to human isolation. The Good Boy says that he is loved because he loves himself, embraces life, does not fear (or appears not to), and is cheerful, but mostly he is loved because he expects others to be glad to see him and to think of him (177). Yeats was himself, like The Good Boy, a person easy to love, naturally cheerful and outgoing. The Baron speaks, in a way that may reveal the limitations of Susan Yeats's love, of the lack of an important type of love, maternal love: "I was never loved more than a little and never for very long . . . after the ordinary, fair enough, mother's love had got so weak in its little pat-pat-patter of the heart" (177).

Other views of love are given, some contradictory. The Baron places love in a Christian context. He is loved because he has been redeemed "by the greatest blood that ever flowed" and so calls all men "by no names but 'Woman' or 'Man' or 'Child,' and always 'friend,' for that goes for all" (178–79). He makes no distinction of persons and loves all; so he is loved. Yeats was a devout Christian and may also have experienced this bond, but he projects here, through the use of the metaphor of the moat by the Squire (a character who appeared at the end of *Sailing, Sailing Swiftly*) a different self of which he was also aware. This self is not loving, is, rather, the reserved one that his father spoke of as having an unsunned well to which no one could penetrate. "My friends don't even love me because they think I love them, they feel happier for not thinking so. They love to think that there is a deep and chilly moat full to the brim, dark as night or bright as steel, always between their wisdom and my folly. . . . But what does it matter as long as they love me?" (180). The lady gives a similar reason as to why she is loved: "I was loved because I never loved . . . because I never gave love a thought" (181).

The next section of the colloquy deals with a second important motif—memory. The particular aspect of the topic treated here is early childhood memories of pictures. Each speaker gives a self-characterizing account of these memories. The experience of creating characters and dialogue for drama enriched the presentation of reminiscence, even though characterization in fiction was not one of Yeats's serious aims. The Baron, who had introduced the Christian aspect of love into the earlier discussion, remembers an appropriate painting called the "Maiden's Prayer." The Squire's memories of paintings, in a home much like Merville must have been, are most extensive and are appropriate to Yeats's own background or to WB's. (The portrait of the Squire may owe something to WB.) The Squire remembers paintings of a farmyard in "Manor House Style" (Grandfather Pollexfen kept over his bed a picture of "Kitely," the manor house that should have been his, and had dreams of restoring the family fortunes); a sportsman (perhaps one like the horseback-riding curate, Grandpapa Yeats); a steeple chase (Uncle George Pollexfen used to ride his own horses in the races and bring them to Merville); and a tomb: "the embroidered name on the tomb was just 'Robert.' " (Yeats's brother Bobbie, who died when Jack was two, was named for his father's brother Robert, who also died young.)

The Squire recounts other early memories which also could have been Yeats's own or WB's. Speaking of his cousins, he says that there seemed to be no happiness in their joking and that he did not know what made them truly happy (187). This view accords with JBY's verbal portraits of his Pollexfen in-laws and WB's memories of childhood at Merville. The Squire tells of a room "a sort of little apologetic cave, a place that made you think of everything but comfort" (188). This accords well with both Lily's and WB's memories of Merville. The Squire also remembers a painting of a ship he liked to think of as sailing to the west "for I hoped some day to sail to the West to a fairyland I often thought of—the United States of America" (190). An uncle is mentioned who would not say more than three words at one time (191). Perhaps most significant is the memory of a fight with a cousin "who had too much to say for himself altogether, and most of it was about my father . . . and most of it was true" (193). Knowledge of the disfavor with which the Pollexfens viewed JBY makes this reference as poignant as the reference to the weakness of the bonds of maternal love. The Squire sums up his ten-page recollection with a statement also very characteristic of Yeats's own relation to events of his early childhood: "and they sank into my store of memory" (195).

Bowsie's memories of childhood reflect another aspect of Yeats's exploration of the "dizzying" multiplicity of his selves. Bowsie represents, as we know from *The Charmed Life*, the sports-loving, theatre-visiting, aspect of Yeats's personality; characteristically, he remembers pictures of an Irish boxer named Heenan and of an actress playing Rosalind. Bowsie grew up in a rented house surrounded by remains of former tenants. These memories may reflect the London lodgings Susan Yeats hated so much. The Good Boy had also seen such pictures.

Other characters' memories may represent other aspects of Yeats's own. The Lady remembers fine, large pictures of

> The Green Vales,
> The round towers,
> The mountains,
> The lakes, and the bright rivers
> Of our dear Land of Ireland.
>   (199)

This hearkening back to the nationalist ideals (and to the language of *Amaranthers*) is placed in an ironic perspective by the Lady's assertion that she saw them on the walls of a bar "where my bold dad did the Macrah Macree Act with all our money" (200). She was brought down there by her "mammy" to shame him into coming home. This bathetic reduction of nationalist subject matter ends the topic of early childhood memories; it may obliquely represent the quarrels over money in the Yeats household, since his father was not, at least in his mother's mind, an adequate provider.

The Lady returns to the book's first major subject—the subject of the colloquies in *The Charmed Life* and of the central experience of *Ah Well*—death. She asks a question to which every speaker responds characteristically: "Did any of you ever think of yourselves dying and how you would like to die?" (200). The responses to her question occupy the rest of the book, which thus returns on itself in the *triskele* fashion. She, when young, had hoped to die in the arms of the actor who played Willie Reilly. Having learned wisdom, the primary theme of all the narratives, she now knows that she will have no choice of a mode of death. She accepts what must come as do admirable characters in all of the narratives, but adds the Christian context more characteristic of the works written in the 1940s: "I die when I must and I hope I die game . . . and die in the hope eternal" (205). This response exemplifies one of Yeats's beliefs about women, that they are intuitively brave and wise and instinctively in tune with the source of eternal wisdom. Like the Baron, she adds a Christian context, a thrust that culminates in the ending of *The Careless Flower*.

Bowsie expresses a poignant wish for a form of death that may reflect feelings of the young Yeats about his mother's neglect; because he thought his mother slighted him, Bowsie dreamed of dying bravely so that at his death his mother would be "splendid" and he could forgive her "all the neglect." He too couches his wish in a religious context, asking God to give him sense and hoping that bravery may follow (206).

The others also express wishes about the circumstances of their deaths, wishes that Yeats might have uttered in his own voice. The Baron would like to die then with that good company (207). The blade hopes to remember "some cheerful expression for the watchers" (211) a hope similar to one raised in *Sligo* when the death of the "motor" driver is discussed. The Good Boy would like to die on a white terrace near a river with tall young people walking through green woods toward him. The description matches the scene of Yeats's first play, *The Deathly Terrace* (1933) and many of the last visionary paintings. The subject of suicide, one of the central concerns of *The Deathly Terrace*, comes up, perhaps brought along by the memory of the scene. The Good Boy rejects the temptation to suicide, like the protagonist of *Ah Well*; he does not drink the waters of forgetfulness, Lethe, on his balustrade, but, like the motor driver in *Sligo*, he is inspired to bravery by a woman: "Come hog, dog, or devil, lady, I know you know, I will die with my fists in front . . . as you cannot help yourself wanting me to" (210).

The Squire, who is now identified with The Good Boy as one of the original pairs of speakers, is seen to be the speaker also of all which went before "Chapter Two." He is now addressed as "M.C., Referee, Bottle Holder, Conscience Handler, Time-keeper, Judge and Starter" and asked to end with his ideas of death. He declines, however, since dawn is coming, and they must leave the park.

The Lady, continuing the Christian context she and the Baron had introduced, ends with a prayer for all the men, including the absent seventh speaker: "[T]he blessing of God is on us all, and on all your ways and my ways—and so farewell, farewell, farewell, farewell." The Squire replies: "Farewell to you also" (212). Neatly rounding on itself, the reminiscence ends with the primary speaker's words, which may be addressed either to characters or reader, a typical Yeats ending.

Although this work contains more discussion than action, Yeats has gone beyond merely "jettisoning memories," as his narrator claimed to do in *Sligo*. His dramatic creation of suitable speakers for his utterances and his creation of a milieu suitable to their utterance—the twilight and dawn states characteristic of his work, which he considered suitable for explorations of semiconscious states—mark this work as an advance in technique over the simple experiments in stream of consciousness we find in *Sligo*.

The book's creation of dream states is innovative. These states are to be explored again in *The Careless Flower*. Yeats's insistence, in "Chapter Two," on the atmosphere of the "half-light," the "pale shadows," the only partial visibility of the characters, and their "flitting" motions indicate that these beings belong to the mental or spiritual world of the first speaker's creative imagination. The use of the seventh speaker reinforces this dimension of the narrative exploration of dream states. At first he seems insubstantial. This "man in the shadows" is described at one point as "a critic weaving from niche to niche in a Valhalla" (144). He is clearly apart from the other speakers, whom he characterizes as "they." His interpolated comments always emphasize his difference from them: "Bravery, dignity, they are always thinking about them" (144), or when the Lady asserts, "Everyone should know that," he replies "No. No. I didn't" (141). The six acknowledge his difference, "Who's that fellow flittering about in the shadows remarking everything he hears?" (142). When he, who had seemed most shadowy, turns out to represent the official and established world, his exit from the park calls into question the terrestrial reality of what is transpiring within its gates. The Baron or The Man-Without-a-Shirt further calls their state as living beings into question when he speaks of "the real ones, the ones I valued when I lived in the same world as them and breathed the same air" (178). Their need to leave the park before dawn may be required because ghosts can only roam at night.

Loftus's comment on WB's *Reveries* may be pertinent to Jack's intentions in *Also*. "The object of such art is not simply to represent human experience, but to move from human experience to a kind of knowledge, emotional and religious, that is beyond purely rational comprehension."[114] Perhaps the introduction of the female speaker, the first in a colloquy, is meant to facilitate the movement into consideration of emotional and religious truth. She speaks first on the ultimate subject of death, which immediately follows the recitals of first memories, as if to imply that we begin dying once we are born. She utters a statement of the primary theme of all the narratives, a profound emotional truth learned from human experience: that she has no choice about her death. She then goes beyond it to assert an emotional and religious truth: that she dies in "the hope of the eternal." It is not only very Irish to view women as vehicles for spiritual truth and emotional verities, but, very typical of Yeats's attitude toward women. JBY had always viewed Susan as instinctive and spiritual. Yeats himself characterized his wife, after her death, as his "May queen," a vernal being to be revered as a representative of the life force. His mother had been the Christian parent, insisting over her husband's objections that the children be taught prayers and go to church. Both familial and nationalist influences would incline Jack Yeats to associate religious truth, and an instinctive connection with first and last things, with women. The importance of these religious and extra-terrestrial dimensions in the last two narratives should not be underrated.

The Careless Flower

The Careless Flower recapitulates and further develops the themes found in the earlier narratives. The primary theme, the rhythms of life theme, is here united with the artistic authenticity theme. Those who can accept the rhythms of life, the paired protagonists Mark and Gaw, drink from the spring of the Careless Flower and become true artists. Those who cannot accept life's rhythms and will not drink from the spring, the foil pair Ralph and Gladys, become imitative storytellers, not authentic artists. Yeats develops the exploration of the nature of the creative process begun in *Ah Well* and continued in *And To You Also* and shows the benefits to creativity of imaginative sympathy. *The Careless Flower* (hereafter *Flower*) also contains an element of the social criticism that appears strongly in the drama.

Structurally, this narrative is more carefully developed than any narrative since *The Charmed Life*; it has four parts, each roughly sixty pages long. Part 1 sets forth the themes and exposition. Part 2 gives an account of the voyage to utopia and the first adventures settling in there. Part 3 (like *And To You Also*) continues the explorations of "less conscious" states and concentrates on the imaginative visions of Mark and Gaw. Part 4 contains the narrative resolution and strongest social criticism. This rich and well-told fabulation is a fitting culmination to Yeats's narratives.

Part 1 most resembles *The Amaranthers*. At the level of the action, Oliver James Gaw, a middle-aged, unemployed intellectual, fallen from the ranks of the professional or middle class but overqualified educationally and socially for the working class, is hired as a "historical lecturer" on a voyage to "sunny seas." The journey is employed as a learning experience as it was in *Amaranthers*, and the principal learning is connected to the theme of acceptance of what comes. Like James Gilfoyle, the protagonist of the earlier narrative, Gaw was the son of an indulgent mother of social pretensions but is now alone in the world. Unlike the young James who has to educate himself, Gaw is middle-aged and educated. As might be expected because of his age, he has a paired protagonist instead of mentors.

The primary theme, the need to consciously surrender to larger forces, is exemplified more in relation to Gaw than to Mark. Gaw, for example, felt, in the opening of the exposition section, that "he had a die to cast, a coin to toss, a chance to take, win or lose" (25). Gaw thinks only of victory and reviews the aspects of fate that brought him this far: the advertisement of the cruise had fallen from a letter box, and Gaw had picked it up; a newsboy in the street stopped, thinking Gaw had signaled for a paper, and Gaw, in his "imaginative charity," bought one; in the "Situations Vacant" was the lecturer advertisement and the name of the interviewer, an old school friend. "But this is fate" (26), he concludes, and accepts it. Having seized the moment, Gaw is equal to the test of strength; he runs the distance to his train in less time than he ever did before. As in *Also,* the theme is placed in a providential context: "Pick up your feet, the good God will put them down again" (26). "Glory" and "lilies of the field" are mentioned, emphasizing the biblical context of the trial.

In the train Gaw accepts advice from a stranger of obscure provenance who then disappears. The brief encounters persist, this one with a "tramp tradesman," another of the perpetual travellers in Yeats's repertoire. The last words of this well-met traveller are

"Plenty good luck, I can't say fairer than that" (28). Gaw is thus established as a man who can profit from chance encounters, and when he meets another "man of the roads," Mark, it seems fitting that he should take to him and try to do a good deed for him.

The mythic resonances of this voyage carry the theme forward. The voyage, or exemplum section of the fabulation, begins in an "ecstasy of dawn." Almost immediately, however, there is foreshadowing that the voyage will not go well. The second steward is a "Jonah" and the passengers come aboard "in a poor draggling hour" (60). A hurricane like the one that impelled James Gilfoyle to his destination in *Amaranthers* strands the four on shore while their ship, the *Scrutineer*, adrift with a wrecked wireless, floats away.

On his way to interview for this job, Gaw had encountered three "old salts" who introduce the artistic authenticity theme which becomes an important part of section three. The old salts are bound for a harbor bar, where they indulge in romantic fantasies like those of the Amaranthers in their club. These three salts imagine voyages for the ships they see moving out of the harbor. They talk of ships and distant places about which they know very little; facts would have spoilt illusion: "That would have soured romance with realism."[115]

The theme of artistic authenticity developed in *Sailing* begins to emerge in the descriptions of the salts' fantasies. The old salts get the fuel for their imaginary adventures out of a magazine and books. Their imagined adventures are described in such clichés as "the short sharp bark of derringers, the upwards slash of the long knife," and take place under the sun or under "burning stars." Occasionally an adventure involved impossible feats of rescuing a woman, but largely, "It was man's world" (21). The visions of the old salts grow out of the boys' adventure stories and the early pirate plays but reflect on them ironically: the three salts know nothing about the sea. Like Tarleton in *Sailing* who instructs good swimmers while not knowing how to swim, the salt named Grey is about to finish his description of what the tug men should have done: "'I've seen it done a—' 'A score of times' he was going to say, when he remembered he'd never seen anything done on the ocean deep" (21). None of them had ever been further from England by salt water than the Isle of Man.

The fragility of the imaginative world of the artist is stressed as it had been in *Amaranthers*. The friends never say much when others are in the bar, or correct each other on an error, because, in the "pellucid atmosphere" required to sustain their illusion, "a jarring correction would have fallen like a piece of faulty masonry in an edifice of fairyland" (22). The masonry reference recalls the fall of the Amaranthers' hotel. It is part of Yeats's theme in *Flower*—as it was in *Amaranthers* and *The Charmed Life*—that the world of romance, precious and sustaining to the spirit as it is, must never be confused with life as it must be lived. The old salts, seeing the *Scrutineer* return to port at the end of the fabulation, understand nothing of the storm that stranded the four passengers on an island or the failure of the journey; they fantasize instead that the ship has been on the Spanish main (195). They are not authentic artists because they do not transform what comes from within. Authentic artists keep their balance. They make the effort to sustain the imaginative life, but this effort, ironically, makes them function more effectively in the world of action than those who do not attempt artistry.

Part 2 demonstrates this truth and then develops it. When four passengers are stranded on an island after a hurricane, only the authentic artists can make use of the visionary opportunity offered to all. The "spring of the careless flower" makes Mark and Gaw boyish, like the old brown man in *Ah Well*, and enables them to perform prodigious feats of climbing as well as to help with the hard labor "down below." Those who cannot sustain an imaginative life, represented on this voyage by Gladys and Ralph, do not cope as well with ordinary life as do the authentic artists. The "fretful ones," the builders of roads and tenders of gardens, depend on the men of the careless flower spring for their spiritual sustenance. It is the mission of the authentic artist, the singer or storyteller, to bring this sustenance, the vision transformed by art, to those unable or unwilling to risk taking the journey to the top of the mountain, the metaphor for the exploration of imaginative life that had ended *The Amaranthers*. Though older, Mark and Gaw can tend the fire and carry down the mountain water from the spring (metaphors for the burning bush and the Pierian spring?); the younger pair, Ralph and Gladys, who, for differing reasons, stay on flat land and refuse to drink the spring's powerful waters, are not successful in their flatland endeavors. Mark tells his tales for them when their own tales falter. He is the artist, the Promethean figure who brings them light and fire. This artistic mission theme is a development of the artistic authenticity theme.

The artistic process as presented in this narrative is mysterious and fascinating. Mark begins his tale with an invention, then the process takes over; the artist is in some way possessed. The tale follows "its own way according to some rule of its own, some law of romance" (109). Yeats's description of the artistic process in Part Three of *Flower* is also an illustration of his concept of "half-memory," explored in *Ah Well* and *And To You Also*. From the top of their mountain, the visionaries, who have now been drinking from the spring for several weeks, appear to be surrounded by the sea. Gaw remembers a childhood holiday by the sea and superimposes this memory on the present reality, in the way Yeats had described in setting forth his theory of half-memory. The light shining on the water in an apparently straight line leads Gaw, by means of memory, to an old boating inn where he looked out the window on a river. Mark, who is a more powerful artist, has visions which generally are more imaginative and metaphoric than Gaw's; he transforms the sea into a prairie and "fancies" an American railway engine on it. Mark realizes his vision was also based on memory, on a memory of posters seen in his boyhood (117–18).

The source of artistic inspiration, the spring, is described in theatre metaphors: "Round three sides in tiers the rocks were laid, making you think of the old fashioned auditorium of a grand old theatre" (110). From his earliest *Broadside* collection, Yeats used theatre metaphors to speak about the artistic process. Even before he began to write fiction, drama interested him. Dramatic groupings characterized his earliest drawings, and his earliest form of play, according to his father, was role playing with dolls.[116] As a young child, he carried the dolls and sets of his dramatic play in a small theatre he called his "farm." His paintings very often use theatrical settings. A ballad singer singing of an event, rather than the event itself, is a common feature of illustrations in *A Broadside*. Yeats's most common metaphor for the balanced, authentic artist was the bareback rider, a theatrical performer. (His prevailing themes include reminders of the importance of maintaining balance between the needs of the audience and artist's need for preserving authenticity, and between imaginative illusion and reality.) Other natural features surrounding the spring are incorporated in the extended theatre metaphor: the waving ferns are seen as plumes on the heads of the ladies in the boxes; the waterfall comes as though out of the middle of the drop scene; a rock is seen as the conductor's old-fashioned box (110).

In the tale or fabulation there are often, in addition to metaphors, mythic resonances, as in *Sailing, Life* or *Also*. In this work, the flower that grows by the spring begins to display mythic powers, putting Mark and Gaw into a visionary state where their creative imaginations are liberated. The flower itself, like the figures on Keats's Grecian urn, is invulnerable to and outside of time, a careless flower:

Just below the jutting rock a flower grew, a single flower on a gently waving stem, rising out of long green leaves. . . . They were . . . always wide spread to catch the spray, which always fell over that flower. The four or five days they had known that flower it had never seemed to change. It was no more full blown than the first day.
    (110)

In its timelessness more appropriate to art than to nature, the flower seems to embody some light within itself (110). Its effect on the two men is to make them also invulnerable to time. The spring water that flows over the flower has time-reversing properties that make the two men healthy and young: "They always now looked as well and hearty as they did the first day they discovered the spring above . . . younger than they had looked any time since they had come to the island" (112). The myth of the Land of the Young is implied.

Those who will not drink from the mythic spring will not take risks; they will not give up the illusion of control. They cannot surrender the will to natural rhythms, nor can they surrender the self. They are unable get outside the bounds of human isolation by means of imaginative sympathy. The qualities Mark and Gaw gain from drinking the water of the spring put them in direct contrast to the nonartists below the mountain who, like those fearful ones James Gilfoyle and the Amaranthers leave behind before making their ascent to the world of imaginative visions, are bound in their solitude and their illusion of the power of the will. These two, Ralph and Gladys, rather than accept the rhythms of the life force, form "plans," while Mark and Gaw "made no plan" (111). Ralph plans to build a path from one side of the island to the other, a path which he describes as a bee-line, "though some of the bee-lines buzzed by the island bees when flowery drunk" were another kind of bee-line (111). The contrast between this path of Ralph's and the line of real bees emphasizes the fact that his is an engineering feat out of harmony with nature. Gladys, too, tries to control nature. As Seamus Heaney has pointed out, the characteristic masculine mode of artistic creation is forging, while the feminine mode is incubation.[117] Ralph and Gladys illustrate these modes. Gladys plans to encircle her house and her hearth with flower-painted stones (106). While this plan is a feminine response and not so destructive of the natural order as Ralph's line-making, forging plan, it is less than ideal in this situation. Her incubating mode serves to close her off from experience, like the bourgeois respectability ringed by experience it fears to enlarge that Ernie O'Malley found typical of his countrymen.

The effects of refusing to surrender the bounds of self, to unite with the forces larger than the self (in this case the spring) have social, as well as artistic, consequences. Ernie O'Malley describes the ring of bourgeois respectability as excluding the artist. In Yeats's literary universe, the nonartist who lacks imaginative sympathy is always fearful or envious of the artist. Ralph and Gladys, nonartists, are fearful; they cannot accept what comes and they cannot understand those who do accept. Seeing the effect on Mark and Gaw of the spring, the source of youth and health as well as the artistic source, the younger pair become anxious. Though each is already nervous away from the security of the known world and its familiar roles, they are made more nervous by the strange phenomenon that Mark and Gaw seem to be getting younger every day. Gladys, for all her limitations, has some of the intuitiveness that Yeats attributes to women; she senses "something magical in the water" and wishes for some, but Ralph assumes the patriarchal role of law-giver and forbids her to drink it. Ultimately conservative, he fears what this change, getting younger, might lead to: "Anyway, let sleeping dogs lie; safety first!" (115) he tells her. They determine to watch Mark and Gaw for alarming changes. The misunderstanding, fear, and envy of the artist by the unsympathetic nonartist, described in *Modern Aspects*, are important motifs in *Flower* and in dramas such as *Apparitions, The Old Sea Road, The Silencer* and *Harlequin's Positions*.

When Ralph comes up to the spring in the opening of part 3, Mark speaks of his own and Gaw's youthfulness and of the spring's virtue, inviting Ralph, metaphorically, to surrender to forces larger than the self and to become an artist; but Ralph, like the Amaranthers' driver in that narrative, refuses the invitation. He characterizes himself and Gladys as conservatives, saying that what's good enough for the father is good enough for the son (or daughter), and that they had got used to the spring down by the house (121). Their refusal to risk, to unite themselves with water, which since *Sailing*, has been a metaphor for the life force in Yeats's work, has an effect on their creativity, their power to tell tales. Like the old salts, they become inauthentic and imitative; their tales, too, have come from "some magazine catering for the thrillable" and lost the power of an original experience transformed through art. As early as 1922, in *Modern Aspects of Irish Art*, Yeats maintained that artists who refuse to seek the authentic vision, but who imitate models, are not true artists. This theme's strongest fictional presentation was in *Sailing.* True artists go to the top of the mountain, like the Amaranthers, surrender the will and the self, and risk all for the vision that sustains them. Yeats's primary and secondary themes blend here; no vision without surrender.

The two artists, who have maintained balance between the two worlds, can function better than the nonartists in the ordinary world. They continue to assist Ralph and Gladys in the world below the mountain, helping with Ralph's "plans," but making it "gay work." The contrast between the two pairs of characters is marked: "the four, the four just men. No, the just man, the very just woman and the two drink-at-the-spring-of-the-Careless-Flower-men" (133).

Ralph's road has clearly become metaphoric. He attempts to control the environment, to build suspension bridges, for example, or to shift a large boulder instead of going around it. He has not given up the ideal of control (*Amaranthers* clearly indicated an artist must) and he is dogged, like a product of his school, even about games. The other three acquiesce in his determination, struggling on with the games, which were originally intended to refresh them, as with a task.

The contrast in the nightly tales told by the four also becomes more marked. Gladys and Ralph make no progress in imaginative sympathy or artistic authenticity. The limitations of Gladys's authenticity, in contrast to that of Mark and Gaw, become clearer as she invents more and more exaggerated events for her protagonist:

But when the next installment came, it came limping. . . . But up on the heights by the signal fire's throne, though the pictures behind the eyes of Mark and Gaw were changing always and had, for each man, his own special set of strong glows, still they never seemed as boisterously bright as Gladys's pirate of the desert had seemed. His dyes were analine dyes.
(135)

Yeats contrasts two ways of creating and sharing, and shows the limiting effects on her artistic sensibility of Gladys's lack of imaginative sympathy.

Mark and Gaw's growth in imaginative sympathy begins to inspire joint visions and, finally, a jointly told tale. As love had been in *And To You Also*, this sympathy is, in *Flower*, the only way out of the solipsistic predicament. Yeats believed in the principle of imaginative sympathy. While aware of human isolation, of the solitary nature of the individual vision—the pictures had for each man his own special set of strong glows—and the limits of language for expressing the private vision to another, Yeats is suggesting here, as in *And To You Also* where love is the means, that the basis for communication is imaginative charity and human comradeship.

There are several sources of the distance to be crossed by these two men, among them class and nationality. Gaw is more handicapped than Mark in his quest for artistic authenticity, since he is English, not Irish, and therefore trapped, like Tarleton of *Sailing*, in an inauthentic culture (one that Yeats thought had too many false traditions). He is also middle-class, like Ambrose Oldbury, one of the paired protagonists in Yeats's drama *The Old Sea Road* who is artistically inferior to a déclassé native Irishman, Michael of the Song. Like Ambrose, Gaw is still struggling to keep on the fringe of middle-class respectability. But Mark, like Michael and like Yeats himself, is Irish, déclassé, an outsider who lives by chance and his wits; so are most of the artists in the Yeats literary universe.

Under the influence of the spring of the careless flower, to which both Mark and Gaw are receptive, they can, unlike Irish Thady and English Jasper of *Sailing*, bridge the gaps of class and nationality. In their joint vision they see various characters going down, or up, a long street "striped with shadows, or striped with lights" (136). Recognition of the necessity for this pattern had represented a gain in wisdom for James Gilfoyle of *The Amaranthers*. In *Flower* this alternation of light and dark becomes a focus of unity for the short tale the two artists tell in turn. They see a man in an adventure plot, moving in and out of the light and dark (like the dancers or those about to die in *The Charmed Life*). He finally gets run down by a fire engine. At the end of his tale their visions diverge. Even good companions like Bowsie and No Matter of *The Charmed Life* cannot go the same path all of the time.

Down below the mountain, Ralph is having a hard time trying to bend nature to his will. His path will not conform to his plan, his preconceived idea of what a road should be. His idea is based on roads he has seen, not on an original insight into nature. Ralph has not made, as Mark and Gaw have, the surrender of the self and will prerequisite to imaginative sympathy and vision. Like Larry in *Sailing,* who gives up his chance for artistic authenticity by imitating carvings, Ralph has no originality and imitates models.

Mark and Gaw try to share their sustaining vision with the two "fretting ones" who cannot adapt themselves to their situation. Mark, the artist who tries to transform his vision for his fellows, now invents the story with which this chapter began. Consciously employing rhetoric to embellish his own invention or gathering (from invention, the first step in classical rhetoric) Mark tells a tale of a traveller like those from *The Charmed Life.*

In Yeats's literary universe, every artist, impelled to try to share his vision, draws on his stored memory, on his own previous work, and then on the work of other artists to embellish his invention. Mark here draws on Yeats's own favorite kinds of literature to "be-jewel" and "be-dizen" his tale: pirate tales and romance tales like those of his own "Theodore," "Black Beard" and "Prince Florizel"; nineteenth-century novels like *The Man in the Iron Mask*; Irish ballads and tales like "The Night Before Larry Was Stretched," "Brennan on the Moor," the "Wild Boar of Benbulben," and the tales of the Boy Cuchulain; utopias like "houses thatched with tuppenny loaves"; and political ballads like "In the Lower Castle Yard" and "The Felons of Our Land" (173–75).

As one artist can understand and appreciate another, especially a more gifted one, Gaw understands Mark's performance and notes the elements that match his own memories: he thinks, however, that only five percent of it touched any memory of Ralph and Gladys, for whom the comfort and shared wisdom are intended. Human experience is essentially incommunicable, except where comradery and imaginative sympathy unite two persons. But eventually the incantatory effect of Mark's "rope of words," his "rigama, rigama, rigama, rigama roleeoh" works for the better, even on

Ralph and Gladys. Language is "mantic" in this interpolated tale, as it was for the signers of the "Poetry is Vertical" manifesto.

The day after Mark's consummate artistic performance, it becomes clear that some new state will soon be entered. His rhetoric comforted Ralph and Gladys, but his shared wisdom has not changed them. Mark and Gaw have another joint vision on Fire Top, the mountain of the spring where they keep a fire going to attract rescuers; this vision confirms the difficulty of setting down one's private experience, let alone communicating it. They see a commercial traveller who has learned wisdom; he prefers being in tune with nature (looking at the fuchsias along the side of the road) to commercial pursuits (looking over his order book). Even this wise traveller, however, cannot set down his vision. In his dream he was told the name of a horse and, though he wakes telling himself he cannot forget it, he cannot remember it by the time he finds a pencil and paper to write it down (178). The failure of the medium of language, the need for another who would write under a nom de plume, is reiterated. This vision is, fittingly, Mark and Gaw's last vision. Gladys, too, sings her ritual song for the last time. Ending part 3, a ship's siren sounds, indicating rescue is at hand; their old ship has sailed back, seen their fire and sent a boat for them.

Yeat's primary theme is reinforced by the differing reactions of the two pairs to the sound of the rescuers. Ralph and Gladys, who have not adapted well to life in this utopia, race to the beach to signal the ship; Mark and Gaw, who have accepted the forces of the universe and benefited from them while living in the same utopia, retreat to Fire Top, cutting away the climbing lines behind them to frustrate pursuit. However, in Yeats's literary universe, the artist cannot always stay in the private world. There is a foreshadowing that someone will follow Mark and Gaw. The exploration of the artistic implications of surrender to forces larger than the self, Yeats's primary theme—and of the corollary themes of the need for authenticity and balance and the need for imaginative sympathy in order to escape human isolation—has been completed; the treatment of the primary theme's social implications is resumed.

The mythic resonances of the fabulation are intensified in part 4 as an almost daemonic figure emerges to wrest the artists from their imaginative haven. A hurricane again ensues. Fear speeds up the boat's crew taking Ralph and Gladys to the ship. As the Captain in *Amaranthers* had observed, men can pull together in a crisis. Captain Lovell shows this truth again when, with a crew of physically crooked men, he returns to the island in the midst of the hurricane to force Mark and Gaw back to the ship. With a preternatural strength imparted by Lovell's Ahab-like determination, the rowers throw themselves into the quest. As in any Yeats utopia, none of these men is subject to another; four volunteers join the captain, and "those five never called out, neither gave nor took an order" (185). As one might expect, the crew's heroics are for naught, however, as the voyage ends disastrously in spite of their success in recovering the marooned ones. The other original passengers had left the ship in the first port after the four had been marooned. The owner had died, and his wealth had been illusory. No one got anything out of the "little ray of sunshine" trip (191).

The social criticism, which had been developed in parts 2 and 3, becomes more sharply critical in part 4 when social relations of the larger world cause the paired protagonists to assume new relations to each other. The social criticism had begun when the four reached the island utopia and had to establish their societal structure. Mark, the outsider, the social inferior of the other three in the larger world, becomes the leader when ability, not pre-established social position, becomes the determiner. There is an analogue to James Barrie's *The Admirable Crichton* in this role reversal. Gaw, the authority figure as the superior member of the crew, accepts Mark's natural superiority and acquiesces when Mark immediately takes charge, his practical ability and imaginative charity having become apparent. The four islanders inherit a house and food stores from a man to whose body they give Christian burial. They do not erect a headstone because Mark, with his imaginative sympathy, senses the man would have wished to preserve his anonymity. Mark becomes their spiritual as well as social leader: "They knew their existence, after water and food, rested on the wisdom of Mark Trimbo" (74). The wisdom of age, the practicality of the man of the road, the imaginative charity toward others, but mostly the capacity for vision equip him for this post.

In keeping with his role as leader/priest, Mark "orchestrates" the dawn of their first day on the island in their new social relation. Dawn is a symbolic moment in any Jack Yeats work. As the light hits a sentinel palm:

Mark was ready, his hands with palms outward, crossed in front of his upward watching face. He threw them wide, then, palms down with fingers spread and hooked, he brought them down in unison with the crash of the bursting song of morning birds. The ancient trick was turned. The trump card of the tropics was up again from the bottom of the pack. The melted gold of day was spilt again.

(76)

Mark also acts as priest/counselor on the island. Speaking of the dead man, Mark says that although they have respected his anonymity by not raising a headstone, he will not be left without prayers, since any sailor who hears of his fate will give him the good thought, "and there's nothing as good as the good thought of a sailor" (84). (Tony Larcson in Yeats's last play *In Sand*—probably written shortly after *Flower*, since it was first offered to the Abbey in 1943 and the fiction was first published in installments in 1940—requests his memorial in the same terms. He wishes to have written in sand "Tony, we have the good thought for you still.") Mark's reaction mirrors Yeats's version of imaginative charity[118] shown in the line from the opening of *Also*: "We have no friends, and all are our friends."

In the realm of social criticism, and in connection with the primary theme, reactions to the rejuvenating powers of the spring rank all four characters on the island on the life-affirming or life-denying scale. In their life-affirming qualities, principally their reaction to the spring of the careless flower found at the top of the mountain, Mark and Gaw unite with natural or providential forces and are clearly the moral superiors of their social superiors Ralph and Gladys. After drinking spring water the two "fire-makers" "were full of joke and boy-out-of-school-ness" (101). The phrasing is reminiscent of the "true boyishness" description of *Ah Well*, where the wisdom of old age causes Dusty Brown to embrace life while the lack of wisdom of youth causes the boy to be attracted to death in the river. Gladys and Ralph both note that Gaw and Mark are as fresh and untired looking as they were when they went up to their labor, but they do not choose to imitate them and rise to their superior level of wisdom.

Mark is so clearly life-affirming that he assumes power benevolently and tries to found an ideal, classless society where no one is subject to another. After his second drink from the spring, in his imaginative charity he thinks that Gladys and Ralph might like to marry. Gaw, who is also life-affirming, agrees with his assessment, and the two oldsters approach the youngsters, individually, about the matter. The two youngsters, products of a paralyzed society, maintain social barriers even on a deserted island. Gladys says she can't marry Ralph because she doesn't "know Ralph's people at all" (106). The same inhibitions that lead her to build a house with a fence around it keep her from embracing life; her house resembles "the box in which most of her life had been boxed away" (107). "Her refusal to drink the magical water is of course the central emblem, embracing her relation to Ralph and to the others and her total inability to imagine anything beyond the restricted pattern laid down for her."[119] She does, however, have some instinct for life; she wants to drink the spring water until Ralph dissuades her. Even though she paints flowers on rocks and sets them all around her living room, closing herself in, her connection to life is more positive than Ralph's. He cannot consider marrying Gladys because he has social as well as engineering "plans"; he is engaged "to a Brazilian girl with a lot of money" (104). Getting and spending limit his life; he has Pollexfen values. Even Gaw, who is more convention-bound than Mark, is more flexible than the young ones. Much of Yeats's social criticism of Ireland centers on this paralysis, this class-bound inability to adjust to new circumstances.

This preoccupation with social differences, or with "getting ahead," also reinforces the barriers to imaginative sympathy and increases human isolation. While the boyish old men, also known as the primrose and the rose, are enjoying their joint or separate visions, the staid old children below are fretting. They were not communicating: "But they both were afraid of the subject of that spring up at Fire Top. Ralph was afraid that Gladys might start again suggesting that he and she should drink of the spring. And Gladys was afraid that Ralph thought she was obstinately thinking about it" (140). Even the forms their fears take are linked to conventional gender roles; he is afraid that his dominance will be lost because of her connection to the life force, and she is afraid that their intimacy will be lost if she displeases him.

Only nature can unite the two groups of the marooned; they all respond to its appeal. The device Yeats uses to unite the four is the song of the birds:

> The thoughts, or whatever they might be called, which passed before Gaw and Mark up at Fire Top, and the thoughts and plans of Gladys and Ralph had between them, as a flock of liaison officers, their quivering, flapping, screaming, laughing, chuckling birds! . . . They loved them on the cliff top. They all loved them down below.
>
> (140–41)

The use of this linking device shows craftsmanship and care. The birds function on several other levels. Introduced by Gaw's vision of a freed thrush, these birds are a symbolic connection to Gladys, whose song they love, and they even inspire Ralph to attempt imitating them.

In keeping with Yeats's social criticism, two songs sung, or attempted, are typical of their singers' status. For example, Mark sings, "in a come-all-ye way," "The Reaper of Glanree," remembering it all as an Irish man of the roads, descendant of the bards, might be expected to. Ralph, "with all the will in the world," can't remember more than one line of his chosen song. This representative of an industrialized, inauthentic culture cannot sing by an act of the will, any more than he can conquer nature by it. The degree to which the four can create art is related to their acceptance of life's rhythms.

The fullest development of one predominant strand of Yeats's social criticism, his view of an ideal world and of nationalism, is contained in Mark's and Gaw's visions in part 3. Mark sees the fall of a Big House. Yeats portrays the paralysis of Ireland in the same guise he used in several late paintings: a dead man under a circus tent watched by a spectator who is the dead man's double. Mark sees a man who tells of the golden warriors of the past who walked that road: "big-built men, bigger than yourself," "wild men," "laughing one laugh." What O'Doherty calls the national myth of regret is operative here, the nationalist harking back to lost heroes like Cuchulain of the laughing lip, to men larger than themselves. These mythic warriors, very like the Fianna, have been seen twice and will be seen again a third time in one of Mark's visions (143–46).

As the "Irish question," even today, is inseparable from the English response to it, Gaw's visions, complementary to those of Mark, are of English history. Gaw's visions go backward in historical time, and they come forward to the present. The first vision is of an eighteenth-century English village with a man in a crimson velvet coat (called "Mr. Chance" by another figure), finding a horse, mounting it, and letting it take him where it will. These horses of chance have been met with from *Amaranthers* through to *Ah Well*. "Velvet Coat" of Gaw's vision uses the horse that chance sent him to rob a coach whose occupants then engage in a ritual sword fight, slashing each other bloodlessly (152). He gives the stolen gold to his mother to buy a new book, and then falls asleep over his bread and bacon. Gaw next sees the same village in the twentieth century, and little has changed. Velvet Coat's descendant, "Brown Hat," has stolen a tandem, sold it, and gone to a gambling casino. These actions seem to represent the exploitative actions of England in modern times. To Irishmen, English culture rests on stolen goods. The passengers in the coach, who fight each other and do nothing about the seizure of their gold, may represent eighteenth-century Irishmen, paralyzed, like their twentieth-century descendants, by internecine strife.

Mark's next Irish visions, by contrast, do not come up to date but go only backwards. The present is not part of the Irish nationalist myth. Ancient Gaelic swordsmen in tunics make a path through wilderness for a beautiful, slim, young woman, the personification of Ireland in its flourishing times. In an idyllic rural setting beloved by the proponents of the myth of regret, the eldest of the four path-makers, the *file* or Gaelic singer perhaps, sings the woman a story: "[H]e began to chime along sort of a song, a story" (163). He tells it rhythmically, beating time with twigs, in a voice "sweet, like wild honey." He begins with that day's events and goes on to tell the past of the people. In the "song-teller's" story, great horsemen, riding horses whose eyes are stars, dismount and play Gaelic games, leaping poles. The beauty of his song brings tears to the eyes of Mark, his artistic descendant.

As Yeats was encouraging his Irish and English readers to do, the two visionary men of the careless flower's spring, one Irish and the other English, transcend their differences. Unprompted by any word of Mark's, Gaw says of these Gaelic heroes: "I saw them well, they are my friends too. Ah, Mark, my old friend of Fire Top" (167). The celebration of friendship on Fire Top may represent an affirmation not merely of the possibility of human communication, but also of the possibility of national cooperation, at least where men are good willed. It would have been an appealing political vision. Gaw, having seen his own visions and these visions of Mark's and having given up his tendency to abuse language (with his "word" tamed), celebrates their friendship "in a lower, more honeyed voice" than Mark had ever heard him use. The next day Mark and Gaw have a joint vision of a great theatre whose drop curtain shows a ship flying no national flag: "Mark and Gaw knew as quickly as they saw she flew none that, had she done so, men armed with knives would have . . . cut away the flag or cut down any defending of it" (169). During the late 1930s, the evils of nationalism were becoming quite apparent.

The most stringent criticism of the class system takes place in part 4. When one leaves utopia, one finds that nothing has changed in the outside world. When the two sympathetically united artists come down from the mountain, the birds which had been their link to the world below are gone. Gaw, less naturally adaptable than Mark, has immediate difficulty on leaving utopia. Gaw takes a chill (a symbol of his inability to adapt to the world he returns to) from which he does not recover. Captain Lovell, who forced them out of their refuge, worries not about Mark, but only about Gaw, who is "a man of too much education to scratch anything with the bare hand anymore" (189). The socioeconomic differences outside of utopia between Gaw, who is trapped by his class code, and Mark, who is a true outsider and déclassé, now assert themselves, as do those between the two of them and the "passengers." Gladys, the intuitive female, nurses Gaw, but their island fellowship is broken. Mark again becomes a servant of those who "having got back to the civilization of their steamer trunks" (192) reassert their property-based social superiority. Though wisest and best equipped for survival, Mark is no longer leader. Death intervenes to help Gaw out of his social predicament. He dies with the memory of the spring and the creative experiences on Fire Top in his mind, saying to Mark "Good spinning, good drinking" (197).

Mark, who is also changed by the Fire Top experience, recognizes the problems involved with going back to the road: "the old road I knew, and the new, the road I know now" (195). However, he longs for Fire Top island. Like Yeats himself, who lived by drawing, Mark draws more of the "Good Luck" cards which were his trademark in the old life, and gets a sailor to help him stow away on a ship bound for the islands.

There are significant artistic and socially critical aspects to Mark's second voyage to Fire Top island. A ship's steward with an interest "in a half spirit world" senses in Mark a kindred soul and befriends him, but Mark refuses to be drawn out (215). His experience of trying unsuccessfully to convey his vision to Ralph and Gladys may have convinced him (as White maintains that trying to communicate with his audience convinced Yeats) that the vision must be forever *sub rosa*. On the island where he is put ashore, Mark wears a bright green handkerchief with a harp in the middle and identifies himself as an Irish exile (218). Thereupon, a stranger of obscure provenance (presumably also Irish) helps him by pointing out a boat he can steal to get to his own island, and leaves him with a cryptic message which may have significance on this metaphoric voyage back to the source of artistic inspiration: "Good

Luck and carve it out. . . . Keep a good heart and fear nothing and remember the old saying 'There's bones in the soup and raisins in cake'" (223). Mark, seizing his chance, like Gaw on the first voyage, takes the boat and drifts away from shore, drinking an elixir from a stone bottle marked "very very old." He jettisons memories: "[A]nd after each mouthful he sat in a dreamless quietude and each time he forgot something, some memory which had now no pleasant use for him" (226). Jettisoning memories is an important part of keeping the flue clean so that one may be a conduit through which the vision can flow. As the Amaranthers discovered, it is necessary to sever all connections, and so, after reaching Fire Top island, he sinks the boat, postpones speaking to the island birds or looking in the house, and climbs up the rock. On top, a young man, involved in a shootout with men in a boat, shoots and wounds Mark. Mark drags himself to the spring, however, followed by the no longer frightened or violent young man.

His last vision at the spring is ambiguous. From one point of view the artist is defeated, because he does not get to drink from the spring. From another point of view he is triumphant, either "saved" or successful in passing on artistic tradition. The young man follows Mark: "Mark did not see him at first. He saw only the spring below him on his path. He cried 'Christ' and it was just an exclamation. And then he cried 'Christ' again, and it was a prayer. 'Ah,' he thought, . . . 'Ah, Christ!'" (239). He sees the young man holding a shell filled with spring water toward him, but refuses to drink and dies. The young man, however, drinks from the spring, washes himself in it, and then, in the ultimate gesture of fellow feeling, cleans the blood from Mark's face with spring water. The significance of this gesture is open to interpretation. Mark, the survivor of the island society in which the social criticism is so clear, repeats the voyage alone, seeking, presumably some higher end, moral or artistic salvation. The spring may be grace, the water of life, the source of artistic inspiration, or all three. He may or may not succeed in passing on to the next generation reverence for the artistic source. The Yeats who wanted viewers to tell themselves the story of his paintings lets the reader resolve the second quest his own way. As he said at the end of *Amaranthers*, each of us will see the world just as each of us likes it to look. The vision is private and the reader's involvement in the aesthetic transaction is the desired goal.[120]

This last narrative represents the thematic culmination of Yeats's fiction. He develops in *The Careless Flower* many of the themes that had been present in the early narratives or introduced in the later ones: the need to seize the moment and to be open to life's opportunities; the need to surrender the self and the will and to immerse oneself in forces larger than the self, accepting one's lack of control; the need to turn inward and be true to one's own vision, to preserve artistic authenticity; the need to protect the vision to sustain the spirit, coupled with the need to prevent illusion from becoming delusion; and the need to escape human isolation through imaginative sympathy, comradeship, and fellow feeling.

These five aspects of Yeats's primary and secondary themes are often treated in similar ways, through the contrast between woman's natural wisdom and man's fear of fear and consequent rigidity, or through the contrast between the Irish or rural intuitive connection with the rhythms of life and the English or urban distance from life caused by a substitution of technological or commercial values for natural values. These themes originated in family experiences and were shaped by the experiences of Irish socialism and nationalism. Taken together, these experiences shaped Yeats's literary universe. The long narratives display remarkable continuity and represent the parallel—and not subordinate—expression of the vision widely recognized in Yeats's paintings.

The last major aspect of Yeats's literary universe is his drama. The plays, too exhibit a continuation of the themes and social criticism in these narratives, showing his literary universe to be remarkably integral.

4. Thematic Continuity in the Drama of Jack B. Yeats

Earlier chapters of this study have explored family and nationalist influences in the formulation of characteristic themes, motifs, and attitudes in the work of Jack Yeats, tracing these themes and motifs from *A Broadside* through his narratives and noting their continuity. Yeats's narrative forms were appropriate for his chosen subjects. For exploring dream states of half-memory in *Sligo* and *And To You Also*, he chose stream of consciousness and then imaginary dialogues or colloquies. For exploring his primary theme of the need to immerse oneself in the rhythms of the universe, and his secondary theme of the importance of the imaginative life and the need for artistic authenticity and balance, in *Sailing, Sailing Swiftly, The Amaranthers, The Charmed Life, Ah Well*, and *The Careless Flower*, he chose the tale, then the fabulation, presenting and exemplifying the ethical ideas his romances were designed to illuminate, and incorporating interpolated tales and colloquies.

Thematic continuity and appropriateness of forms also characterize Yeats's drama. He was always experimental in his forms, testing the limits of existing modes, seeking those most useful for expressing his private vision. He described himself as a spear head, pressing forward and barely aware of other artists less experimental than he. Yet he was not a primitive. He understood the need to master one's technique and to be aware of what other artists were doing. But he abhorred convention, seeing in it a lazy approach for painter/writer and viewer/reader, an attempt at "shorthand" that prevented the aesthetic transaction from touching deeply either artist or appreciative audience. He mistrusted language, seeing it as a poor mechanism for expressing deeply emotional experience. All of these attitudes, with his early experiences of personal isolation and his later experiences of cultural and social isolation, produced unusual literature. His fiction became more powerful as he explored his private fantasies, impelled by fellow feeling to share his deepest experiences of escaping the prison of self by transcendence, by cultivation of the vision of the unity of all being, and by an enjoyment of the sense of immersion in forces larger than the self. His drama was not as positively influenced by his attitudes and experiences as his fiction.

Ruby Cohn makes an observation about a playwright's use of language that is useful in diagnosing why Yeats's plays were not successful drama: "In the famous Saussurian distinction between the signifier and the signified, the realistic playwright seeks a transparent signifier, so that the spectator looks through it to the signified. The linguistically conscious playwright, in contrast, points to the signifier itself as an object of dramatic validity."[1]

Yeats was linguistically conscious. In his fiction, particularly in *Sligo*, which he described as perhaps the last book ever to be written, since words were becoming useless as a medium of communication, he demonstrates this consciousness. Yet, as "an object of dramatic validity," Yeats's language fails him, perhaps because he so profoundly mistrusted it. If there is little dramatic action in a play, the consequent focus on speech requires an extremely finely tuned linguistic instrument. Yeats's dramatic speech, while often "poetic" in its use of figurative language, is neither concentrated enough, nor strongly rhythmical enough, to carry the weight in the way that Eliot's or Fry's or Beckett's dramatic language can. His language, although skillful and appropriate to his experimental fictional forms, does not always serve the needs of his dramatic forms.

Yeats's themes are consistent, from the first decade of the century to the major fiction and drama written alternately through the

1930s and 40s, but they are often more skillfully embodied in the narratives than in the plays. Though all of the fiction was published, only four plays "for the larger theatre" were published in his lifetime: *Apparitions*, a volume of three plays, in 1933, and *La La Noo*, in 1943. *In Sand* was published posthumously in 1964.

Only three of his plays were ever performed, and when they were, they puzzled audiences. Yeats's vision may have been too private for the theatre goer, although not for the reader. His tendencies (present since the early puppet theatre) to concentrate on reported rather than portrayed action, and to have his characters talk majestically and do little, do not always make for effective theatre.

Yeats insisted that if *La La Noo*, the second of his plays to be performed, was "acted," it was "fatal." He wanted dialogue to flow from one actor to another, with each becoming "nothing but an agent" and putting all of Yeats into his words.[2] This concentration on speech (since his actors were to be merely vehicles for his words), rather than on action, mars the plays in which the language is not adequate. His wish (like his brother's) for a select audience, who would enter into the aesthetic transaction as fully as the ideal viewer of his painting described in *Modern Aspects*, may have led Yeats to ignore too many conventions, to despise as "shorthand" for a lazy playwright and audience what is necessary in as ephemeral a transaction as a performance.

Robin Skelton says that Yeats's late drama "frees itself from the conventions of the drama of its time, breaks all the laws of unity, and challenges all contemporary preconceptions of what is dramatic."[3] Although Skelton sees this unconventionality as a positive value of Yeats's plays, the same unconventionality limited their audience. Few members of the Irish public, at whom the drama's social criticism is aimed, saw or read the plays until 1971, when Skelton himself published them as the collected plays.

Yet Yeats loved the theatre, attended performances regularly, and liked "action" theatre, particularly melodrama. His one known aesthetic pronouncement on drama was that he preferred "crook drama" to theatre that made the audience "think too hard." He hated George Bernard Shaw's talky, intellectual drama, and it is supremely ironic that audiences find his own plays too talky. He wanted them to be performed. He thoroughly enjoyed attending rehearsals, to watch the performance take shape; he enjoyed giving the performances of his early juvenile drama and enabling children to give their own live performances by means of his toy theatres. Closet drama was not his goal.

Whatever limitations the privacy of his vision, his plays' unconventionality, and his consequent lack of performance experience placed on Yeats's development as playwright, his sense of himself as an outsider, a traveller without a ticket, had a positive value for his drama. It made him a good social critic. The same nationalism for which he had been praised in *A Broadside*, when his views were in tune with popular ideals, is expressed in his later drama through the outsider's criticism of the society which had failed to live up to his ideals. The prevailing preoccupation of the drama for the larger theatre (the use of the term indicates that he regarded it as different only in size from the puppet theatre of his early works) is the paralysis of Ireland, a subject he shared with a primarily nondramatic Irish writer, James Joyce. The socio-political subtext in Yeats's drama is its most noteworthy aspect: with thematic consistency, he continues to assert in his drama that the Irish, individually and collectively, must adapt to changed conditions and must value the contribution to society of the artist, the man of vision.

Plays for the Miniature Theatre

Thematically, Jack B. Yeats's plays for the miniature stage provide for the interpreter of his late plays, as his *Guardian* pieces do for the reader of his later fiction, or as his illustrations do for the viewer of his late paintings, an example of a strikingly similar and realistic use of some of the same materials later to be transformed by his creative imagination. Marilyn Gaddis Rose says of this thematic continuity and transformation: "In terms of sophistication and development, these latter are at the far end of the spectrum from the plays for the miniature stage. But the themes remain the same."[4] Yeats is exploring in drama, as in fiction, the primary theme that humans need to surrender the will to forces larger than the self, to accept the rhythms of life, and the secondary theme that artists need to preserve the authenticity of their inner vision while attempting, in the face of a consciousness of the limits of language as a medium of communication, to communicate the vison for those less favored than the artist. While the early drama Yeats was conventional in the forms used for this exploration , in the late drama he searches for new forms. Although Yeats's father did not live to know the late plays, he saw his son's potential in the early plays: "In my mind he will some day surprise the world with serious plays; working with these puppets and his mimic theater he is forced to study the broad effects. It is so easy to lose oneself in the details. If you catch the dog you catch the fleas."[5]

In an essay written for Gordon Craig's *The Mask*, Yeats made a revealing statement about the absence of dramatic action in his plays for the miniature stage: "I write all my plays with as little movement for the figures as possible, they slide into their place; I fix them upon slides of thin lath ... and unfold the plot by dia-logue—though most of my characters do little but talk, and walk, majestically, I have had some characters of whose *business* I am very proud" (italics in original).[6] He continues these composition habits in the later plays, where characters are broadly outlined, dramatic action is minimized, and the plot unfolds by dialogue. One is reminded of WB's alleged wish to put his actors in barrels so that his words would be highlighted.

Yeats's first experience of serious theatre may have contributed to his tendency to rely on dramatic speech. In contrast to the music hall and melodrama he viewed in Sligo, the drama he witnessed in the clubhouse at Bedford Park, when he first returned to his father's home in London, was consciously "aesthetic." "Poetic non-natural-istic drama, which could not be staged in the contemporary com-mercial theater,"[7] it had a lasting influence on the conception of drama that emerged in Yeats's late plays. The early plays, however, are quite straightforwardly melodramatic.

Their literary forebears were the plays for miniature stage beloved of Robert Louis Stevenson. Yeats tells us in *The Mask* essay that the whole idea of his theatre was suggested by "those fine old penny plain and twopence coloured plays of our grandfathers." His comment on these plays is that they were "exciting," and his own plays are filled with exciting adventure. Even if the characters often speak about actions rather than performing them, the reported action is usually exciting. Like the early fiction, these plays appeal to a young audience.

Timothy Coombewest or Esmeralda Grande, Yeats's first, unpublished, play (1900), has a tale for young boys to identify with—the tale of Tim, a farmer's boy who prospers. He becomes a cabin boy on a pirate ship, inherits a huge, pineapple-shaped emerald, "Esmeralda Grande," and gets the girl of his choice, Marjorie Morning. The tone is that of a romantic comedy, but there is a characteristic theme: the struggle for riches wears out a life in vain. Timothy, who has not sought fortune, who has given himself up to the rhythms of life, gets the emerald.

Yeats's incantatory use of language is a striking feature of this play. Captain Blackbeard makes the crew swear by a series of Gaelic place names which produces a hypnotic effect, a "mantic language." The suppression of Irish place names was particularly deplored by the Gaelic Revivalists. The place names represent for Irish writers a reminder of deep cultural truths, a form of access to the mother earth, in a country that regards itself as female, not, as does the England of John Bull or the United States of Uncle Sam, as male. To swear by these places would be to swear a deep oath. In all of Yeats's work the place names are beloved for their symbolic value as well as their sound.

In the next year, 1901, Yeats published a bloodthirsty melodrama. *James Flaunty, or The Terror of the Western Seas*, opens with the pirate, Flaunty, flaunting boldly and beating back, with his sword, a crowd of beachcombers who are threatening the wandering seaman, Pine. The play ends with a role reversal as Pine, in a Sidney Carton-like gesture, sacrifices himself for his original defender, Flaunty. This play for the miniature stage is Yeats's first published book.

James Flaunty exhibits Yeats's fascination with the pirate motif and his early social criticism following traditional nationalist lines. Tempted by the British Navy to betray the pirates to them, Flaunty acts as a double agent, and attempts to betray the naval brig to the pirates. In good socialist and nationalist fashion, Flaunty sides with the underdog when the pirate Gillen reminds him: "They have money and a king behind them, but we have nothing but the living we can claw off these coasts." Flaunty replies: "Yes, by the old trade and the merchants of the old trade I am with you."[8] This oath is similar in its phrasing to "The Adventurer's Oath" from *Esmeralda Grande* which the pirate crew is made to repeat: "By the old trade and the merchants of the old trade / We swear to stand by Captain Blackbeard the Second" (28). Much of Yeats's drama shows a tendency to use incantatory language. Characters have attributive names in the plays, as they did in the narratives: "Flaunty" is a boastful flaunter and the *shuler* (wanderer) "Pine" pines for home.

Like the villains in *Esmeralda Grande*, Pine has struggled vainly in life, but unlike them, he achieves his final goal by acceptance, by sacrificing his life. Perhaps his achievement is intended to reflect the central Christian paradox. The significance, or insignificance, of death is a major theme in Yeats's fiction, particularly in *Ah Well* and *And To You Also*. Christian elements become more pronounced in the late works; *The Careless Flower*, for example, his last published fiction, has a strikingly Christian ending, one in which a possible Christ figure performs ritual cleansing gestures at the death of the protagonist. Although the tone of *James Flaunty* is darker than that of *Esmeralda Grande*, its ending is not dark. Pine is tranquil in the face of death, since he expects to get his wish to go home: "To-night I'll be on Sligo Quay" (47). Like the protagonist of a later play, *Rattle,* Pine experiences peace in surrendering his will to larger forces in the universe.

In the Christmas season of 1901 Yeats produced a much lighter play, *Onct More's First Circus*, which exhibits a different, but no less characteristic, style and subject. The circus motif replaces the pirate one. Where James Flaunty had uttered a melodramatic rhetoric ("They cannot tame the eaglet, let it once feel the long sweep of its pinions, and they cannot tame James Flaunty but in death" [46]), the clowns of this spectacle, Tuffcake and Cream, delight in knock-about word play:

> *Tuff:* I am going to ask you a riddle.
> *Cream:* He's going to ask me a riddle, boo boo.
> *Tuff:* How many wells make a river?
> *Cream:* How many wells? I dunno.
> *Tuff:* Then I suppose I must tell you—one if it's big enough. Now I will ask you another riddle.
> *Cream:* Now he'll ask me another riddle, boo boo.
> *Tuff:* If a boy and ½ with a boot and ½ takes an hour and ½ to walk a mile and ½—How many days will it take 6 boys to walk to London?
> *Cream:* One if it's long enough.
> (51)

Both the melodramatic rhetoric of the pirate plays and the music hall patter/ circus clown routines of this spectacle persist as speech patterns into the late plays. The first half of this play ends with the unfilled promise of an "himpersonation" of an Irish Ballad Singer, a performer dear to Yeats's heart. Its illustrations exhibit common motifs: a tumbling bareback rider, two male bareback riders, and a female rider. The spectacle "Ride of All Nations," which forms the last half of *Onct More's First Circus*, must have had its progenitors in the Wild West shows Yeats frequented in his Earl's Court days. Familiar figures such as cowboys, red Indians, ancient Romans, and jockeys parade.

The graphic artist's interest in costume and stage design is shown in the second version of this play by sketches of three changes of costume for Tuffcake and Cream: two sailor costumes, two Hamlet costumes, and two ancient Roman costumes are given in *Onct More's Great Circus: Second Year* (1902) for the two paired clowns, one short and heavy, one tall and thin. Similar sketches give us an insight into *La La Noo*, an enigmatic late play.

Yeats's persistent fascination with design and costume was gratified when Elkin Mathews, a neighbor from Bedford Park who published all Yeats's plays and books for children, brought out an edition of *The Treasure of the Garden*, in 1902, with a stage and pages of scenes and characters to be constructed, as in plays "penny plain and two pence coloured." Hilary Pyle indicates that Yeats continued to hand-color batches of the loose scenes for assembly by the purchaser, and sheets of characters for cutting out and mounting, as Mathews asked for them.[9] He was so interested in this aspect of theatre that in 1912 he wrote two articles, one in Gordon Craig's journal *The Mask* (quoted earlier) and another in *The Music Review*,[10] describing elaborately how he constructed the stages, characters, and sets for actual performances. In these articles, the early Bedford Park influence can be seen; designer and costume designer worked closely with the playwright in the dramas staged at its clubhouse. The "Directions" for *The Treasure of the Garden* (performed in October 1902) are very elaborate, filling more than a page of text in the collected plays, and dealing with lighting effects and how to speak the lines as well as with graphic matters. Yeats's interest in production was always keen; his are not closet dramas.

Fascination with the pirate motif resurfaces in *The Treasure of the Garden*. The title page shows the hero Willie McGowan (the surname is the same as that of Yeats's pseudonym in *A Broadside*), "The Man Hunter of the Gulph," standing on the prow of his ship firing his pistol and waving his sword. Looking much like James Flaunty, or Theodore from *A Broadside*, McGowan is outlined against the sky, with sails of another ship visible. In the Prologue, McGowan reports lively action, swashbuckling enough to thrill any school boy. The characters in these plays do talk as "majestically" as Yeats had said. While it is melodramatic, their speech is also appropriate to their roles. Ruminating in the Irish idiom on the "horrid trade" which spares few ("fifteen men left out of forty that was my darling crew" [63]), McGowan reveals the fundamental good nature that many of Yeats's outsiders exhibit when he decides to give up his ship and go back to Connaught.

Hilary Pyle comments on the amount of personal reference in these early plays. Yeats uses a Gaelic place name, "Carrick na gat," as a character's surname; the locale for the play is Poolthoia, a pseudonym for Rosses Point, as the illustrations of Ben Bulben indicate. He uses real Sligo surnames such as McGowan (the surname of James Flaunty's sweetheart in that play) and Gillen (the family name of a pilot who worked for the Pollexfen shipping firm in Sligo) as surnames for other characters. Pyle concludes that the miniature plays were a form of personal release.[11]

They are not, however, merely private plays. *Treasure* deals with a public Irish problem, the moral responsibility for embarking emigrants in ships known to be unseaworthy. In Yeats's play, the prospective emigrants seek reassurance since, as Yeats seeks to remind his audience, one ship, *The Maid of Galway*, actually sank with all the emigrants on board. Willie McGowan, who was too tender-hearted to continue as a pirate after losing twenty-five men from his pirate crew, refuses to be captain of a doomed emigrant ship. A ballad singer in the play underlines the moral correctness of McGowan's decision by songs that deal with related public themes— the sorrow caused by emigration and the memory of exiled Irish heroes:

> Oh, rise up, Willy Reilly, and come along with me,
> I mean for to go with you and leave this coun-te-rie,
> To leave my father's dwelling, his houses and fine land;
> And away goes Willy Reilly and his dear Colleen Bawn.

and

> We drink the memory of the brave, the faithful, and the few!
> Some lie far off beyond the wave, some sleep in Ireland, too;
> All, all are gone, but still lives on the fame of those who died.
> All true men, like you, men, remember them with pride! (66)

These two Irish ballads continue to haunt Yeats's creative imagination, appearing, for example, in *And To You Also* whose one female character is obsessed with Willy Reilly.

Both irony and the nationalist ethic, which were strong in his work even as early as 1902, persist into the late plays. In *Treasure* it is Willie McGowan, who refused to struggle for immoral gain, who finds the treasure. (Similarly Timothy Coombewest in *Esmeralda Grande*, who was not seeking it, found the emerald.) The exploitative character Henderson dies in pursuit of the treasure. In a further irony, the faithful Willie plans to share his find with Jessie, his faithless sweetheart who is already dead as a result of her greedy pursuit of the money to be gained out of the emigrants' plight. While the emigrants and the crew are all saved, Jessie and old Henderson both die.

The primary theme of the need for surrender to the larger forces in the universe, in this case Providence, is emerging in the early drama. This play is more melodrama than romantic comedy, as it does not end in a happy marriage but in a punishment of the evil characters and a reward of the good. Jessie Henderson "earns" her fate by the following speech to Willie after his refusal to do her father's evil work:

> You've made a pretty pickle of yourself young man. I did mean to marry you, and so I will still, Willie, if you'll go back to my father and make all square with him again. I don't seem, Willie, as if I could ever marry a poor man; but I don't care a tosser for dad—and that's God's truth. You make some money—with him or without him—and I'm yours, dear sweetheart.
> (65)

In her evil, money-grasping ways, Jessie is unlike most of Yeats's women who are innocent and intuitively wise, according to the nationalist ideal. She is a far cry from faithful "Marjorie Morning" or James Flaunty's "Nance," but not too far from "La Lolita," the wife of the protagonist in the next play, *The Scourge of the Gulph* (published in 1903). "La Lolita" must have been a significant name in Yeats's private mythology, for it is also the name of the wife of Theodore the Pirate in *A Broadside*. This femme fatale causes both the flogging of Joe Miles (the Scourge of the Gulph who "spoke saucy" to her) and the death of her husband. The latter is attempting to carry out Lolita's last wishes by burying her head on the Island of Plumes when the revengeful Miles shoots him.

There is yet more irony in this play in that Miles, thinking he will obtain treasure as well as revenge, gets only "an empty skull, a black box, a dead skipper!" and asks himself, at the end of the play: "Have I done anything or nothing?" (80). The ironic spirit of this play is much like that of *Treasure*, where the money Willie wants to win for Jessie comes to him only after her death, "In this compressed saga of violence, we find sea-faring Anglo-Irish, deprived of their moral bearings by a critical situation in a tropic locale, responding by inappropriate reflexes. Survival in a new situation calls for a new code—but these characters . . . can carry out only rituals relevant in their old society."[12] Characters in the narratives, such as *The Careless Flower,* and in dramas, such as *Apparitions, The Old Sea Road* and *Rattle,* are similarly unable to adapt and so are doomed to frustration. The adaptation message to the Anglo-Irish which forms an important part of Yeats's social criticism, introduced in these early dramas, is part of his larger theme of acceptance of larger forces. The motif of paralysis, of the self-destruction of those who cannot adapt, is the opposite pole of Yeats's social criticism.

Neither this theme nor the irony of *Treasure* and *Scourge* characterizes the last, unpublished, plays for the miniature theatre, which return to a more straightforward entertainment suitable to his juvenile audience. He knew his audience's taste well enough to entertain them with a pantomime. The last entertainments given at Strete were all pantomimes and "Galanty Shows." *The Wonderful Travellers or the Gamesome Princes and the Pursuing Policeman,* one of Yeats's own favorites that he called in his sketch "the Mysterious Travellers," was performed at Christmas 1903 and 1904 and featured special effects such as a clown who smoked a real pipe and a tall cylindrical letter box which opened to reveal another clown. The humor here is much like that of Tuffcake and Cream; there are puns, sight gags, and Punch-and-Judy-style knockabouts featuring clown and pantaloon (the gamesome princes) "Dude," "Old Buffer" and other victims of the hoax, as well as the "Pursuing Policeman" and "Mystery," a mime who shakes his head but doesn't speak. *James Dance or The Unfortunate Ship's Boy* was also done in 1904 as a pantomime.

Much of this miniature theatre was taken seriously by critics in those pre-movie and pre-television days. Gordon Craig, for example, used the toy theatre as a stick with which to beat adult theatre: "In England we possess the best Toy Theatres and the worst of grown-up Theatres. We consider that Pollock's Theatre is the best

Toy Theatre in the world, and that Beerbohm Tree's Theatre is the worst grown-up theatre in the world."[13] An article published in this same issue of *The Mask* alleges of *Scourge of the Gulph*: "In this masterpiece things happen. In Dramas of this century things don't happen."[14] The article ends with an exhortation to buy Yeats's works, including *A Broadside*.

In the book review section of this same issue, "H.M." reviews the first critical book on Yeats, Ernest Marriott's *Jack B. Yeats, His Pictorial and Dramatic Art*. In the section on Yeats's "dramatic art" Ernest Marriott relates this drama for children to the Irish drama, alleging that the plays have literary quality which can be attributed to "the fanciful simplicity and directness of phrase which we find in the work of the better-known dramatists of the Irish movement."[15] Marriott also speaks of Yeats's transformation of melodrama: "For subjects he uses figures of ancient popular melodrama, but there is a difference when they have passed through his alembic. They have been broken to pieces, trimmed here and there, glued up again, carved afresh into something new and strange and made to fall in harmony with their backgrounds with a rhythm and balance of pose which makes for absolute dramatic congruity."[16] Marriott's monograph was first read to the Manchester Literary Club and was printed in *The Manchester Quarterly* for July 1911. Because Yeats's sketches (including those for his joint travelogue with Synge) and his short fiction pieces had appeared in Manchester, his work was better known there than in London.

Quotations from Marriott's monograph, as well as reviewer's comments from *The Speaker*, *The Manchester Guardian*, *The Daily News*, *The Dublin Express* and *The Academy*, were used as publisher's blurbs in the five books Mathews published. These comments relate Yeats's plays to older melodrama traditions or to the Celtic revival. A quotation in *Academy and Literature* maintains that they belong to the tradition "before playwrights became self-conscious and before poets aimed to please the high foreheads in the stalls."[17]

Yeats did find positive value in the less self-conscious tradition of melodrama, and he understood the characteristics of this form. In one of the early prose pieces from the *Life in Manchester* series he wrote, "The Melodrama Audience," Yeats mentioned melodrama's tendency to exploit visual and verbal devices for revealing character. Yeats understood that costume is one clue for character identification, and he used it consistently, even in the late plays. The "lady villainess" in the melodrama he describes is "gorgeously clothed"; the ingenue wears "a garden hat." His stage directions, even for the later plays, are very precise and written with the graphic artist's eye for the total scene as well as for the identifying function of costume.

Another form of identifier he understood is characteristic speech. In "The Melodrama Audience" he comments on the audience's reaction to the opening speech of a character: "That, I hope, told us all what to expect from him."[18] The heroes of Yeats's early plays speak "majestically," and villains are less impressive in their rhetoric. Turning against convention as he found less consensus in society and against individualism as he saw unity to be a more important goal, Yeats abandoned the identifier of characteristic speech in his later plays.

Where Yeats did not differentiate characters' speeches, we may assume this device to be deliberate. We know that Yeats was aware of verbal identifiers of character and that in his early work, where outlines had to be sharpened and broadened for a relatively unsophisticated audience, he used these identifiers. If in the later drama he chose not to employ these clues, we may assume that he made an artistic choice, designed to achieve another effect. In the late fiction, Yeats does not identify speakers in a colloquy because he wishes to stress the Modernist sense of the breakdown of societal consensus, the relative unimportance of personal identity, and the imitative character of most human speech. In the late drama, failing to use such clues as speech patterns is equally deliberate, and reflects his desire to emphasize unity and de-emphasize individual human differences in his vision of the ideal world. However, an audience needs more clues than a reader.

Yeats's early melodramas were seen to be in opposition to contemporary commercial theatre; his later plays also opposed commercial theatre practices. The later dramas, like the late paintings and fiction, have passed through what Marriott called the "alembic" of Yeats's mind. His creative imagination transformed melodrama in his later plays as it had transformed linear progressive narrative in the fiction, and representational art techniques in the painting. The basic form of the late plays is melodrama, but with a quizzically ironic tone like that of *Treasure* and *Scourge*.

Neither the late nor the early dramas are constructed in a way that would be accepted in commercial theatre. Even the Abbey, which had started out as experimental theatre, consigned the Yeats plays they performed to the Peacock, the smaller of their two spaces; there the audience expected more esoteric works. Part of the reason for the nonaligned and noncommercial quality of Yeats's plays is his scorn of the values he found in the age and in Ireland. No son of John Butler Yeats, the Irish landlord turned Bedford Park bohemian, would aspire to commercial success; nor would a revolutionary nationalist sell out to the middle class which defeated his social ideals and whose conservative representatives attempted to control theatre by censorship.

Another reason the plays would not be produced in commercial theatres is that Yeats tested the limits of his dramatic form, as he had his fictional and painterly forms, to express his private vision. He became interested in themes difficult to embody in drama, themes Christine Brooke-Rose has called "the insignificance of the real," with reality seen as "both fortuitous and determined."[19] As in the late fiction, Yeats was concerned in the late drama to explore the nature of reality, chance, and randomness. This search for "the real" was particularly acute for writers working in Ireland at the time. Speaking of Flann O'Brien's hovering between the real and the surreal, Seamus Deane says: "One gains from his books the sense of a normal society in which the hope of revolutionary change has become a surrealist neurosis. They infer a degree of political disillusion which is total. It leads in the end to a transfer of democracy from the world in which he lives to the art by which he lives more intensely than he can in the so-called 'real.'"[20] Yeats's disillusion was equally great and it led to his explorations of the nature of reality in drama and fiction as well as in his almost surreal later paintings. As Brooke-Rose maintains, when empirical reality is insecure, interest in the unreal (or the surreal) grows. Artists become interested in dream states or in worlds within. When the prevalent cultural metaphor is no longer that of order or organic unity, but that of entropy, as it has become since Freud and Einstein have transformed our notions of the self and the universe, the real becomes unreal.[21] In *The Deathly Terrace*, his first play for the "larger" theatre, Yeats focuses this interest on the world of cinema, that twentieth-century medium of melodrama and the unreal. Yet he does not neglect the primary narrative theme of the need for immersion in the rhythms of life. Even the motifs and the language used for exploring the theme are similar to those used in the narratives.

The Deathly Terrace

At the opening of *The Deathly Terrace*, while two men struggle on a terrace for possession of a revolver with which one of them is attempting to commit suicide, a woman's voice sings offstage: "Blow breezes blow, the stream runs fast, / The rapids are near, and the daylight's past!" (95). Her song places the mortal struggle onstage into the larger perspective of the human need to immerse the self in life's rhythms. This unpublished play was roughly contemporaneous with *Sailing, Sailing Swiftly* and uses the same metaphor for life—the stream. There are also strong thematic similarities to *Ah Well*, in that the play is concerned with death and attempted suicide; the same attitude—suicide is a betrayal of the life force—pervades, and, at first, the suicide is prevented. In act 3 the would-be suicide, while telling the type of traveller's tale common in Yeats's fiction, employs the hyperbolic language used in the opening of *Ah Well* to describe the "way of space," the transcendence of the self:

I have been among the gales of the mountain top, and among the lacey rollers of the beaches. I have journeyed over all the worlds, either in body or in spirit and sometimes in both. . . . Time has no meaning to me, I am imbedded in time, and floating in eternity. . . . And I have stepped from

the fragment of one star to the nucleuary fragment of another, and I have looked at myself so doing.
(106)

Although the hyperbolic language is the language used in *Ah Well*, the transcendent states of the speakers—out of body, out of time— are the states also explored in *Amaranthers, And To You Also*, and *The Careless Flower*. The daylight motif of this opening song is developed in the play's imagery, as it would later be in *The Careless Flower*, and there are other linguistic similarities between this play, what was written before it, and what follows it.

In its exploration of themes related to artistry, this early play resembles the later fiction. For example, the exchanges between individual characters and the characters' informal autobiographies assert the power of the imagination over reality. This continuing theme is dealt with, finally, in the tales of Mark and Gaw in *The Careless Flower*. The explicit exploration of the role of the artist as the sharer of the vision and nurturer of the imaginative life in act 2 of this play takes up a theme used almost two decades earlier in *A Broadside* and still being explored two decades later in Yeats's last published narrative. It is a subject John Butler Yeats never tired of discussing; resolving the potential conflicts in establishing a proper relation of artist to audience and to truth troubled his younger son all his life. The artist is both a bringer of truth and a purveyor of illusion to an audience; he or she must therefore establish a proper relation both to truth and to the audience. Like the bareback rider Yeats used as a symbol of artistic authenticity in *A Broadside*, the true artist must never pander to audience expectations and has an obligation to his own vision of the truth which may not meet audience expectations; yet, the artist depends on the audience. While looking at the rushes of their filming, Sheila Delgarvay, the actress, expresses this conflict: "I find this a bit low brow. If I had my absolute way there would be nothing in this picture but pure, straight, noble, refining drama of Life seen once and seen nobly acted by a natural nobility." Andy, the erstwhile director, replies: "This is a Trade Show not an intellectual treat." To which Sheila recaps: "I don't care, I feel, I feel as if I was standing where two clouds meet, the golden cloud of prosperity and the pale blue cloud of Art like a polished dagger of beauty leaping, by its own volition, from the scabbard of crepe-bound dull-witted obscurity" (100). (The golden cloud of prosperity is a good metaphor for Pollexfen ambitions, as Papa expressed them, while the polished dagger of beauty and pale blue cloud of Art are good metaphors for Yeats ambitions.) Not only Sheila and Andy are concerned with pleasing the audience. Cameramen, actors, and others all discuss what material in the rushes will "go" commercially in much the same terms that Yeats had used to explore audience expectations in "The Melodrama Audience." Aware of what would "go," Yeats, at some level, avoided writing or painting it, seeking Art instead. By the 1930s he had come to consider that the polished dagger of beauty had to make great leaps to escape from dull-witted obscurity, the dull-wits constituting the majority of Irish society.

The exploration of illusion and reality in *The Deathly Terrace*, the first play for the larger theatre, resembles metatheatre: a film is being made within the play. None of the would-be film-makers in this play actually knows how to make a film. They are playing roles while making it, cameramen and director as well as actors. Even the corpse is not real. Although "Nardock" has pretended to kill himself, in an absurdist fashion he walks off the deathly terrace at the end of act 1.

There are more layers of illusion to pierce. The film world is false, but so is the world Nardock opposes to it, "the old style." Although Hilary Pyle thinks Yeats is "satirizing artificiality and advocating unfettered life in the old-fashioned style,"[22] this old style world is equally false. The very subsoil of Nardock's estate, the earth that supports the deathly terrace, is used for creating illusion. A prospector has found in it "some mineral which . . . justifies its existence by lending itself to all forms of adulteration. It never appears under its own name. It is a stretcher created by the great upheavals of the world for the purpose of making, perhaps, tooth powder go further, or face powder cover a larger face, without costing the manufacturers of these articles too much" (105). The commercial world deplored in "The Flat Iron" has taken over, and "the old style" is a fiction too.

In this play's universe, reality is problematic; names as indicators of internal reality, or even of continuity, are no more to be relied on than they would be in the universe of *The Charmed Life*. The house attached to Nardock's deathly terrace is constantly being re-named: "I will re-name the house—SHARK'S BELLY HALL [since he escaped from his debts by appearing to be in the belly of the sharks which are seen just beyond the terrace]—The old name was Casa Amarillo ex Now or Never ex Merry Widow ex Lord Jim ex Tara Boom de A ex El Casa Viejo, so you see it has always been changing like leaves changing" (105). Nardock's very name is changeable: "[T]he name I go under now is not my name. It is an assumed name. Assumed for the purposes of confusion" (106).

Even geography cannot be counted on. Cities are changing their nature. "Paris. Pleasant city, but it was not what it is. And it is not what it was." Perhaps it is "a neverwaser, but an alwaysiser, or a will be like Cork, or a don't-want-to-be-but-can't-help-being like New York, or a muffled sob like London" (106). Layer upon layer of illusion is uncovered, and Nardock's world is no less artificial than the world of the film whose illusion he pierces by rising from the dead.

The exploration of reality is continued in a familiar Yeatsean mode: the conversation of a male pair of travellers. Nardock and Andy converse on the deathly terrace, and the fabulous tales they tell there are somewhat akin to the panoramic visions of Mark and Gaw, after the latter have drunk from the spring of the careless flower. Nardock claims to have been everywhere, invented every-thing, and found all systems wanting. Andy claims his life was dedicated to luck by his father, and that chance, not premeditation, ruled it. Reality is fortuitous. Therefore, the two propose to live by luck, lowering a crab pot over the side of the terrace and taking up what comes to them, "hilariously welcoming the gifts of the Gods" (111). (This manner of subsistence is similar to that of the coach that fed itself in *The Amaranthers*.) Meanwhile, while they are proposing this charmed life, reality obtrudes in the form of the circling sharks and Sheila Delgarvay rowing toward them.

The familiar motif of the failure of language is taken up while

Sheila is approaching them: "It's a superstition, using words for speech, and I suppose the day will come when it'll be found out, like most superstitions. . . . When all speech dies at last the sniff superior will be the last comment, because of course you can sniff flowers silently if you like" (114). Sheila illustrates this point with a yellow rose at the end of the play.

Thus, the end comes full circle to the beginning. Sheila, wearing the same dress she wore in the film, comes to the terrace again in a boat. Nardock again fakes suicide and leaves the terrace, this time taking Andy with him to the charmed life (like Mark and Gaw retreating up their mountain in the face of "rescue" in the tale written two decades later). Sheila, using the alternation of light and dark imagery which opens the play (and features prominently in *The Careless Flower*) repeats her melodramatic speech from act 1 ("[N]ight with its velvet pall will fall over all") and punctures her own overblown farewell to "the days that are no more. Music, Poetry, the Arts" (118) by saying, as the sun sinks, "Ah so, flop, ends the tropic day. That gets me" (119). Sinking to the ground, she twiddles her flower silently, perhaps uttering "the sniff superior."

Through this puzzling play Yeats is exploring two of the prevailing themes of his literary universe: (1) that it is necessary for an individual to accept chance and to seek unity in acceptance of the larger forces in the universe, and (2) that telling a tale, sharing the imaginative vision, is both a necessary and worthwhile act to sustain imaginative and social life. Andy, who has lived by chance, by chance meets Nardock, who has become involved with a larger force, "that vital principle which caused the creation of the world." Together, this male pair of travellers and outsiders goes from this real/unreal world to pursue their imaginative vision. Skelton suggests that, in Yeats's literary universe at least, spiritual goodness can spring from an acceptance of the life of the intuition and the imagination.[23]

The themes of this play—that it is necessary to preserve artistic authenticity, to preserve the life of the imagination, and to seek union with the vital principle that caused the creation of the world—are central to the fiction as well as to *The Deathly Terrace*. There is thematic continuity as well as formal development away from the melodrama used in the early pirate plays in this first play for the larger theatre. Although it was never produced and was not published until Robin Skelton included it in the *Collected Plays*, it is an important play to study in an attempt to trace themes in Yeats's universe.

Apparitions

The next three plays were published together in 1933 and should be looked at together. Their primary importance is their social criticism. The notes for intended performance tell us that the overture to the title play, *Apparitions*, was to be the highly ironic anti-war ballad, "Johnny, I Hardly Knew Ye." The theme of this ballad, that society sends young men off to war and is unmoved when they return unrecognizable and helpless ("You haven't an arm, you haven't a leg; you'll have to be put with a bowl to beg") matches the theme of this play: "The worm-like sufferings of another . . . are a joy untold to the observer from the Olympian heights of safety . . . in the front row of the best seats, which surround the arena . . . where the victim's heart throbs" (139). The illusion of distance insulates.

Like *The Deathly Terrace*, *Apparitions* is also a play about dramatic illusion and role-playing, and is also metatheatre, but at its end a fiction is being written, rather than a film being made. The apparition of the title is a fake; the play's setting is the town of "Pullickborough," which one character calls "Pull-leg-borough" early in the play; and the plot is a double leg pull, the subject of discussion between Nardock and Andy in *The Deathly Terrace*. Other familiar themes and motifs emerge in this play's exploration of the nature of reality. The attitude toward language—its inadequacy to express meaning—is found in the play's statement of its primary theme. This statement, a somewhat classic definition of comic distance, is bungled by a writer, playing the role of a waiter, who has also played the role of the apparition. He dictates his attempts at the statement to a clerk at a typewriter (literature is speech written down), amending it as he goes and commenting on its inadequacies:

Chapter eight. "As turns the Worm at Eventide." Quotation mark and "anonymous." In my last chapter I beguiled the reader, and I trust I did beguile him, for the worm-like sufferings of another, are as balm and wormwood—no, not that—not wormwood; balm and—balm and—balm and what? I've lost it. Sufferings of another are a joy untold to the observer from the safe vantage place of—no, not vantage place, it sounds like some sort of silly joke about lawn tennis—"love all" and that sort of thing—a joy untold to the observer from the Olympian heights of safety in the front— oh dear, oh dear! in the front row of the best seats, which surround the arena. That's not very good. I'll come back to it and alter it later on. Surround the arena, where the victim's heart throbs. In short, in my last I described the indignities I had put up with from bull-necked, ignorant, inaesthetic clods. But the point in my career at which I had now arrived will show the reader what . . .
(139)

Just at the point where the author, like Sheila Delgarvay, is about to be carried away by his own role playing, Yeats has the clerk interrupt him, telling him she loves him because he's so funny. His response, "Well, that's useful, anyway," ends the play. This reaction is typical of the comic responses to life of Yeats's characters. As Mr. No Matter comments in *The Charmed Life*, "Seeing funny things is a protection."

The stage directions for the action following this last speech accent the play's exploration of the nature of reality (a subject of *The Deathly Terrace*) and its concern with the role of the artist. The latter theme is dealt with in the two companion plays of the *Apparitions* volume. In a gesture typical of expressionist or anti-realist theatre, the actor who had played the multiple roles of waiter/apparition/writer, and who had earlier set up the stage, becomes a stagehand again by putting on white gloves. He puts down a card, signaling, in the music hall/vaudeville tradition, the end of a turn or act. He then changes from stagehand back to actor by throwing the gloves on the table and seizing the mask he had worn as "the apparition" and putting it on the back of his head so that it is seen by the audience as he exits from the arena, or circus ring. His disappearance into the audience breaks the illusion of distance. The victim, the artist, turns not only on his tormentor, the societal representative in the play, but on the audience which had assumed it was in the Olympian heights of safety in the front row of the best seats.

The play has a peculiarly Irish tone; it is written in what David Krause calls "the profane spirit of Irish comedy."[24] While some of the humor of the play is dialogue at the level of Tuffcake and Cream, the clowns from *Onct More's First Circus*, sometimes the clowning is serious. Yeats, who used the clown figure in his painting as a metaphor for the artist, is aware of the psychological and aesthetic dimensions of playing roles. Krause's examination of "redemptive profanations" is useful in the social context of this comedy. The Irish anti-hero, defeated from the start, must learn to live cheerfully and resourcefully with defeat. By using his wit, the helpless rogue occasionally defeats the repressive authority figures, achieving through mockery a release from the repression. In this comedy of unmasking, two comic servants (Charlie the silent barber and Jimmy the silent waiter) successfully mock their repressive social superiors, both the Anglo-Irish Ascendancy types (Squire Everton, the big-game hunter, and Albermarl, the retired colonial official) and the equally repressive middle class, in this case made up of former revolutionaries.

The play's arena setting enhances the social criticism, as well as the exploration of the nature of reality suggested by its title, by emphasizing the microcosmic dimensions of the play's world. The circus ring is one of Yeats's favorite metaphors. The seven characters gathered to defeat the apparition, like the seven speakers in the colloquies of the fiction, represent various elements of the Irish society of the 1930s. In this play, five are obsessed with respectability. In addition to the squire and the retired official, there are the three former revolutionaries: Phil Poleaxe, a gunman; Bill Scott, a sentimental failed soldier of fortune and gambler; and Erick Parlbury, a big-mouthed "Labour speaker" who talks in slogans. The two remaining selected men are Charlie, the rogue anti-hero and rebellious artist; and "Little Livid," who occupies a slightly more complex position in this anarchic comedy of worms turning. Livid is a clown, an ex-music hall performer who mocks the others during the course of the play, yet is himself mocked and tricked. Perhaps, at the level of comedy, he is the trickster tricked, and at the level of social criticism he is the artist who accepted repressive conditions. The eighth character, Jimmy, plays multiple roles, but is not part of the select group.

The comedy's temporary suspension of the social order takes place on Halloween (the Celtic "Samhain"), the night of pranks as well as of apparitions. The vehicle of humiliation, as well as its target, is the desire to maintain face. The group is gathered as "seven hearts as brave as any as ever beat in any part of the entire world together at the same time," and they are surrounded by "the watching eyes of the inhabitants of this part of the world" (123). Selected for their physical courage, they are to face down a ghost that has appeared in this pub ever since a former owner committed suicide on October 30th. The treatment of the recurring apparition is not tragic, as in WB's *Purgatory*, but comic; the seven are gathered to "scotch a ghost or goblin, or whatever it is," and they know before midnight that they have come one night too late, on October 31. They agree to go through with the intended action in order not to make a laughingstock of themselves, to keep their error to themselves. Obsessed with appearances, they agree to Charles's proposition to "wait in the dark for whatever may come, like the lot of bloody humbugs we are" (130).

The consequences of the specter's appearance are also treated comically. The brave defenders of society sit still and do nothing. The hair of each man who has made a brave speech turns white, proving, as Charlie maintains, "you're a poor lot; if your hearts are brave your heads aren't" (131). The unmasking continues beyond exposing the sham of courage to expose the sham of community. This attitude toward community is influenced, no doubt, by political events in Ireland. After the common enemy, the British, left, the Irish turned on each other in the Civil War. The same attitude toward community is expressed in *The Amaranthers*, in the Captain/ Philosopher's assertions that, while men can temporarily unite against danger, they separate again as soon as danger has passed. In this comedy, as in the vision of Mark in *The Careless Flower* where the coach passengers turn on each other and allow the robber to escape, men do not even unite in danger; furthermore, each acquiesces in what he thinks is the trick played on all of the others, under the assumption that he alone is not being tricked. Charlie, the formerly silent barber who is addressed as "worm," becomes the worm turned in this anarchic comedy, which Jimmy later calls "As turns the Worm at Eventide." Having told the "lot of old hear-me-outs" what he really thinks of them, Charlie asserts the play's main social criticism, that none of these "images" is going to do anything (133). They are all paralyzed, as is the country. He further insults them and, by offering to cover up their white hair, the symbol of their cowardice, makes them acquiesce in his trickery.

The social criticism of this play is clear. Yeats's picture of Irish paralysis is similar to Joyce's. Instead of acting in behalf of the community by putting the ghost (Ireland's history?) to rest, this self-elected, quasi-governmental body merely files a report. Both the Ascendancy types and the former gunmen and social revolutionaries who comprise the government of Ireland in the 1930s are obsessed with respectability. Only outsiders, artists like Charlie and Jimmy, and perhaps Little Livid, can see the sham.

Although the Ascendancy types behave badly in *Apparitions*, they are equaled by their former enemies, the revolutionaries. The labor speaker and journalist, Parlbury, represents what the social revolutionary has become in the Ireland of the 1930s; he is a mouther of slogans, co-opted by the conservative, small-land-holding class. As such, he comes in for special abuse. He is reviled by Charlie as a reader of Shaw. (Shaw, an Irishman who moved to London and ignored the plight at home, was, in Yeats's estimation, a fake or co-opted socialist.) Together the Squire and co-opted revolutionary keep Irish society in paralysis. They are reviled for it bitterly by Charlie: "Even Comrade Commune Parlbury couldn't get himself to join a general riot with the object of putting me where the good niggers go. And Old Toffee wouldn't let you; he'd veto anything that had any kind of a jump to it. ... Toff Everton, the man who invented standing still and reading yesterday's paper to-morrow evening" (133). In addition to their failure to act collectively for the general good, these six men betray each other in the hope of individual gain. Yeats's profound disillusion with Irish leadership includes disgust at its propensity for greed and betrayal.

Charlie isolates another important aspect of this trilogy's social criticism, the role of the artist: "But I'll show you how Art can put right the mistakes of nature" (133). The role that Ireland offers the artist now is to return a flattering image of itself. Disarming the suspicions of each, and appearing to offer each immunity from what he observes to be the plight of the others, the artist shows up the sham of community; while he inks each man's hair red, that man looks around the table at the others, subsiding into solitary laughter (135). The comedy's final unmasking takes place when the "artist" shows them his work of art, themselves. Disclaiming reforming intent, he says he is "just holding the mirror up to nature" (133).

The play's parable of society's rejection of the artist has significant details, revealed in another of the informal autobiographies by which characters in Yeats's narratives and plays justify their views of life. In this instance a character tells of his father's, not his own, fate. Old Charlie Charles, whose prodigious memory and training of apprentices associate him with the Gaelic bard or *file*, had been rejected in his role as oral transmitter of culture by a customer who says that he does not care for the story. Old Charlie next tries the role of prophet, giving the customer a tip on the winner for the "Gold Vase," but he is again rejected (131). The reaction of the true artist to rejection is both immediate and lasting: "It cut the old man to the quick. He never took any notice of anything again. That fatheaded old tool-chest killed an artist that day. I had my lesson, too. I've never troubled any of you old fat-heads with my talk the few times any of you have sat in my chairs, and that's not often, with your safety razors!" (132). Scorned as an outmoded functionary by an industrial society and demoted from his role as counsellor to governors in Gaelic society by a bureaucracy that wants him to be only a skilled craftsman, the modern Irish artist takes his revenge by showing society's flaws.

Yeats was not the only Irish artist to feel this disillusion about his role in society. Speaking of Flann O'Brien's "simultaneous separation from the literary revival and from nationalism," Seamus Deane, himself a poet as well as a critic, says: "No one of the authors [of the 30s and 40s] escapes the disillusion which followed upon the collapse of nationalism and the poverty of the period between 1930 and 1955. Ireland ceased to be a mythological centre and became a provincial backwater."[25]

In the second play in this volume, *The Old Sea Road*, Yeats continues his socio-political criticism and criticism of the role assigned to the artist in Irish society. He also continues to present an aspect of the primary theme—the need to accept change, to give up attempts at control, and to accept life's rhythms—primarily, in this play, through the Anglo-Irish figure, Ambrose Oldbury. It gradually emerges that Ambrose's practical joking is desperate, an attempt to rebel against the bleakness of his life by finding something funny, a typical device in Yeats's literary universe. The play seems also to be exploring the question asked in *The Charmed Life*: "When the curtain falls on fun, what then my children?" Yeats's answer: "Then we, you and I, must take what comes" (6). Ambrose has not learned to do this; he is still struggling. One of the play's "sub-rosa" social themes is that the Anglo-Irish must give up the political struggle to retain control of Ireland, as well as the individual struggle to retain control of personal destiny.

Yeats uses the outsider motif and the device of pairing male characters who reveal each other through dialogue. Ambrose Oldbury represents one half of the primary pair. An Anglo-Irishman, he is rather déclassé, like Gaw in *The Careless Flower*. A traveller, like Yeats's fictional protagonists—James of *The Amaranthers*, Bowsie of *The Charmed Life*, Dusty Brown of *Ah Well*, and Mark of *The Careless Flower*—Ambrose is also the Yeats "outsider" figure. Ambrose is warned by the policeman, who in deference to his social standing calls him "Captain," that the people of the village are too ignorant to understand his joking. He is an outsider, culturally and socially, from the native Irish, the "ignorant" people of the village.

The other half of the primary pair is "Michael of the Song," who, as an artist, is also an outsider in this society. On the level of Yeats's social criticism, Michael's encounters with the townspeople have been no more satisfactory than those of Ambrose. His art, like that of the elder Charlie Charles in *Apparitions*, is rejected. He says that his song (which at twenty-one verses long may be another reflection of the prodigious memory of the Gaelic *file*) was intended to get the people interested in him, but "as soon as I hit the second verse of my song the unfortunate people thought it was personal and they never let me finish, and they'd give me neither bite nor sup" (150). Modern Ireland, as in *Apparitions*, is not ready for any personal criticism; it will pay the artist for nothing but a flattering self-image. In a neat trick of psychological displacement, the very melodeon on which Michael played his song is "heartbroken." To carry on the tradition of oral poetry and song he had obtained the instrument from another travelling artist in Kerry, the heart of the Gaelic southwest, as the price of one of his own songs. Now he has thrown the instrument into the tide. Socially, Michael represents the plight of the dispossessed native artist, reduced in ability and social position from the status of his Gaelic forebears, and he blames that old villain in Yeats's work, "the commercial instinct," for souring the times. There is also a back-hand slap at censorship presented through Michael when Josephine, the school mistress, representative of the conservative educational establishment, reproaches him for speaking to a student about philosophy. She hopes Michael didn't tell him anything that wasn't good for him (151), a sad commentary on the educational mentality of Ireland in the 30s.

Not only the educational establishment rejects the outsider. Michael has apparently had many brushes with other forms of the establishment, since he has developed the useful "gift" of recognizing a plain-clothes policeman. "Authority . . . linked with convenience," in the form of the postman and the policeman, offers Michael nothing. The postman, speaking for the progressive town says: "Oh, there's nothing for you, me bold feller" (152). Only his tradition is left to Michael, his memories of better days. When a student, the one to whom he had spoken of philosophy, offers to give Michael supper in Cahirmahone, the more traditional of the two villages, Michael refuses and, betraying his disillusion, asks only for "a touch of a poem, . . . My Dark Rosaleen, Iween, sheen, has been?" (152). This nationalist ballad, which Yeats had placed near the end of *A Broadside*, keeps Michael's attention. When Ambrose returns, however, the two outcasts—one the remnant of the Ascendancy rake, reduced to a practical joker, and the other the remnant of the native aristocratic bard, reduced to a singing dancing-master—unite for the play's significant action. Both utter aspects of the play's social criticism. Recognizing each other as soulmates (Ambrose recognizes Michael's similar exclusion and addresses him as "old son"), they agree that the people around them are "the limit." The two outsiders have been rejected by both the progressive town, Jacksport, and the conservative village, Cahirmahone. They react in ways that exhibit Yeats's criticism of both traditions in modern Ireland.

Ambrose speaks Yeats's social criticism of the native Irish while admitting some of Michael's criticism of his own class. Being less resilient (as the Anglo-Irish Gaw was less resilient than Mark in *The Careless Flower*), Ambrose sees himself as "full to the brim" ("everything is sticking to me . . . I'm the end of everything") and wants to open his mouth and "swallow the wave." Stung by Michael's rebuke that he has lost the instinct for jokes, that he is too urbane, Ambrose admits that he is "smothered" by his heritage. (Like many of the Anglo-Irish, he has too much intellectual and social baggage.) However, he claims (using a claim with which Yeats would be sympathetic) that his jokes have failed "because the material I had to work on [the people of Ireland] was too materialistic" (155). The native Irish have become middle class. Ambrose, accused of frivolity and loss of connection with instinctual life, in turn rebukes Michael, the native Irishman and representative of the Gaelic tradition, with being a "dead centre." The conservatism of the native tradition contributes to the paralysis of Ireland as much as the baggage-ridden stagnation of the Ascendancy tradition. Ambrose rebukes Michael for his resignation and offers to show him something he's never seen before: "Man upright defying the slings and arrows and getting away with it" (155). The Anglo-Irish generally found the native patience unfathomable and regressive.

Yet Ambrose betrays the insecurity of his class, the sense of being patronized by the representative of the older tradition, by saying "and then perhaps you won't be giving me your airs, your high and mighty airs" (155). In a showy gesture, he burns all his money, the baggage of his class, and exults in his freedom from tradition:

> I'm on the road
> Rattling the stones
> Over the bones of
> The old ones
> Dead and gone.
>   (157)

Michael, who has known the disadvantage of this sort of freedom, continues his own criticism. He refuses Ambrose's offer of community, his offer to walk "the roads of the world with you," by saying, "Well, thank you, but I wouldn't walk the Heavenly paths with a man so little in sense as yourself." He denigrates Ambrose's histrionic gesture by asking if he couldn't have experienced freedom "without all that fire-burning business?" (157). Neither patience nor rebellion seems to work. Ambrose, rejected yet again, the permanent outsider as an Anglo-Irishman (with or without his property) whom the native Irish still scorn, takes up the suicidal implications of his Hamlet allusion; he will respond to slings and arrows by suicide. Having said he had "two jokes left," he offers Michael a drink. With his back to Michael but seen by the audience, he empties a bottle into his silver flask, and they both drink. As he slumps, he leans over on Michael's breast, uniting them in death as they never were united in life. Michael accepts their union and forgives him the poisoning, asking: "Would it be any offense if I said a prayer for you?" (158).

As in *Apparitions*, Yeats's real targets are both the paralysis of Ireland and its moral hypocrisy. The two deaths go unnoticed (like the death in Breugel's "Icarus") by Nolan and Dolan, the workers on the old sea road who represent the "moral hypocrisy of the community,"[26] and by officialdom, the postman. The deaths of Ambrose and Michael will have little impact, finally, on the community, largely because of the essential passivity represented by Nolan and Dolan's "genial way of life . . . their good-natured obtuseness."[27] Some notice is taken by the more admirable characters in the play. The ballad-singer mourns both and an intuitively wise peasant woman (like Synge's Nora or Pegeen Mike) ends the play by mourning Michael, the "lovely man" (162). But the reaction of the other community representatives has been hypocritical. When the peasant from the bog sees the two bodies and goes to alert the establishment, the postman tries to pretend to the woman and child that no deaths have occurred. The publican, another hypocrite, represents the decline of the tradition of true hospitality and the rise of the "commercial instinct"; he only pretends to foster community. The principal target, however, is certainly Ireland's stagnation.[28] Paralyzed Ireland has ostracized its two best traditional elements while hypocritically striving for a limited concept of progress.

Ambrose's suicide and murder of Michael are related negatively to Yeats's primary theme, that man should immerse himself in the rhythms of life: suicide is a crime against the life force. Robin Skelton, however thinks that the play's primary emphasis is on man's struggle to shape life; he sees the play as an ontological parable. He finds Ambrose, whose surname, Oldbury, "is an obvious indication of his character as a death bringer," to be "one who challenges, by means of his jokes, the validity of life itself."[29] In his introduction to the collected plays, Skelton says that *The Old Sea Road*, bitterer than *Apparitions*, is about a cosmic joke: "The last practical joke of Ambrose is murder and suicide; it is hinted that this is as much a deception as his two previous practical jokes. . . . The inconsequence of the play is marked. It is so organized as to suggest the wayward fluctuant progress of life, and the finally desperate attempt of man to give it shape, even by mocking and denying it."[30] Skelton's interpretation neglects several elements in the play. Michael has the last word—"Would it be any offense if I said a prayer for you?"—and Ambrose accepts his prayer. These two actions suggest Yeats's essentially Christian theme, the necessity of surrender of the will to a higher power, a thematic ending similar to the end of *The Careless Flower*; Yeats's universe is not given shape by man.

The final commentary of the play, spoken by the ballad singer and the woman (both vehicles for truth in Yeats's work) neglects Ambrose and focuses on Michael's sad end, indicating that he is the focal character and reinforcing the emphasis on Yeats's social and artistic themes. The ballad singer claims that society, in the form of the policeman, has laid low "great creatures like this one (looking down on Michael's face)" (162). The play's focus is not on Ambrose's ontological relation to the primary theme but on Michael's; its social criticism is strong. Ambrose is acting as a representative of his class, the Anglo-Irish Ascendancy, which committed social suicide. The real tragedy is that the native Irish tradition died along with it, equally repressed, as Yeats believed, by the "commercial instincts" of the "paudeens" (to borrow WB's word) who took over and betrayed the social and aesthetic ideals of the Rising. Only the powerless but life-affirming characters, the peasant woman and the ballad singer, understand and value Michael's "song," the artist's contribution to society.

The third play in this volume, *Rattle*, which takes its title from Ambrose's song about "rattling the stones over the bones of the old ones dead and gone," continues Yeats's social criticism by showing ineffectual Anglo-Irish destroying their inheritance, as Ambrose had destroyed his money in a pointless attempt to be free of his "baggage," his traditions and his guilt. There are strong thematic similarities in all three plays; Yeats develops his social criticism through the three works and accentuates it by his stage directions for music. The ironic ballad about indifference, "Johnny, I Hardly Knew Ye," is appropriate to *Apparitions*. The romantic song "Believe Me If All Those Endearing Young Charms," with its theme of the attempt to maintain a belief in an ideal, is appropriate to *The Old Sea Road*. The third song, "Let Erin Remember," reinforces the monitory thrust of *Rattle* with its emphasis on the consequences in the twentieth century of the unjust actions of the characters' forebears. The twentieth-century Anglo-Irish in this play were reaping the harvest their eighteenth-century ancestors had sown.

To convey his social criticism artistically, as he had done since *A Broadside*, Yeats creates a dramatic fabulation. He shows the Irish social situation in the first part of the play—the exposition—and transposes it to a utopian tropical island in the second portion of the play, the equivalent of the exemplum found in the narratives. Even critics as sensitive as Robin Skelton, who calls the play "formless,"³¹ have failed to see the commentary created by the play's form, the connection between its two halves, by not taking into account the patterns of the major narratives. The social implications of the inheritance question ("The myth of sudden inheritance becomes that of undeserved death"³²) has also been misinterpreted by critics not taking into account the social ideals of *A Broadside*.

The first phase of the action of *Rattle* shows the inability of five heirs to dispose of a wharfinger firm. One of the heirs claims to have inherited from his eighteenth-century forebear, the founder of the firm, the instinct for telling when the end of a business was near: "I detect the rattle in the throat. I can always tell. It's an instinct" (168). There are several resonances in the title: the death rattle of a society and the rattle of the stones over the bones of the old ones in an attempt to escape tradition. Picking up the first resonance in nostalgic fashion, Yeats portrays the inheritors as inferior to their forebears. They are either unable or unwilling to run the inherited business themselves. There are several causes of their incapacity: (1) their ancestors had not prepared them properly to assume their role; (2) they are essentially frivolous; (3) they are unaware of the change in their position; and, most seriously in Yeats's universe (4) they are unable to adapt. From the early play, *The Treasure of the Garden*, Yeats has shown a paralyzed Irish society unable to adapt.

In *Rattle*, one of the characters voices the clearest expression of Yeats's solution to the problem of dealing with an unavoidable change, immersing oneself in the larger forces of the universe. Yeats is still exhorting his class, much as he did in *A Broadside*, but to a different course of action. Using the metaphor of the flow and ebb of the tide, familiar from *Sailing, Sailing Swiftly* which was written at about this time, William, one of the heirs, comments on a piece of broken wood drifting: "But there is some symbol there. Perhaps this vagrant wood is to show that the rhythm that cannot be mastered can be enjoyed until it laps you gently into a state of static bliss with a number of other pieces of drift" (184). Like the young Yeats who regretted not spending more time peering into the water from the Sligo bridge, or the narrator of *Sligo* who learned to accept the rain by not resisting it, William objects to interfering with "the steady ebb and flow, flow and ebb of the tide up and down this river, just at our doorstep as we might say" (183).

The heirs, however, unable to accept change, demonstrate in the first half of the play those qualities which doom one of their number, the youngest and bravest, to death on a tropical island in the play's second half. Speaking of her lack of preparation for managing the inherited enterprise, the one female heir correctly identifies the first cause of their plight when she laments her own lack of education, blaming her father: "[S]o had father neglected our education, with his ridiculous ideas about the young learning whatever they wished, and leaving the rest unlearned" (169–70). Yeats, his brother, or his sisters might have laid the same charge against their father.

These scions of the Ascendancy are too frivolous to be interested in or capable of holding on to what was grasped for them in the eighteenth century. This charge, from Maria Edgeworth's *Castle Rackrent* on, was a preoccupation in Anglo-Irish literature. This cause of the Anglo-Irish plight has as much personal resonance for Yeats as the first cause does. His Pollexfen-Middleton ancestors were similarly involved in a shipping company, through multiple intermarriages like those of the Gardynes (Guardians?) and Golbacks (Goldbacks?) of this play. His grandfather's inability to manage the family business led to Yeats's return from Sligo to his father's home in London. At the time of his grandfather's death the young boy may have witnessed scenes similar to those in the play. He may also be criticizing his own father's inability to manage his

inherited estate, impoverishing his sons by mortgages while insisting that Willie, his "heir," refuse a paying job and take up the
intellectual pursuits of the gentry. Anglo-Irish frivolity in dealing
with inheritance has immense significance for Yeats. Ambrose Oldbury in *The Old Sea Road*, frivously burning his money and claiming to rattle the stones over the bones of those dead and gone,
reflects the second cause of the Ascendancy plight; Alec Gardyne,
the most frivolous of the heirs in this play, represents it too, with
his scheme for selling the freehold of the wharfingering firm for a
cinema site. His lack of business acumen is shown by his schemes
for bringing in an audience by barge and his naive and frivolous
notion that the only things needed to consummate a business deal
are dinner at a "slap-up restaurant," port, and a cigar (172).

Predictably, the heirs' schemes come to naught, reflecting the
third and fourth causes of their plight, their lack of awareness and
inability to adapt. Placing their trust in the inalienability of class
privileges, they assume that they can manipulate the new middle
class by flattery and offers of social inclusion. They also assume
that, given time, they could manage anything. Although he has just
eaten a rich meal, Alec claims to be depleted, "But no doubt, if I
had a long rest somewhere, I could lay out a plan of some sort"
(183). He says this even after the businessman has told them that
their scheme will not work, that no one could make it a paying
proposition (178); he exhibits the Anglo-Irish tendency to confuse
postponement of the consideration of a problem with its solution.
Like the land the Anglo-Irish depended on for maintaining themselves, the freehold is worth nothing without proper management.
The outsider, the hoped-for rescuer, comments shrewdly on their
situation: "No, what you really want is something that will pay you
a nice income, at least equal to what the wharf has been producing
in the past, and will be amusing to all in some way. So that your
romantic complexes, if there are such things, go on all right" (179).
Not surprisingly, these improperly educated, frivolous, imaginatively impoverished representatives of "the commercial interests"
can think of nothing to do but let the wharf go on as it is, promoting
the clerks to run it for them. Like "Toff Everton" of *Apparitions*,

"who invented standing still and reading yesterday's paper tomorrow evening" (133), or like the displaced Irish in *Scourge of the Gulph*, they can think of nothing better to do than go on as before, depending, in this case, on social inferiors. They exhibit the faults of absentee landlords.

In the exemplum section, the more serious consequences of the inheritance of colonialism begin to manifest themselves. Ted has been informed that his father has bequeathed him property in a "far away land," "lands, forests and lakes." Not a commercial enterprise (which had at least taken time, effort and talent to run, however unfairly the founders had been aided by restrictive laws), this inheritance of real property has more culpability attached to it. Yeats's socialist sympathies are still strong. Exhibiting the indecisiveness, or awareness of guilt, which makes action impossible, Ted's father had tried the Anglo-Irish solution of half-measures and postponement. He had bequeathed the property to the state for ten years, at the end of which time it was to go back to his heirs. This situation may represent the benign neglect absentee landlords often showed Ireland when they were too busy elsewhere to try to run their own affairs.

The representatives of "Packawana," the faraway land, suddenly arrive to give Ted his inheritance by conducting a mystifying ceremony that serves as the transition from the exposition to the exemplum. The imagery functions here as a bridge between the real and the visionary, as it does in *The Careless Flower*. There is tide and wave imagery, symbolic rose imagery, and color imagery. At the end of act 2, the Captain strews "eight golden-yellow-rose-like flowers" in a half-circle about the doorway through which the Packawanians and Ted have walked after the ceremony. (This circle of roses had been portrayed in a significant *Broadside* drawing.) No one dares to cross the half-circle, indicating their awareness that a ritual action has taken place. In act 3 the importance of these roses becomes clearer. The glade in which Ted and Dr. Canty, the Packawana interpreter, are standing is filled with trees whose flowers are bright yellow, "like giant evening primroses" (194). Yeats had previously alerted the audience to the importance of the color when a wharf-hand had cried "Fever colour, yaller, quarantine, fever" and Canty had replied "Yes, fever. The fever that flows forever in the blood of the people of Packawana" (189). The Packawanian sailors are all wearing yellow jackets, and "Captain For More" wears yellow trousers, a gold belt, and gold epaulets. A "golden" sun is sinking, and Ted is told he is to remain with them until the sun sets, when he will be free. It becomes gradually clear that this freedom is illusory, that many Packawanians in addition to the Captain are "for more," and that the "fever" in the blood of Packawana people can have dangerous consequences, as gunshots ring out and come closer to the glade. Ted's status as "guest of the nation" begins to resemble that of the hostage in O'Connor's story of that name; he, too, becomes a sacrificial victim.

There are more mythic resonances similar to those in *Sailing, Sailing Swiftly*, published in the same year. On the island Ted is given an elixir, as are characters in that fiction, and he is fed a ritual meal from a basket adorned with "golden yellow flowers," gold being a symbol of his greed as well as of their fever. He is given a "wine that flows while grass grows and water runs. It's the wine of gladness, it's the wine of a sort of sub-madness, as though a walker on a tight rope over a forest walked with ease. . . . Ease and elegancy, with safety, painted to look like danger" (196). The tightrope walker is an excellent metaphor for the Anglo-Irish in general and for Ted in this situation. They had to balance between the claims of the native people and their sense of the claims of their ancestors. This elixir Ted is given also appears in Yeats's fiction, where it is often a metaphor for the imaginative life or (with its references to grass growing and water flowing) for acceptance of rhythms of life larger than the self. Here it apparently has to do with Ted's education to accept his fate, as it does in *Amaranthers*, the narrative published just after the *Apparitions* volume. Ted does not want to know much and does not take action, behaving like a representative of his paralyzed class—not distinguishing between safety and danger, waiting to be exterminated by the natives, and whiling away the time eating, drinking, and being preoccupied with the trappings of rank: the collar, the cape, and the palanquin in which he will be carried by native bearers. Although in a more extreme form, as befits a fabulation, Ted's actions resemble those of the Anglo-Irish in Elizabeth Bowen's Irish novels.

Familiar Yeats subjects come up while Ted is waiting. As in Yeats's early plays, there is more disquisition than action, and what action there is takes place offstage and is reported by characters who "speak majestically." The question of place names arises, a question with particular relevance in Ireland, where Gaelic place names survived long after other cultural landmarks had disappeared and represented to the Irish an important link to the deep truths of an older culture. Ted asks Canty about the name of the capital and is told its name is "Pannikin." He is astonished at this, since a pannikin is a tin basin for food. Canty's reply is Yeats's clearest exposition of the persistent use of Gaelic place names as resistance to oppression, and of the use of Gaelic as the key to a revolutionary culture. Irish historian Owen Dudley Edwards, in an essay on "The Burden of Irish History," speaks succinctly of the two languages the oppressed native Irish used, "one for purposes of communication to the rulers, one among themselves."[33] Here is Dr. Canty's version of the same phenomenon:

But some visitor, long ago, before your father's time, I believe, said "it looks like a pannikin to me . . .". The people were amused and so they called it Pannikin. That is, if anyone who is not a Pakawanian asks, they say "Pannikin." The people themselves, we ourselves are too fond and proud to give the city a name that is a fixed name. Some call it sometimes "that foolish place"; "that fond place"; "the friendly place"; "that oblique place"; "that everything of a place." You will notice, as you become more deeply involved in the ideas of the place, that adjectives are substituted for proper names very often. Not proper adjectives, but changing and various ones. (197)

This passage is the key to Yeats's treatment of names and language in the later narratives. Its naming situation is similar to the situation Brian Friel treats in his play *Translations*, the recording or transliterating of place names for the first Ordinance Survey by British Royal Engineers. In Friel's play, while trying to record "Ban na hAbhann," which means "mouth of the river," for example, the engineer says, "Let's leave it alone. There's no English equivalent for a sound like that," and they settle on "Burnfoot."[34] "Pannikin" isn't much worse than "Burnfoot" and its meaning is of little relevance to people who will continue, among themselves, to call a place by the old name. The renaming, as Friel's engineer and Ted both discover, cuts two ways. The engineer has a sense of destroying an important order, an older and perhaps better one: "I had moved into a consciousness that wasn't striving or agitated, but at its ease and with its own convictions and assurance."[35] Ted discovers a tranquility and acceptance of the rhythms of life in Packawana, symbolized by the Order of the Wave. Friel's engineer, like Ted, is unable to be as ruthless as his father, "the perfect colonial servant." He learns, as Ted does, that, as attractive as the country might be, he would always be an outsider: "Even if I did speak Irish I'd always be an outsider here, wouldn't I? I may learn the password but the language of the tribe will always elude me, won't it? The private core will always be ... hermetic, won't it?"[36] (ellipsis in original). Yeats, who himself studied hard to learn Gaelic, must have come to somewhat the same conclusion. An outsider, like Ambrose in *The Old Sea Road*, he was always alienated from Michael of the Song and his native counterparts.

In alluding to what Friel's engineer calls the "hermetic" core of the language, Yeats's Dr. Canty touches on a quality of the older language which modern scholars call the "aspective" character of Gaelic, its tendency to consider properties of things in denominating them, a tendency to express states, or aspects, rather than actions.[37] If the states are always changing, fixed names are pointless, as Nardock in *The Deathly Terrace* would claim. A different order of perception is at work here, to which language is the key. The depiction of states was a more important concern to Yeats than was the portrayal of actions.

Utopia is a familiar motif that arises while Ted and his interpreter are waiting for the bearers to come to take Ted to the last part of the Ceremony of the Wave. Canty's treatment of utopians reflects Yeats's profound disillusion with the revolutionary ideal. The utopians who come to Packawana with their abstract ideals, their "sort of fit-up" utopias, are deported to an island Canty calls "Renaygia" (Renegia?) where they enjoy "a sort of sterile beauty" (199). Although he claims to have no utopian expectations of Packawana, Ted betrays some which are remarkably like those held by a younger Yeats. They also resemble the conditions in utopias portrayed in *In Sand* and in *Ah Well*:

I am sure it is a place where intellectuality and good fellowship are blended. . . . And I suppose you have some fine schools, perhaps where only the best of everything is taught under the freest possible conditions? . . . And Picture Galleries where the best native work is shown side by side with examples of the oldest and the most modern from the rest of the world.

(202)

Although these speculations on many familiar themes have taken place, holding up the dramatic action in a way that may be unacceptable in the theatre, the inheritance question remains primary in this play. The suppression of a culture, as well as the seizure of land and the exploitation of natural resources, is a crime of colonialism for which Ted must expiate. Canty encourages Ted to make a will. Like the Anglo-Irish he represents, Ted leaves half of his property to the country (which has, as in Ireland, wrested it from him by force of arms) but the other half to his relatives, perpetuating the struggle for ownership of the land. While the Ascendancy did not keep quite half of Ireland for the United Kingdom, they kept a substantial portion, and one with important cultural associations as well as natural resources. The perpetuation of the struggle is still apparent almost sixty years after Yeats published these plays advocating relinquishment of the struggle for control of Ireland.

The relinquishment of the struggle for control of personal destiny is portrayed symbolically in the play. The theme of acceptance of chance is emphasized, along with the desirability of uncertainty:

Canty: "Let you remain uncertain. It's your best hold . . ."
Ted: "Well I have always liked uncertainty. Even when a little boy I used to like not to be told where I was going. . . . And I delighted in having an old uncle holding a small present in each of his hands and making me choose which I'd have."

Canty: Weren't you sometimes disappointed?"
Ted: "Yes, of course—sometimes. But never enough to want to cry off
   with my chance."
Canty: "You had the spirit! Heroes are like that."

While Canty and Ted discuss heroism, Ted's relinquishment (like Ambrose's burning of his money) brings peace. Freed at his own request from the Wave Collar, which Canty calls "the old harness," Ted dies quietly. In tune with the ebb and flow now, he is reported by Canty to be "Zaappah (Gone forward)" (206). Death, to Yeats, is a change of state. The expected bearers, also wearing the Wave Collars and blood-red cloaks with which Ted had been invested, now appear to carry Ted in his palanquin, moving in "a quiet swing, as to a known ceremonial" (206). With Ted's death, the ritual sacrifice of expiation for wrongful inheritance has taken place. The expected ceremonial will actually be his funeral.

The three plays published in *Apparitions* are thematically related in their treatment of contemporary Irish society and of the role of the outsider, the artist and the Anglo-Irishman, in that society. These plays make use of much of the early material of *A Broadside* and introduce several themes to be developed in the later fiction.

The true revenant in the entire volume of *Apparitions* is Irish history, and the plays are social problem plays. Instead of writing a realistic, well-made play after the fashion of Ibsen, however, Yeats chose an anti-realist mode. The plays are a type of dramatic fabulation. In the metatheatrical *Apparitions*, Yeats shows us contemporary Irish society unable to deal with its own past. The seven representative men chosen to confront the apparition fail; the artist has set up an apparition to show them their own paralysis and lack of community after the society collectively rejects the artist's vision of the truth. Yeats wanted these plays staged in an arena to show the audience that its indifference was part of the problem. In *The Old Sea Road* societal indifference was again attacked. When the two travellers, one representing the Gaelic tradition and one the Ascendancy tradition, die on the road, the community, represented by Nolan and Dolan, is indifferent. The official figures behave as badly and ineffectually as in *Apparitions*, and they are charged by the artist, the Ballad Singer, with being responsible for the death of the old artistic tradition. The actual murderer, who commits suicide at the same time, is the Ascendancy rake. The Anglo-Irish guilt is the principal problem in *Rattle*, the third play in the trilogy, which shows us the frivolous heirs to an estate, ill-prepared by education and temperament to manage their inheritance because they are out of touch with the instincts and traditions which established their heritage. One of the heirs is shown paying with his life for colonial guilt. The tone of this social criticism has changed from that of *A Broadside*, where an insider appeals to his own group; it is more like that of the narratives where an outsider shows both the paralysis of the society and its rejection of the vision of the artist. In a prophetic drawing at the end of *A Broadside*, the artist watches sadly while unheeding passersby ignore his chalked message "Up Kerry!"

The Silencer

The next play is also a social problem play in which the society silences the artist whose message it doesn't want to hear. The villain this time is not an Anglo-Irishman, but one of the other group of villains from *Apparations*, a former revolutionary and die-hard gunman: "The Silencer." The artist in this play, however, is himself more culpable than those in the *Apparitions* volume, and demonstrates his participation in the paralysis and garrulousness of the society.

This play, which was neither published by Yeats nor performed, has the full title *The Silencer or Farewell Speech* and has close affinities with *Sligo* in its attitudes toward language. Its protagonist, Hartigan, is called "Chatagain" by the other characters, and his tendency to "speak majestically" and at length, a tendency that might be extended to the Irish in general, is the cause of his trouble. Although the play is set in London, Hartigan is an Irishman who represents Irish oratory in excess. The societal paralysis we have seen in the *Apparitions* volume results, in this play, from the tendency to talk too much while doing nothing. Hartigan bewitches his auditors with his incantatory language. His hearers are also fascinated by his power of expression, by the artist's powers of representing what is locked up within inexpressive man (220). The society is willing to use the artist's gift and manipulate him for its own ends. A "con" man appeals to his sense of injustice: "Now, you're a gifted man; you have speech and you're getting nothing out of it. It's a gift, I tell you. Used properly it leads its owner to what they call Fame and Fortune. Why some of that you told me about the Copra days was a poem. Like a Hymn. But with more to it! You come along of me this afternoon and use your gift" (224–25).

The plight of the artist, unsure of his role and unappreciated, is as central to *The Silencer* as to *Apparitions* and *The Old Sea Road*. When fired by his employer for doing too well his job of entertaining clients, Hartigan, like the artist in modern Ireland, is "bewildered." His employer feels bad about Hartigan's plight and accepts some responsibility for it. But Hartigan, too, is to blame, as he demonstrates in losing a messenger job by talking too much. The artist turns scornfully on an inarticulate hearer:

You are listening to me because you have nothing to say yourself . . . You have forgotten you have a tongue. . . . You love the sound of me and you hate the sense. . . . You are speechless because I talk for you. You think you speak yourself. You think I echo your thoughts. You have no thoughts; you never had thoughts. . . . You have never existed in your own right. You exist now in mine. . . . By my lips you live; by their stillness you pass away or back again into your solidity of a poised dust mote. You could wish yourself alive but you will never do it.
(232–33)

At the level of social criticism, Hartigan represents both the artist adrift in a society which has no role for him and the artist as target of the former revolutionaries, like Parlbury in *Apparitions*. Hill, "The Silencer," represents the gunman, the noble outsider of revolutionary days, who has become excessive. Now as powerless and bewildered as the artist, the second type of outsider has become the die-hard Avenger, obsessed with trying to punish the man whose rhetoric betrayed his comrades.

Another aspect of Yeats's criticism of modern Ireland concentrates on its violence and desire for revenge. Hill the Avenger is the least sympathetic character in the play, reflecting Yeats's detestation of violence, and his awareness that vengeance is often mistaken in its target. Speaking like the blindest of the IRA avengers who appear in O'Casey's plays (and in the fiction of O'Connor, O'Faolain, and other Irish writers of the time), Hill says melodramatically: "I know what I want with Hartigan. I'm to settle up with him. There's no one to do it but me, and I'll do it if I swing" (230). We know what Yeats thinks of revenge from the situation of Miles, the Pirate of *The Scourge of the Gulph*, who, after getting "his fierce revenge" on the captain, asks, "Have I done anything or nothing?" (80). A less violent character, Sam, tries to dissuade Hill from revenge by saying that "the bloody old fool" didn't mean to get them arrested and that "the boys don't think he did anything willingly on them." Hill replies, using all of the clichés of post-Troubles rhetoric, that Hartigan's talking "is going to be his death now," claiming that he is not going to see Hartigan free for three years while his friends are in jail: "I'm Truth and Justice. . . . A life for a life, I always said. . . . I'm not a man, I'm an Avenger" (230). This surrender of one's humanity, thinking with a gun and resisting logic often results in unjust revenge. When Sam, who claims responsibility for introducing "Chatagain" into the scene, asks Hill why he isn't ready to give himself up to justice after getting Hartigan, he is met with the blind iteration: "I'm Truth and Justice." Hill's revenge resembles what Yeats called elsewhere the envy of the cripple for the man who can jump; it is clearly aimed at the artist whom he calls "your gifted friend" (231). This focus is reminiscent of a speech actually made by a general from the Abbey stage: "We have been deserted, at the present time and all through the fight put up in the country, by our poets and our literary men." This resentment of artists by "men of action" seemed to Yeats to be all too common an attitude in Ireland in the thirties. Unlike the noble revolutionaries of *A Broadside*, gunmen like "Hill the Spiller" seemed motivated only by violence, enemies of the life force that the artist represents. As shown by his petition to Synge for a ballad "not too bloody" to use in *A Broadside*, Yeats had always abhorred violence. Disenchanted with the sort of blind patriotism which was used to mask a liking for violence, Yeats portrays Hill as a petty, revengeful man.

The sentimentality of the violent man's need for signs of forgiveness, which had been touched on in *Rattle*, is developed in this play. Ironically, in act 3, Hill's revenge has begun to haunt him. He frequents seances, seeking forgiveness from Hartigan's ghost. The fraudulent seance (perhaps a dig at WB's occult preoccupations) is exposed and broken up by Sam, the "shell-back." Hill sees Hartigan's ghost and begs its forgiveness, but, bored by the ghost's explanation of life in the spirit world, berates him with what Yeats called the self-mutilated man's envy of the artist: "You're a nasty . . . insincere old chat. . . . You think you're somebody, and you think you're everybody. There's nothing behind you but gas. . . . You don't know nothing about Truth and Justice, but I do. And I wish now I'd shot you twice instead of once. It'd be a pleasure" (245). He takes that pleasure metaphorically and shoots the dictaphone through which Hartigan's ghost speaks in fake seances, although he cannot succeed in shooting the ghost since his aimed gun will not fire.

A farcical ending takes place, with law enforcers as the butt of the joke. Fancy Dress Constables, whose antics would do justice to Tuffcake and Cream, defraud the complaining landlord and release Hill (who continues to watch obsessively the ghost he alone can see). Earlier criticism of the law had come when Hill first shot Hartigan; while the criminals, Hill and Sam, were escaping, the policeman, as in *The Old Sea Road*, was merely concerned with irrelevant details, taking down with his pencil and pad the witness's "name in full" and so forth.

There are also some random endorsements of familiar values, as when Hartigan speaks admiringly of seamen who stood up to their troubles, who lived and died game (212). This same admiration of fortitude is present in Yeats's presentation of Ambrose Oldbury in *The Old Sea Road*, of Ted in *Rattle*, of Mark and Gaw in *The Careless Flower*, of the traveller in *Ah Well*, and the woman in *And To You Also*.

In the speeches of this play Skelton finds the essence of Yeats's beliefs, and he thinks *The Silencer* most explicitly presents Yeats's attitudes. He finds exhortations to see the unity of life, and the attitude that death is not "a conclusion," but "a continuance and a change of perspective."[38] Although these and other theme statements are presented in the play, their ironic context makes them less than satisfactory as explicit statements of Yeats's values. The social criticism is more worthy of attention than the metaphysical speculation, but neither is skillfully embodied in dramatic action.

Harlequin's Positions

Harlequin's Positions, the first of Yeats's plays for the "larger theatre" to be performed, was done in 1939 by the Abbey Experimental Theatre under the direction of Ria Mooney. Anne Yeats designed the sets. A play in five acts, with successfully staged action, it deals with some of the same themes and motifs as the five plays previously discussed—particularly with the need for acceptance of what comes, of what chance, personified in the Harlequin, brings—and embodies some of the same social criticism particularly of the paralysis of Ireland. Characterized as "a play of war's alarums" (a phrase that may be mocking his brother's poem "Politics"), it was written about 1938 and accepted for performance at the Abbey's experimental theatre, The Peacock, in January 1939, just before the outbreak of World War II.[39] Ironically, this acceptance occurred in the month of WB's death; the end of WB's great career at the Abbey coincides with the beginning of Jack's brief one.

This play's criticism of the paralysis of Ireland, a condition more ominous as Europe moved into war, is sharper than that of the earlier plays. As often in Yeats's work, a travelling stranger comes into a settled community and stirs up action. This stranger, Alfred Clonboise, identifies himself with Harlequin, one of the witty servants or *zanni* of the *commedia dell'arte* who were the plot weavers, and whose bat or wooden sword was the ancestor of the "slapstick." The Harlequin was a frequent figure in *A Broadside*. Hilary Pyle, describing Yeats's trip to New York in 1904, tells us that the Sicilian puppet theatre performances he saw there influenced his creative imagination. Alfred's stirring up of activity in *Harlequin's*

Positions, which may represent the inevitability of the war's en-
croachment, had an effect on the play's paralyzed Irish characters.
They seem, at first, capable of beginning an action, although they
cannot, due to the paralysis of their society, complete one.

Appropriately, in a play produced in 1939, the Harlequin also
stirs up conflicting attitudes toward violence. Some characters'
comments on violence continue the social criticism of *The Silencer*.
In speaking of cycles of violence in South America, Alfred, representing the nonviolent view, says: "Civilization always seems to arrive at a point, and stay there for a while, where blood-shedding
isn't the cure for all troubles. Then, in a moment, we have passed
that point and we are all at each other's throats again" (263). In
Ireland, contemplating Europe in 1939, this must have seemed a
correct analysis. The characters speculate on heroes, war, and violence and decide violence against civilians is the most shocking
type:

> *Annie:* It must be terrible to see perfectly ordinary people who say
> "that's a good day" and "goodbye now" killed in their ordinary
> clothes.
> *Claire:* Yes, the clothes make a difference. I think even a postman killed
> suddenly, with a bomb perhaps out of the sky, would look less terri-
> fying than an ordinary laboring man.
> *Alfred:* Naval sailors, officers and men, even heaped dead would look
> less terrible to me than one Merchant Seaman or a Merchant Sea
> Captain, lying dead on his bridge.
> (263)

Many civilians contemplating this war must have had similar
feelings.

No matter how nonviolent the stranger, the reaction to the presence of an outsider in a settled society is often violent, and some of
this play's characters espouse violence. The first character Alfred's
presence stimulates to consider violence is Johnnie, who (like Hill
the Spiller) reacts negatively to eloquence. The outsider is an artist,
and Johnnie wants to act violently against him, since he has brought
a world "too strange, too abnormal, too wonderful altogether, like
yourself with your duels and your parrots, and first of all your harle-

quin's positions and all your old talk" (268). This speech is reminiscent of the speech of the "man of action" in *The Silencer*, yet Johnnie is passive, a defender of the status quo. He wants all his eggs in one basket (literally) and recommends that his friend Annie put the money she receives from the sale of land for a cinema (dream of the heirs in *Rattle*) into "something safe, low, certain, steady interest" (270). Alfred mocks him, and, through him, the paralyzed Irish society and the impossible Anglo-Irish dream of financial security without labor (also mocked in *Rattle* by the businessman). Alfred/Harlequin says: "It must be wonderful to have enough and plenty as you say, just coming in from something safe. Sit in a garden and watch the roses bloom, with, perhaps a gentle river tinkling at the foot of the garden, a little music coming from a distant native musician, with a harp under some umbrageous trees. All in a green shade" (270).

Yeats's portrait of Johnnie, and his society, in this play, is not all mockery. Johnnie has the Anglo-Irish virtues Yeats admired: he is "the kindest person in Droleen" (264), and he stands to his troubles well (270) (like Ted Golback and Ambrose Oldbury). Encouragingly, Alfred tells him that he only has got to shake himself a bit: "Shake into harness and then nothing'll stop you. ... You've got education [neither Yeats nor the heirs in *Rattle* had received an education] and determination. ... It's better than a lot of mouldy capital" (270).

Alfred criticizes not only paralysis, but also provincialism, saying that the people in town who believe they're "miracles" only think so because they've stayed at home: "Oh, yes, that's always so in little places. But have they ever proved it? Could they prove it here?" (271). Johnnie is not easily shaken out of his complacency, though, defending his "hole in the coast." He is tempted by glory—by the desire to show the town what he could do "if circumstances came my way" (271)—but is incapable of action. Like the heirs in *Rattle*, he is naive and unimaginative; he is unable to conceive any greater scheme for achieving fame and fortune than attracting tourists to the bathing places of the town. Like those Anglo-Irish whom Yeats is warning, he clings to the dream of a better past and lapses into a nostalgic discussion of how much better the weather, and the drink, used to be in times gone by. He unconsciously reveals the current social, cultural and intellectual poverty of the town by discussing its main attractions: films, hurley, and a living freak with a wry-neck.

Alfred's Harlequin has better luck stirring up Annie Jennings; the women of Ireland in Yeats's plays seem to be more able than the men to adapt to circumstances, to take what chance brings their way. Having received the cheque from her share of the cinema, Annie acts. The porter, a representative of the passive town, comments: "But it was at that instant she heard of an opportunity from some family dying, or backing out, and she got a whole row of cabins, for half nothing, from Liverpool, going a voyage into the wide world. Only start at once. With that girl it was always quick work, like her mother before her" (275).

The porters, who form a sort of chorus to the action, are another pair, like Nolan and Dolan of *The Old Sea Road*, who represent the conservative mores of the community and its apathy. Having reflected the town's astonishment at anyone's ability to move at all ("Aren't the old ladies very lively now to go trotting off on the wide ocean?"), one porter reveals their usual apathy by wishing "to be doing nothing all day . . . but wandering on the green hills round the town" (275). Alfred's mockery is close to the mark. These Irish are bound by lethargy. Even the aunts marvel at their own sudden activity: "I can't get over Annie stirring us all up like this on the spur of the moment. I didn't think we had it in us" (279).

However, before the women can complete their action, the stagnation and fear of risk-taking reassert themselves as "war's alarms" intervene. There is, as in *The Silencer*, still too much talk in the land. Rumors that war has broken out cannot be confirmed because the telegrapher (a fit representative of "commercial instincts," those villains of Yeats's literary universe) has to take care of "pig jobbers." The men in the town—porter, guard, and clerk—are too fearful to accede to the ladies' wish to be "just going out into the wide world pleasing ourselves" (281). When Annie, exhibiting her first act of bad judgment, asks Johnnie's advice, he replies with the stay-at-home's fear; if they couldn't get news at the junction, they'd have their luggage stuck there. The porter, reflecting the town's paralysis and provincialism, takes the luggage out of the train. Although Harlequin almost provoked Annie into taking some new action, he cannot overcome the paralysis of this rural Ireland. There will be only fantasies of travel, like the porters' fantasy of how they would walk to America "if the Atlantic was to run dry itself, . . . and it's the two of us would wheel the old barrow for you" (283). They too are tempted by glory: "We'd make a great name of ourselves. We'd be like the heroes and great ladies of the ancient line of Heroes in Great Ireland of old" (283). Trapped by their history, which Joyce's Stephen Dedalus, the prototypical Irish artist, called a nightmare from which he was trying to awake, these Irish will talk endlessly of doing, but will do nothing. Annie resignedly accepts her defeat: "I think we best go back now" (285), and all the ladies leave.

Paralysis reasserts itself as the men, Johnnie and the porters, continue their talking, in which the fabulous and naive combine. Returning to the subject of violence and war, arguing about whether or not war is glorious, they continue the endless Irish debate about heroes:

> *2nd porter:* They say 'tis a glorious thing to be swinging a sword through the skulls of the people, but I don't believe it . . .
> *1st porter:* Isn't it better for a man to die for something when he must, most times, die for nothing.
> (285)

They discuss the brief span of the glory of heroes and the first porter sums up with an ironic denunciation of political rhetoric, of talk without action (like the ones in *Apparitions* and *In Sand*): "Ah, say, say, say, they'd say anything. . . . You'd think dying was the finish of a glory, a winning post, to listen to the talk off a platform, by a barrel head, before a market cross" (285). He then utters a comic denunciation of his partner, who claims he would be able to find some glory Johnnie would die for "if" he had "the gift of speech." He says: "Take no notice of that man. He isn't right. He's always got his head in the clouds and his feet in the old bog hole" (286), an apt description of the men of this paralyzed town.

Reinforcing the denunciation of speech without action, Harlequin appears, having heard that the trip was not to take place:

> *Alfred:* "Some wild tales of Wars, or rumours of Wars, . . . has altered your people's plans?"
> *Johnnie:* "I suppose we might say it's that, men?" . . .
> *1st porter:* "Strong rumours."
> *2nd porter:* "Imminent."
>   (286)

but the Harlequin mocks them again:

> *Alfred:* Where the bullets whistling fly / Comes the sadder, fainter cry, / Help us brothers ere we die / Of—Ennui.
>   (287)

Finally, having failed to stir them up, Alfred/Harlequin quite accurately predicts Ireland's neutrality and its resulting isolation and provincialism. The speech represents both Yeats's own disillusion with the failure of the socialist ideal of his brand of nationalism and the ambivalent attitude toward his country which underlies much of his late work:

I had hoped that there would be less suffering in the world of the future than in the old world. But even still there seems to be much suffering in many lands. Evil distribution, or at any rate wrong distribution of necessities and luxuries too. I predict, however, that this country of Ireland will never see any great suffering again. Peace and quiet ways beside the beautiful waters of the Broad Atlantic. Of course, flying, aviation, will gradually bring other lands nearer. But visitors from other climes will just pause here, birds of passage, long enough to open their purses and distribute some of their wealth and then fly on again to Europe. The people of this country will then draw the curtains, light the lamp, will switch on the Shannon Scheme and prepare to spend the evening in happy quiet with a book or in searching for the root of some strange Gaelic word, heard during the daytime in the market place. The far-away worlds will clash and fight for empty nothings. Money, Power, Variety. But here in Portnadroleen the wise inhabitants like ole Brer Rabbit will just keep on "saying nuffin."
    (288–89)

Those who, wisely or not, will not struggle for money or power will certainly not have variety and will stick in the "old hole in a coast," as Johnnie described his town earlier, and may die of Ennui. (The play *La La Noo* also reflects Yeats's ambivalence on Irish provincialism, passivity, and neutrality.)

The derided citizens now close ranks against the Harlequin, remove his revolver from his pocket, examine his credentials as a traveller, and warn him: "You haven't been here long enough to hear everything yet" (290). The only action of which they are capable is defense of the status quo. Alfred goes off, comically excluded. Act 5 reestablishes the irony of the play:

> *Guard:* "Has the day passed off here as usual?"
> *1st porter:* "Much the same."
> *Guard:* "There's a stop press piece of news here that says that the rumour of war in the Middle East is denied authoritatively."
> (294).

Harlequin was right. The ladies could have taken their trip on the wide world, it seems, had not the men preferred things to stay "much the same."

La La Noo

The next play, *La La Noo*, performed by the National Theatre Society in the Abbey in 1942, also deals with paralysis, provincialism, and breaking out of stagnation. According to Hilary Pyle, "Audience and actors were slightly baffled by *La La Noo*."[40] Robin Skelton finds that the nudity "in the heart of the play cannot be fitted into any thematic pattern."[41] Seen in the context of other Yeats plays, and with some knowledge of the fiction and *A Broadside*, the play's meaning is clear, and the nudity highlighted by the title points to its central subject, risk taking, accepting what chance brings.

The play's final judgment on risk taking is related both to Yeats's primary theme, the need to accept what comes, and to his social criticism of Ireland's paralysis. The stranger, as in *Harlequin's Positions* often the initiator of action in a Yeats play, in speaking of nudity encourages risk taking in a timid and untravelled publican:

> *Stanger:* The English pronounce it nude . . . the French say Le Nu.
> *Publican:* La Noo.

Stranger: Le Nu.
Publican: La Noo. La La Noo. French! That's French! If Schoolmaster was
    to hear me now talking French he'd rise out of the old mountainy
    graveyard where they left him. La La Noo. La La Noo.
Stranger: You'd soon pick up any language. It's only a matter of taking
    fences and having no fear.
    (314)

As in *The Silencer* and *Harlequin's Positions*, many Irish in Yeats's
plays confuse language and experience; they talk well, but they do
not act. The play's social criticism points out the paralysis of the
Irish; they do not fear language, but they fear experience. The Irish
Yeats portrays are full of fear and will not take fences. The social
criticism that the desire to experience the strange and extraordinary will be overcome by timidity and provincialism has been
made before, in *Harlequin's Positions*. In *La La Noo* the publican
desires to sing out or speak: "I'd like well this minute to be able to
stand up and give out a good song to you, or perhaps some great
speech from a classic man of the old times" (310). He is encouraged
by the stranger, as Johnnie and Annie had been by the Harlequin,
but like the steward in *Amaranthers* cannot act to achieve his desire. Unlike most of Yeats's Irish, he cannot even speak well.

Although he encourages learning of foreign languages and risk
taking, the stranger's later speeches reflects Yeats's ambivalence
about provincialism. Are the sheltered places better than the busy
ones? When do neutrality, receptivity, and passivity become stagnation? (The Harlequin's assessment of Ireland's neutrality in the previous play reflects a similar ambivalence.) The stranger thinks the
publican's area should be healthy, since there is nothing to worry
its inhabitants (300). Isolation may be a blessing, he asserts, because most of the people travelling aren't "fit to be walking a road
with honest men, it's what the half of them ought to be in a sack,
with a stone in it, in an old bog hole" (301). When the publican tries
to assert that the roads encourage progress—"Before there were
any roads in the country the people were very benighted"—the
stranger replies: "Ah, but they had great innocence and kind hearts.
It is the big cities of the world that spoil the humanity in the people

and turn it into nothing but envy, obstruction and throat-cutting in the way of business" (301). The Yeats of "A Flat Iron" would have agreed. This idealization of the rural, which is a part of the national-ist peasant ideal espoused in *A Broadside* and *Modern Aspects*, had been introduced in *The Old Sea Road*, where the more modern and cosmopolitan "Jacksport" was unfavorably compared to the more traditional "Cahirmahone." (Part of Yeats's nostalgia for the iso-lated rural villages involved a love of horses and a hatred of cars. The role of "transport" in extending civilization/spoiling nature was discussed in *Harlequin's Positions*, as were the values/limita-tions of isolation and neutrality.) When, in the opening of act 2 of *La La Noo*, the publican repeats his complaints about the backward-ness of the place, the stranger is explicit: "Isn't it better so. There's nothing to be ashamed of, to be in a quiet place. You ought to thank God for it" (309).

The stranger is sympathetic, however, when the publican ex-presses his frustration with the boredom of isolation (which the Harlequin had named as the price of neutrality): "It's just that a man that would be growing old thinks that if he'd once cut a lump of a stick out of a hedge, put on the brogues and rattled over the bogs and far away, he'd have something to be thinking about even if it gave him a sour stomach" (310). When the publican claims, "If I could get away and see some excitement, and some of the great scenery of the world, then, maybe, I would come here and be con-tented to draw down my own excitement out of the heavens or up out of the deep sea" (315), the stranger encourages him to trust his own instincts and test his own theory that he has divinatory powers. The publican is held back not only by ignorance and the poverty of his surroundings, but also by superstition: "Ah, no sir, I wouldn't like to have anything to do with them old things. It isn't right" (315). The picture of paralyzed Ireland gained from the *Apparitions* vol-ume and reinforced in *The Silencer* and *Harlequin's Positions*, where characters speak a great deal but do nothing, reappears in *La La Noo*, but with more complexity. During a cataclysmic war, the values of isolation and neutrality are enhanced, even if paralysis is their price.

The play's climactic action calls into question the value of fear-lessness and risk taking. When the ladies, who have come in from the road twice—each time prevented by the rain from travelling on—are about to miss their bus, the stranger shows his risk-taking instinct. Although he has never driven a lorry, and is warned by the fearful stay-at-home publican that lorries are "very headstrong" and the road dangerous, he insists that he will drive the ladies to the bus (318). While the stranger is attempting to master the mode of transport at his disposal, the publican again exhibits his ambivalence about the risks associated with gaining experience by delivering a soliloquy on modes of transport. Expressing the conservative view that "slow and steady might be better in the end," the publican deplores the speed of the lorry, just as the stranger crashes into a tree. Like the Harlequin who is run out of town when it is discovered that he carries a gun, the stranger comes to a bad end, although the community needs his example of risk taking as an antidote to its stagnation.

While the stranger is attempting heroic action on the road, the publican and the ladies are, ironically, discussing heroes. The publican disclaims the validity of the heroic deed, and asserts the supremacy of the word, attributing to the artist the creation of the hero, and dissociating language from experience: "But if it wasn't that you'd heard them and their deeds told out so well you mightn't think so much of them. They had poets and old shanachies to tell out their great deeds, and it was the poets that had the great thoughts. . . . They could sketch a small thing, so that it'd look like a gold banner shining above a mountain" (323). This championship of the artist's contribution to society is part of Yeats's theme in the narratives, particularly in *The Careless Flower*, and is also complementary to the social criticism from the *Apparitions* volume, where the contemporary displacement of the artist is a prominent theme. The play thus fits into several thematic patterns.

The play's end, like that of *Harlequin's Positions*, exhibits situation irony. The publican, who had planned a cheerful night with his neighbor the smith and the stranger, is left with the corpse of his would-be guest, waiting for his neighbor: "The three of us—

here for the night" (325). In tone, this play is most like *The Scourge of the Gulph* where the pirate anti-hero asks: "Have I done anything or nothing?" Marilyn Gaddis Rose's assertion that there is a randomly cruel universe in Yeats's plays[42] fits these two plays best, as does her assertion in another essay that Yeats, in his use of existential irony, anticipates the theatre of the absurd by nearly a decade.[43] There is indeed an existential irony here when the seventh woman reveals, after the stranger's death, that she can drive a lorry. Like Annie in *Harlequin's Positions*, and like most women in Yeats's writing, she is more able than the protective males who, by trying to do things for her that she can do herself, unnecessarily inhibit her. Yeats often exhibits feminist sympathies.

In this play he feminizes a previous pattern: instead of the usual grouping of seven men found in Yeats's narratives and other plays, in *La La Noo* we have seven women. Although Skelton thinks the women cannot be schematized, the group of seven can be broken into four social groups based on the costume sketches which accompany the play. The 1st, 2nd, and 3rd women form the first group; the 4th woman stands alone; the 5th and 6th form the third group; and the 7th is alone. Their dress, always an identifier in a Yeats play, marks them out from each other. Just as dress marks the stranger as an Anglo-Irishman, déclassé and a traveller though he may be, dress indicates that the women differ in class. Yeats's costume sketches, which Skelton reproduces in his collection but does not emphasize in his interpretation, indicate clearly these four groupings. The first three women, "well and neatly dressed" according to the stage directions, are drawn as elegant urban types with dressy hats, coats, and shoes. The 4th woman has "worn clothes, ragged shawl and broken boots"; she is rural poor. The 5th and 6th women have "neat shoes" and "fawny" shawls, marking them as well-to-do country women. The 7th woman, who drives the lorry at the play's end, is country gentry, wearing "workman-like heather tweed" and a "grey felt hat." In the first production she had to sit on a shooting stick,[44] to reinforce the identity of her social group of country gentry.

The speech of the women, far from being as undifferentiated as the speech in the narratives, is the same kind of identifier Yeats spoke of in the early "Melodrama Audience" piece. The words were so important to him, as to WB, that he insisted that "dialogue must flow from one actor to another, each becoming nothing but an agent and putting all of Yeats into his words."[45] Although he did not urge actors to rehearse in barrels, Yeats did not want the players to act, saying that "acting" would be "fatal" to this play. The women group naturally and speak as befits their origins and educational level, the 4th woman being most colloquial, the 7th most briskly competent and authoritative, the first three most aware of their social roles, and the 5th and 6th most in touch with nature. In dialogue passages the alliances and oppositions of the groups are apparent. This characterization of minor persons in the chorus is skillfully done. As a group they represent all the segments of society that demand heroic action but desert the hero when he fails. Individually, the characters are socially identifiable, realistic, active speakers whose dialogue reveals conflicting opinions.

As a group, they also perform a plot function; the women's re-entrances serve to point up the stages in the publican/stranger dialogue which is the play's central action. There may be a symbolic level to the action as Skelton suggests,[46] and the women's enforced nudity while they wait for their clothes to dry can have metaphysical implications, but their recurrent absences from the stage point to the centrality of the dialogue between the male pair, a very typical pattern in Yeats's literary universe. The thematic continuity and social criticism represented by the men's discussions of heroism, of the value of taking risks, and of going outside the ring of known experience are the exposition of the play's theme. The stranger's attempt at heroic action and its reception by the chorus of women constitute the exemplum. The themes of heroism and risk taking had been discussed by the chorus of porters in *Harlequin's Positions*. As in Synge's *Playboy*, hearing the tale of heroic action performed in the past is preferable to witnessing action performed in the present. The Breughel-like indifference to the stranger's death is similar to the community's reaction in *The Old Sea Road*. These thematic similarities link this play to the ones which preceded it, and support the thesis that *La La Noo*, too, is a social criticism play whose theme Yeats presented through a dramatic fabulation, as ironically and subtly as he had presented his social insights since *A Broadside*.

In Sand

In Sand, the most obviously political play since *Rattle*, also had the largest audience to affect by its social criticism. Generally, there is a strong connection between nationalism and Irish theatre in the twentieth century,[47] and Yeats's plays have good examples of sophisticated nationalist themes. Taken together with its prologue, *The Green Wave*, this play sums up almost all of Yeats's important themes.

The "Conversation Piece," *The Green Wave*, recapitulates Yeats's aesthetic theories. It was performed in 1964 and published with the play in the Mac Gowran edition,[48] but was not performed at the Abbey Experimental Theatre in 1949. Yeats himself said in a 1948 letter that it seemed to him to have more to do with the play than he had thought in 1943 when he first submitted it to the Abbey. The familiar male pair, "1st Elderly Man and 2nd Elderly Man" talk about a painting of a green wave. (In Yeats's accompanying drawing they are in a studio much like his own studio where Ann Russell, John Rothenstein, John Berger, and others tell of visiting him.) The second man likes paintings to mean something, wants to know what the wave means, and wants to know it at once, so he will not waste time trying to figure it out. Asserting that the wave means "just to be," the first elderly man's reply to this question asserts Yeats's ideal of private meaning or sub rosa art.

> *1st Elderly Man:* If that wave could speak it might say, "I'm an Irish wave and the Irish are generally supposed to answer questions by asking questions," and the wave might ask you what was the meaning of yourself!
>
> *2nd Elderly Man:* Agreed! Agreed! The wave could do that. If the wave could speak, but I wouldn't tell him—not that.
>
> *1st Elderly Man:* You're quite right to keep it to yourself.
> (330)

Yeats also meant his work "just to be," and kept its meaning to himself.

The theme of a proper acceptance of death is prominent in the first part of *In Sand* (1943) as it was in *Ah Well*, the narrative published just before it, in 1942. By the time this play was performed, Cottie and Lily had died. Willie and Lollie had died in 1939 and 1940, probably near the time both works were written. Jack Yeats, seventy-eight when *In Sand* was produced, had outlived all of his close relations and was, no doubt, thinking about his own death. Robin Skelton finds in *The Green Wave* "a key to the Socratic stance of Jack Yeats' drama. He is presenting us, in all his mature works with green waves that disturb us with questions, first as to their nature and then as to ours. . . . [O]ur knowledge of life's meaning and of the meaning of ourselves can only be achieved by humourful and affectionate acceptance of the whole of the business of living and dying."[49] Anthony Larcson, who dies in the first act of *In Sand*, may be seen as raisonneur since he shares many qualities with Yeats. He jokes in the face of death; seeing funny things is a protection for him as well as for the protagonist in *Sligo*. As Skelton remarks, "The final irony is that the event which traps us, death, is not the trap we have supposed it to be and that the glory we desire is not the glory we suppose; the desire itself is the glory."[50] Like the characters in *And To You Also*, Tony has imagined his own death, "a hero's death"; his version of the hero's death resembles that of the characters in *The Charmed Life* as well as the imaginative version of *And To You Also*, dying on a quay wall, "after saving a beautiful little girl child from the dark waters" (334). Expressing Yeats's own gently ironic humor, Larcson has decided against this version of his death because he could not satisfy himself with his imagined last words.

Acceptance of the rhythms of life extends beyond one's personal death. Larcson also decided against the type of memorial he had read of in a poem of "Old Tom Hood," called "Forget-me-not" which ended with "Six tons of sculptural marble / As a small forget-me-not" (334). He chose instead a memorial more in tune with Yeats's primary theme of the need to accept the rhythms of life and of forces larger than the self. A "nice little girl of about ten years of age" is to write, in sand, the words "Tony, we have the good thought for you still." She is to write it just above the water's edge, on the far strand, "just after the last of the low water spring tide" (336). (We know that this tide was dear to Yeats; he had entitled one of his well-known paintings with those words, as early as 1906.) Writing a memorial in sand is a particularly apposite action for a character in the Yeats universe, an action related to the primary theme of acceptance of life's rhythms, since death was only a change of state, and since being incorporated into the rhythms of life, often represented by the tide, was life's goal. A memorial constantly in flux, one in union with the wave—which from the first tale, *Sailing, Sailing Swiftly,* to the play *Rattle* is used as a metaphor for life—was a very appropriate choice. Brian O'Doherty finds this action particularly appropriate to the political meaning he finds in Yeats's work: that myth is superior to history. He sees this grasp of Ireland's myth as central to *In Sand* and, indeed, to all of Yeats's work:

Yeats's sensitivity to gesture is visible in all his work, and is seen par excellence in his play *In Sand*. The writing of a simple memorial on the sand is passed from one generation to another, survives its meaning, and becomes mysterious on a (literally) foreign shore. Myth is proved superior to history. Writing on sand becomes more durable than on marble, testifying, as Jack Yeats's work always does, to the survival of the intimate over the "important" things. This concern with gesture is the key to Jack Yeats's universe, and to the country whose mythologies he so powerfully reenacts.[51]

The most striking aspect of Yeats's presentation of his theme is the imagery. Besides the writing on sand imagery, there is the wave imagery. Even the foolish mayor uses the wave imagery which dominates this play as it did *Rattle*. He speaks of the "hours which keep coming toward them [those in mid-life] like waves of the sea, some with crests of glistening foam on them and some dark as blood, no two waves alike" (341). Robin Skelton relates the title of the Prologue to a picture of "The Green Wave" that Yeats published in the 1937 revival of *A Broadside*. This painting, having red as well as green pigment in it "contrives to suggest the current of life itself, the tide of the blood."[52] Although Skelton does not note their similarity, this double pigmentation inspired the mayor's description of the waves. This metaphoric substitution of the waves for hours of life is characteristic of Yeats's creative imagination from *Sailing, Sailing Swiftly* through *Rattle*. Wisdom, for Yeats, cannot be gained by thought, plans, or an act of the will. The ability to accept what the wave brings is the mark of a wise man in Yeats's literary universe. James in *Amaranthers* struggles to learn how; Bowsie in *A Charmed Life* survives because he knows how to accept what the wave brings. The "choruses" in *A Charmed Life*, *And To You Also*, and other works chart the need for acceptance even of apparent randomness. In Yeats's last published narrative, *The Careless Flower*, Mark alone of the four characters stranded on the island can truly accept what the wave has brought.

In this play, Yeats experiments with projecting acceptance beyond the span of life and links acceptance to imaginative sympathy and respect for tradition. By choosing a memorial that is itself subject to the tide, Larcson accepts the workings of the larger force of the tide even for his memory.[53] The little girl, the executor of the will, and the spectators are to wait until the tide washes out the words. Tony will be remembered only if the chosen little girl, or someone else, writes them again. The "good thought" is dependent on human connection and a reverence for tradition. The importance of tradition, of a right relation to the past or a sense of place and past, is another typical Yeats attitude stressed in act 2. The values of the old ways are often asserted in Yeats's work. Although too great a reverence for tradition can lead to stagnation, tradition is usually good. Alice, whom Larcson has not known and who has not known him, remains connected to him by her imaginative sympathy, by her respect for his memory and for tradition; so she repeats the prescribed ritual act. As an adult she says: "And whenever I find myself on a sea strand for all the years that have gone by I write to encourage Tony. I looked on him as a good friend" (344). Others who see the message also write it, preserving the tradition. Ten years after her marriage, when she and her husband (whom she would not have met without Larcson's legacy) have been almost around the world, he observes that Tony must be remembered round the world now all the time and that a great many people, far more than they ever knew anything about, must have written his memorial words (349). A sailor, on the island where Alice spends her last days, also writes the message, linking those two themes he counsels: acceptance of chance and respect for tradition. At the end of the play two lovers write, for luck, "what we have always written: Tony-we-have-the-good-thought-for-you-still," because "the old things are best" (375).

The repetition of this ritual act functions structurally in the play as well as thematically. The device resembles the use of the linking ballad refrain in *Sailing, Sailing Swiftly*. It ties together the thematic material—the meditation on death, on the need for acceptance of life's rhythms, and on tradition—with the social criticism. Both political and social themes are introduced in act 1. Oldgrove, Larcson's friend, reminds him that he had grand ideas "that would have shaken up all the old Bank Managers of this place," but they were never put into operation because he was too kind to upset anyone. Oldgrove, too, would have liked to disturb the status quo; indeed he "would have shaken this exquisite old town upside down, including their worships the Mayor and the Councillors" (337). In death, Larcson is less kind; his memorial shakes up the town worthies; the mayor considers it a "criticism of our bad old ways" (341). The satire of political rhetoric begun in *Apparitions* reappears in act 1 Scene 2, for example, where Larcson's dying wishes are carried out. The mayor, a character like Parlbury in *Apparitions*, makes a pompous speech, which takes up the entire scene. Appearing first after the mayor's pompous speech, the writing in sand terminates, at the end of the play, a long political satire on colonialism, similar in theme to *Rattle* but lighter in tone. The consequences of colonialism here are less lethal than in the earlier play, and the emphasis is on the strength of native traditions to withstand colonizing efforts; this strength had been alluded to in the place names dialogue and asserted by Ted's ritual death in *Rattle*, but here it is explicit.

Much of this criticism is familiar anti-colonialism. The island in this play, like Ireland, had been a colony ruled from afar. The sailor tells the visitor in act 3 at governors came and went. None seems to have governed successfully, since they could not adapt to new conditions. Some of them, like Ralph in *The Careless Flower* were unable to enjoy the "Earthly Paradise"; they were "full of biz, doing things, making roads cutting straight up into the country." Like Ralph, who tried to make straight roads and who could not adapt to nature, they accomplished little, since a burst of rain often came and washed out their roadway. Other governors were repressive, cutting down the flowering trees because the scented flowers which the girls put in their hair made them "too attractive." These latter sort sound suspiciously like parish priests in rural Ireland. The last sort of all were "great on improving us," perhaps like the masters of the National Schools, the conservative educational establishment satirized in *The Old Sea Road*. The natives were largely undisturbed by these governmental attempts. They reacted as the Irish did to political and cultural oppression, by getting sly: "This is the slyest Island on all the seas" (360). The visitor's own attempts to control the island are an exemplum of what the sailor had been explicating. With the new governor, he tries to bring order to a "higgledy-piggledy" state, but his attempt is useless. An ironic contrast is generated between the triumph of Tony's memorial message and the failure of the "New Governor's" slogans. Unlike the sailor who has learned to accept the rhythms of life, the visitor does not realize that "the island insists on retaining its own dreamy gentle identity and that no Governor can alter it."[54]

Another aspect of colonialism Yeats had stressed in *Rattle* is its effect on the colonizer. This governor appears as insecure as those of whom the sailor told the visitor. He carries a revolver with one bullet in it. He is threatened by Alice's writing in the sand, just before her death, and he is frustrated by the fact that the tide washed out her writing before his attendant could learn what she wrote. The world he projects is somewhat like that of 1984. The censorship of Ireland is certainly Yeats's target here. The governor has drawn up a list of slogans (no doubt in Newspeak) and the visitor recommends that " anything outside that list, any free-lance slogan

[is] to be barred absolutely" (362). (One of the slogans which is permitted is "Art for Art's sake" [363].) The sly island has learned to cope, like the natives in *Rattle* and in Brian Friel's *Translations* who go on using place names in the original, not the imposed, language. As the sailor had told the unheeding visitor, the natives survive and mock their oppressors "by various dubious tricks." When the governor hired a man with a horse-drawn brush to eliminate the scurrilous slogans, those not in sympathy with authority would send the sweeper to a distant beach to remove something shocking there while they would write all over the beach near the town. The would-be conquerors, like Ted in *Rattle*, would never know what was going on among the natives.

Yeats's political satire turns on revolutions and on political rhetoric, the topic of act 1. The visitor proposes a coup before the return of the steamship captain, an almost mythical being who brings governors and takes them away. Parodying the colonialist's sense of mission, the visitor senses that this island is his "Spiritual Home" and that he has been brought here for "some special end." He has a desire to help others, and the governor assures him that he will find many to help, "Even if they themselves do not realize it" (362). The visitor proposes to make the island an independent state. The way in which he and the new governor go about setting up this state is the most obvious satire in Yeats's work and shows his disillusion with the behavior of those who had taken over the revolutionary nationalist movement in which he had once believed. The governor will become "Chief" and the visitor "the Evident—you know, self-evident" (364). The would-be forgers of a state decide they need a Constitution, an army, and a flag; a motor road (although they have no cars); a swimming pool to attract the youth (although they only paint a sign "Swimming Pool" near a natural pool); a picture gallery; a race course (though they have no race horses); and a library: "Firstly a Reference Library (we won't have *Who's Who*, I'm not in it), a ready-reckoner and the poets, and we will want an Atlas. Then in the Library Proper, some fiction, crime tales" (368). The revolutionaries recognize that everyone is impressed by solemnity, so they will be solemn; the national motto will be "By Trial

and Error"; and they'll have an "Incognito Rule" by which the
evident and the chief can become "invisible in law, at will." While
they have decreed themselves as invisible it will be a criminal offense for any citizen to say "I see you, Evident." or "I see you, Chief"
(368).

While some aspects of this projected coup are merely funny—
the poets in the reference library, or people fighting over what
pictures are hung, but not which books are shelved—many, like
the "Incognito Rule," are bitingly satiric. The constitution will be
"retrospective" and known only to themselves. The parliament will
meet in an "Old Ceremonial Double War Canoe" (to keep the
Rights and Lefts equal and keep Parliament floating "on an even
keel"); members will have to wear their best clothes to make them
"careful," while the evident and the chief will be allowed to wear
swim suits. The description of this situation would do justice to
another Irish patriot, Jonathan Swift:

> You and I will sit in the middle and the representatives of the two parties
> each in their own canoe, and you know how cranky these old war canoes
> are. If the number in one canoe exceeds the number in the other the
> whole concern will begin to tip over and I will then of course have my
> vote for what I think best, and should by any chance, owing to the different
> weight of individuals, there be any difficulty about trimming the two ca-
> noes, I will use you as a trimmer.
>
> (370)

The political satire becomes more biting as the revolutionaries
align themselves to the old villains, "the commercial interests." At
first these interests are supportive of revolution. The problem of
persuading the former colonial power (represented by the steamship captain) to let go of the island, for example, is solved by the
commercial interests, represented by the hotel. They know that the
captain is tired, the crew is escaping wives in other ports, and the
brokers' men can be bought off. This cynical assessment reflects
fairly closely the actual English/Irish situation at the time of the
Treaty. The problem of what "the people up in the hills" will think
about the new state is dismissed with a typically "colonialist" de-
humanizing disclaimer: "I don't think that they think as we under-

stand the word. Their thought processes are of quite a different order to ours I do believe. But like the climate here, they are benign. Benignity is one of the most difficult things to deal with in a subject people. . . . You see, they don't realize they are a subject people at all" (373). Neither did the Irish. With typical colonial disdain for the culture of the natives, the visitor and the new governor, although they understand only "a word or two" of the language, are going, with all the self-confidence of the worst type of colonial officials, to meet the most important people, "the stratums and cliques among the higher classes," the leaders of "the Mountainy Society" (373) and win them over with ceremony. One can imagine what the inhabitants of "the slyest Island on all the seas" would do in response to that approach.

Their belief in ceremonial (the evident wears a white tie and tails while "symbolizing Democracy") is akin to that of the heirs in *Rattle* who expect to convert businessmen with good dinners; Ted dies as a result of his belief in the power of ceremonial, a victim of the revolution closing in on him. The colonialist dismissals of another culture's "thought processes," language, and form of civilization, their "Mountainy Society," are accurately caught. Just as the visitor is launching into a rehearsal of his speech, the rhetoric of which outdoes even the mayor's speech in act 1, the commercial interests, on whom the revolutionaries are totally reliant, call off the revolution. The tourists are here. The bitterest stroke of the satire is reserved for the aspect of the failure of the revolution most disillusioning for Yeats: commercial interests dominate, no matter who are the nominal masters. Deserted by the "Receptionist of the Hotel," the visitor goes in to "change" (375).

The conservatism and political indifference of the natives are stressed as much as the effects of colonialism. The people simply continue to ignore the law. When two native lovers write for luck, "what we have always written: Tony-we-have-good-thought-for-you-still" the following exchange takes place:

> *Governor:* Is this taken from the list of Permitted Writings put up on the tree there?

Brown Girl: No, Governor.
Governor: Did you read the notice?
Brown Girl: Yes, Governor.
Governor: Well, why do you think I put it up?
Brown Girl: Oh, I thought you just put it up for putting up.
   (375)

Urged by the Brown Girl, who assures him there's no harm in this saying that always brings good luck, the governor also writes the saying in the sand. Realizing he has disobeyed his own "ukase," he tries to commit suicide with the revolver he carries for that purpose. The lovers prevent him and console him with the play's last words: "The tide is coming in now fast, look, look, the waters are covering up and washing away everything that we have written" (376). This return to the initial situation is an aesthetically pleasing as well as a typically ironic Yeats ending. He would agree with Robbe-Grillet: "The world is neither meaningful nor absurd. It quite simply is."[55] He would add: "Accept the rhythms of life. It is pointless to oppose them." The tide washes away all.

   Robin Skelton finds this attitude "strangely non-occidental, somewhat oriental." His description accords with the view of the narratives given here, the roots of which may be found in Yeats's indifference to the classic Western tradition. Skelton says that the meaning of *In Sand* is "life is a flux of illusions, death is a subterfuge of life; the dream is as powerful as the fact. . . . This wonderful creature, man, once released from his bondage to rents and revenues, once able to let chance, providence, and fantasy move him along its natural path, may find sorrow and solitude, but will also find strength, and a kind of security, free from dogmas about art, politics, or meaning."[56] This statement of the central theme of this play is reminiscent of the ideals of John Butler Yeats, for whom freedom from dogmas about art or politics was an essential condition of true humanity. Ideals absorbed from his unorthodox father, as well as his own disillusion with conventional political and social ideals after the failure of the revolutionary nationalist ideal, motivated Yeats to become the spear head of his own self-characterizing metaphor. Moving away from "the schematized philosophy of the symbolist drama" as well as from the "social naturalism" of Galsworthy and the "rationalism" of Shaw; belonging to no school of thought or art; and unlike other Irish dramatists except, perhaps, Fitzmaurice,[57] Jack Yeats went his own way, as his sister Lollie noted, breaking dramatic conventions, as reviewers of *In Sand* observed.

Yeats's drama fits into his literary universe; the body of it, although little known, represents a unified political and aesthetic statement. Like his ballad collection and his narratives, his dramas represent a continuing effort on the part of a gifted artist to present his vision of the world, testing forms and selecting elements which best served that vision. His primary theme, that life's rhythms must be accepted, that struggling to set up systems or place controls on the flux is self-defeating, has both an ethical and a political dimension which make it relevant to his sense of place and past, to the Irish social conditions which produced this sense, and to the enduring human condition.

Conclusion

Looking at the entire corpus of Jack Yeats's writing illuminates each work. Although this method is useful in examining the work of all writers, it is particularly necessary to look at all of Yeats's work because it is thematically unified and because he so often reused material. Describing his "literary universe" by tracing recurrent themes, one can see that his themes convey social, political and philosophical insights.

His primary theme—that one must learn to accept change, chance, and randomness and to escape the prison of self by immersing oneself in forces larger than the individual—has both ethical and social implications. The way to personal fulfillment and ethical behavior is to seize the day, to take risks and to strive to get outside the self. One can most easily transcend the self by contemplating nature, particularly water, whose ebb and flow is an accessible analogue to the rhythms of life. Having become more aware of the forces of the universe in this way, one should attempt to become immersed in these forces by seeking the visionary state. Insofar as is possible, given the essential isolation of the individual and the limits of language to express the visionary, one should attempt to communicate one's glimpses of this larger life to others. The artist is the one who consistently attempts to communicate this vision. Since this attempt is the most important human activity, it gives a dignity to the artist that should be acknowledged by society.

The way to national fulfillment and responsible societal behavior is to respect tradition, not to be imprisoned in it; to risk change, not to fear it; and to accept, as gracefully as possible, what is inevitable, particularly in the economic and social realms, where those who have must be ready to acknowledge the legitimate aspirations of those who have not.

Yeats attained these social and philosophical insights because of familial and nationalist influences. Growing up an outsider in his own family gave him an especially strong need to seek unity with some sustaining force outside the self. He did not expect to find comfort in human relationships. Growing up in communities which contributed to his sense of isolation made him anxious to feel allied with a tradition and a nation. He needed a sense of place and past. He found them through the Irish nationalist movement, in its most socialist and revolutionary wing. The abortive attempts of his countrymen to achieve those social and national ideals in which he profoundly believed had a great influence on his work. Before the failure of the nationalist dream he wrote in traditional forms, but afterwards, like Modernist writers who shared his sense of disillusion and isolation and of the failure of authority, he began to experiment with form. In fiction, he used forms like the tale and the fabulation, a form that emphasized the visionary ethical insight. In drama, he attempted to transcend melodrama and to avoid both the well-made play and the realist problem play. In all of these works he emphasized the same ideals and maintained artistry and aesthetic distance by using irony, allusion, metaphor, and symbol. His was a consciously sub rosa art, and he expected the audience to enter actively into the aesthetic transaction.

Many of his subjects—death and the proper human response to it, artistic authenticity and the need to preserve the imaginative life, language and its limitations for expressing the artistic vision—are universal. Many themes are specifically Irish, exhorting his countrymen, and particularly his own group, the Anglo-Irish, to accept political and social change gracefully; to preserve tradition, but not to become stagnant by overvaluing it; to keep in touch with nature and resist both urbanization and commercialization of values; and to arise from the paralysis of their society by acting instead of talking endlessly in a self-deluding rhetoric.

Many of the devices he used for expressing his vision in his mature work can be traced in his early work, published and unpublished, where they can sometimes be seen more clearly than in the later work. The wave is the dominant image in many narratives and dramas, and the circus ring is a common metaphor. Ballads and ballad refrains, often taken from *A Broadside*, function structurally and often ironically in narrative and drama. Even his early work shows carefully crafted endings; the circular is preferred as a narrative motion to the linear.

Yeats's artistry and seriousness as a writer have often been overlooked or denied. His social criticism has not been sufficiently appreciated. Perhaps because he was a spear head, his literary innovations were not recognized in his lifetime. Thirty-five years after his death, he is known as a painter, one of Ireland's national painters. He deserves to be better known as a writer, one of Ireland's national writers.

Appendix

Jack Yeats's niece, Anne Yeats, has stored these works from her uncle's personal library in her home in Dalkey.

The Author (1956), a journal for members of the "Society of Dramatists."

Today (1917), containing WB's *At the Hawk's Well* and an article on Masefield.

The Irish Review (1911), in which he is listed as a contributor among such acknowledged writers as AE, Padraic Colum, Lord Dunsany, Douglas Hyde, George Moore, and James Stephens.

transition, An International Quarterly for Creative Experiment, (1929 and other years) edited by Eugene Jolas and published by Sylvia Beach's "Shakespeare and Company." One issue contained poems of Hart Crane, an essay by Stuart Gilbert on the Aeolus Episode, and a portion of Joyce's *Work in Progress*. In 1931 this journal published the critical manifesto, "Poetry is Vertical," signed by MacGreevy and Beckett, among others, and an essay by William Carlos Williams, "The Novel is Dead. Long Live the Novel."

The Music Review (1921), containing Jack Yeats's essay "A Theatre for Everyman."

The Mask (1912–25), Gordon Craig's journal of experimental drama, which stated, "*The Mask* believes in the Theatre and in the Drama whether written, acted, sung or spoken . . . its strange air . . . its queer ways . . . ALL." Jack Yeats contributed several articles to this journal.

The Dublin Magazine (1924–54), "A Quarterly Review of Literature, Science and Art" edited by "Seumas O'Sullivan." Notable issues of this quarterly contain work by James Stephens, John Masefield, and Jack Yeats (July–September 1923); a review of *The Amaranthers* (July–September 1936); extracts from *The Careless Flower* (October–December 1940 and January–March 1942); and a review of *Ah Well* by Vivian Mercier (January–March, 1943).

The New Alliance (1940–44), also containing extracts from *The Careless Flower*.

The Envoy (1951), containing work of Patrick Kavanagh, Arland Usher, Anthony Cronin, and Denis Johnston, and a special Joyce issue.

The Bell (1941–42), edited by Sean O'Faolain, with Frank O'Connor as poetry editor. This journal featured, in a single issue, Denis Johnston, Elizabeth Bowen, Patrick Kavanagh, and Austin Clarke and published selections from *Ah Well*.

Irish Writing (1957), featuring Brendan Behan's *The Big House*, a chapter of Austin Clarke's *Autobiography* and an article by Donald Davie on Thomas Kinsella.

The Arrow (1939), a commemorative number with articles by John Masefield, Austin Clarke, Gordon Bottomley, Edmund Dulac, John Rothenstein, Oliver St. John Gogarty, and Lennox Robinson.

Samhain (1901–16), the publication of The Abbey with WB's *Beltaine*, and *On the Boiler*.

The Little Review (1917–21), edited by Ezra Pound, which called itself "A Magazine of the Arts Making no Compromise with the Public Taste." It was also inscribed "The Magazine That Is Read by Those Who Write the Others." These issues contain work by Ezra Pound, T. S. Eliot, Wyndham Lewis, WB Yeats, James Joyce, William Carlos Williams, Arthur Symons, Lady Gregory, Ford Madox Hueffer, Wallace Stevens, Amy Lowell, Carl Sandburg, Sherwood Anderson, Marianne Moore, Kenneth Burke, and Jean Cocteau.

Notes

Introduction

1. I use the term "universe" in the sense implied by Jameson in his statement: "One branch of modern criticism aims at reconstructing creative universes by the thematic method." Fredric Jameson, *The Prison-House of Language* (Princeton: Princeton University Press, 1972), p. 134.

Chapter 1

1. Hilary Pyle, *Jack B. Yeats: A Biography* (London: Routledge and Kegan Paul, 1970), p. 124.
2. William M. Murphy, *Prodigal Father* (Ithaca: Cornell University Press, 1978), p. 523.
3. Pyle, p. 172.
4. David Lynch, *Yeats: The Poetics of the Self* (Chicago: University of Chicago Press, 1979).
5. Helen Vendler, "JBY," *The New Yorker* (8 January 1979), p. 66.
6. Murphy, p. 43.
7. Vendler, p. 66.
8. Murphy, p. 77.
9. Lynch, p. 182.
10. Vendler, p. 68.
11. Pyle, p. 11.
12. Murphy, p. 51.
13. Murphy, p. 116.
14. Douglas N. Archibald, *John Butler Yeats* (Lewisburg, PA: Bucknell University Press, 1974), pp. 40, 46.
15. Pyle, pp. 29–30.
16. Ibid., p. 29.
17. Murphy, p. 162.

18. Ibid., p. 623, note 174.
19. Vendler, p. 70.
20. Murphy, p. 412.
21. Lynch, p. 64.
22. Murphy, p. 436.
23. Pyle, p. 20.
24. Archibald, p. 30.
25. Murphy, p. 244.
26. Ibid., p. 348.
27. Ibid., p. 215.
28. Pyle, p. 58.
29. Ibid.
30. Murphy, p. 436.
31. Pyle, p. 39.
32. Edward Sheehy, "Jack B. Yeats," *The Dublin Magazine* (July-September, 1945), p. 39.

Chapter 2

1. James Plunkett, *The Gems She Wore: A Book of Irish Places* (London: Hutchinson and Company, 1972), p. 15.
2. Ann Saddlemyer, "The Cult of the Celt: Pan-Celticism in the Nineties," in *The World of W. B. Yeats*, ed. Skelton and Saddlemyer (Seattle: University of Washington Press, 1967), p. 3.
3. Ann Saddlemyer, "A Share in the Dignity of the World: J. M. Synge's Aesthetic Theory," *The World of W. B. Yeats*, p. 214.
4. Murphy, *Prodigal Father*, p. 113.
5. Richard J. Loftus, *Nationalism in Modern Anglo-Irish Poetry* (Madison: University of Wisconsin Press, 1964), p. 281.
6. Ann Saddlemyer, "The Noble and the Beggar-man: Yeats and Literary Nationalism," in *The World of W. B. Yeats,* p. 6.
7. Loftus, p. 282.
8. David Krause, "The De-Yeatsification Cabal," *Irish Literary Supplement* (Spring 1989), pp. 5–6.
9. Sheehy, "Jack B. Yeats," p. 41.
10. R. F. Foster, *Modern Ireland 1600–1972* (London: Viking Penguin, (1989), pp. 452–3.
11. David H. Greene, "Synge and the Irish," *Colby Library Quarterly* (February 1957), p. 159.
12. Saddlemyer, "The Noble and the Beggar-man," p. 21.
13. Foster, p. 548.

14. Ernie O'Malley, "Introduction to the Catalogue for the Exhibition held in the National College of Art, Dublin, June–July 1945," in *Jack B. Yeats 1871–1957* (Sligo: Sligo County Library and Museum, 1963), p. 9.

15. Mairin Allen, "Jack B. Yeats: An Impression," *Capuchin Annual* (1933), pp. 579–80.

16. C. P. Curran, "The Yeats Exhibition," *Capuchin Annual* (1945), p. 102.

17. Augustine Martin, *Anglo-Irish Literature* (Dublin: Department of Foreign Affairs, 1980), p. 45.

18. Brian Inglis, *The Story of Ireland* (London: Faber and Faber, 1965), p. 244.

19. Seamus Deane, *A Short History of Irish Literature* (Indiana: University of Notre Dame Press, 1986), p. 7.

20. Martha B. Caldwell, *Jack Butler Yeats: Painter of Life in the West of Ireland* (Ann Arbor: University Microfilms, 1971), p. 8.

21. George Russell (AE) quoted in Caldwell, p. 46.

22. Foster, pp. 446–48.

23. Deane, p. 17.

24. Foster, p. 38.

25. Terry Eagleton, *Criticism and Ideology* (London: Verso Editions, 1978), p. 55.

26. Foster, p. 450.

27. Wayne E. Hall, *Shadowy Heroes: Irish Literature of the 1890s* (Syracuse: Syracuse University Press, 1980), p. 47.

28. Pyle, *A Biography*, p. 118.

29. Peter Costello, *The Heart Grown Brutal* (Dublin: Gill and Macmillan, 1977), p. 135.

30. Deane, p. 75.

31. Costello, p. 18.

32. Loftus, p. 6.

33. Ibid., p. 237.

34. Hall, p. 39.

35. Archibald, *John Butler Yeats*, p. 31.

36. George Russell (AE), "An Artist of Gaelic Ireland," reprinted from the *Freeman's Journal*, Dublin (23 October 1901), in the private papers of Jack B. Yeats.

37. Pyle, p. 54.

38. Ibid., p. 119.

39. Deane, p. 8.

40. Pyle, p. 14.

41. W. B. Yeats, "Reveries over Childhood and Youth" in *The Autobiography of William Butler Yeats* (New York: Collier Books, 1965), p. 4.

42. Allen Carric, "Captain Jack B. Yeats: A Pirate of the Old School," *The Mask* (July 1912), p. 44.

43. Jack B. Yeats, "How Jack B. Yeats Produced His Plays for the Miniature Stage," *The Mask* (July 1912) p. 52.

44. Pyle, p. 74.

45. O'Malley, p. 5.

46. W. B. Yeats, p. 16.

47. Foster, p. 454.

48. "H. M.," "Book Reviews," *The Mask* (July 1912), p. 77.

49. Sheehy, p. 39.

50. Thomas MacGreevy, "Yeats and O'Malley," in *Jack B. Yeats, 1871–1957,* p. 3.

51. Pyle, p. 89.

52. Murphy, p. 450.

53. Ibid., p. 455.

54. Foster, pp. 456–57.

55. Anne Yeats, *Broadside Characters* (Dublin: Cuala Press, 1971).

56. Hall, p. xiii.

57. Murphy, p. 244.

58. Costello, p. 28.

59. Pyle, p. 15.

60. Curran, "The Yeats Exhibition," p. 104.

61. C. P. Curran, "Jack B. Yeats, RHA," *Studies* (March 1941), p. 80.

62. Pyle, p. 97.

63. Ibid., p. 98.

64. James White, "Introduction," *Jack B. Yeats: Drawings and Paintings, A Centenary Exhibition* (London: Martin Secker and Warburg, 1971), p. 12.

65. Yeats, "How Jack B. Yeats Produced His Plays," p. 52.

66. Pyle, pp. 99 and 110.

67. White, p. 14.

68. Ibid.

69. Hall, p. xii.

70. Hilary Pyle, "Catalogue Notes" in *A Centenary Exhibition*, p. 148.

71. Jack B. Yeats, "Ireland and Painting," *New Ireland* (18 February 1922), p. 172.

72. Ibid., p. 171.

73. Pyle, *A Biography*, p. 108.

74. Murphy, p. 244.

75. Pyle, *A Biography*, p. 104.

76. Ibid., p. 103.

77. Caldwell, p. 26.

78. Pyle, *A Biography*, p. 103.

79. F. S. L. Lyons, *Ireland Since the Famine* (London: Weidenfeld and Nicholson, 1971), p. 404.

80. Foster, p. 495.

81. Lyons, pp. 413–15.

82. Foster, p. 508.

83. Pyle, *A Biography*, p. 119.

84. Caldwell, p. 26.

85. Eamon de Valera, "Introduction," in *Modern Aspects*, inside front cover.

86. Yeats, *Modern Aspects*, pp. 1–2. Cited parenthetically for the next few pages.

87. Caldwell, p. 72.

88. Murphy, p. 209.

89. Jack B. Yeats, "Ireland and Painting," *New Ireland* (25 February 1922), pp. 189–90.

90. Jack B. Yeats, "A Painter's Life," *The Listener* (September 1937), p. 455.

Chapter 3

1. Jack B. Yeats, *The Careless Flower* (London: Pilot Press Ltd.,1947), p. 173.

2. James Mays, "Jack B. Yeats: Some Comments on His Books," *Irish University Review* 2 (Spring 1972), p. 35.

3. Roger McHugh, *Jack B. Yeats: A Centenary Gathering* (Dublin: Dolmen Press, 1971), p. 18.

4. John Pilling, "The Living Ginger: Jack B. Yeats's *The Charmed Life*," *Journal of Beckett Studies* 2 (Summer 1977), p. 56.

5. Marilyn Gaddis Rose, "The Sterne Ways of Beckett and Jack B. Yeats," *Dublin University Review* (1972), p. 164.

6. Katherine Slater Gittes, "The Canterbury Tales and the Arabic Frame Tradition," *PMLA* 98 (March 1983), p. 240.

7. Ibid., pp. 239–40.

8. John Rothenstein, "Visits to Jack Yeats," *The New English Review* (July 1946), p. 43.

9. Ibid., p. 44.

10. John Butler Yeats in a letter to W. B. Yeats, 1902, quoted in Curran, "The Yeats Exhibition," p. 103.

11. John B. Yeats, "The Education of Jack B. Yeats," *Christian Science Monitor* (November 2, 1920), p. 5.

12. Joseph F. Connelly, "Jack Yeats: Entertaining the Common Man," *Eire-Ireland* 17 (Winter 1982), 153.

13. Anne Clissman, "Brian O'Nolan," The Macmillan Dictionary of Irish Literature. (London: Macmillan, 1979), p. 541.

14. Pamela Berger, "Many-Shaped: Art, Archaeology, and the Tain," *Eire-Ireland* 17 (Winter 1982), 13.

15. Anthony Cronin, *Heritage Now* (New York: St. Martin's Press,1982), p.14.

16. Ibid., p. 13.

17. A. Norman Jeffares, *Anglo-Irish Literature* (Dublin: Gill and Macmillan, 1982), p. 268.

18. T. G. Rosenthal, *The Masters* 40 (London: Knowledge Publications, 1966), p. 3.

19. Conversation with Anne Yeats, July 1982.

20. Yeats, *Modern Aspects*, p. 10.

21. Quoted in Roger Shattuck, "Life Before Language," *The New York Times Book Review* (April 1, 1984), pp. 1 and 31.

22. Pilling, p. 56.

23. Rosenthal, p. 5.

24. Mays, p. 37.

25. McHugh, *A Centenary Gathering*, p. 17.

26. Marilyn Gaddis Rose, *Jack B. Yeats: Painter and Poet* (Berne: Herbert Lang, 1972), pp. 21–22.

27. Pyle, *Biography*, p. 126.

28. Yeats, *Modern Aspects*, p. 3.

29. Pyle, *Biography*, p. 128.

30. Jack B. Yeats, *Sligo* (London: Wishart and Co., 1931). All page references are to this original edition.

31. Quoted in Shattuck, p. 31.

32. McHugh, A Centenary Gathering, p. 12.

33. Mays, p. 37.

34. Jack B. Yeats, "Irish Authors": 36 *Easons' Bulletin* 4 (October 1948), p. 3.

35. Ibid.

36. Sean O'Faolain, "Jack B. Yeats," *The Bell* 1 (January 1941), 36.

37. Yeats, *Modern Aspects*, pp. 5–6.

38. O'Faolain, p. 34.

39. *Studies: An Irish Quarterly Review* 30 (March 1941), 75.

40. O'Faolain, pp. 33, 36.

41. Pyle, *Biography*, pp. 175–76 and Caldwell, pp. 157–59.

42. Undated letter from Masefield in the collection of Anne Yeats, examined July 1985.

43. Pyle, *Biography*, p. 74.

44. Ibid., p. 91.

45. Eugene Mason, *Today* 4 (June 1917), 133.

46. Pyle, *Biography*, p. 119.

47. Costello, p. 187.

48. John Masefield, "Mr. Jack B. Yeats," *The Dublin Magazine* 1 (August 1923), 4.

49. Sheehy, pp. 39–41.

50. Ibid., p. 40.

51. Unpublished letter of 29 December 1913 in the collection of Anne Yeats, examined July 1985.

52. Ihab Hassan, "The Dismemberment of Orpheus," in *Learners and Discerners* (Charlottesville: University of Virginia Press,1964), p. 139.

53. John Butler Yeats, *Further Letters of John Butler Yeats*, selected by Lennox Robinson (Dundrum: Cuala Press, 1920), p. 13.

54. Hassan, p. 153.

55. Ibid., p. 152.

56. Ruby Cohn, "Inexhaustible Beckett: An Introduction," in *Samuel Beckett: A Collection of Criticism* (New York: McGraw Hill, 1975), p. 2

57. O'Faolain, p. 36.

58. Mays, p. 35.

59. Ibid., p. 38.

60. Ibid., pp. 37–38.

61. Yeats, *Modern Aspects*, p. 2.

62. Sheehy, p. 40.

63. Yeats, *Modern Aspects*, p. 4.

64. Mays, pp. 38–39.

65. Sheehy, p. 41.

66. Pyle, *Biography*, p. 145.

67. Ibid., p. 144.

68. Mary McCarthy, "Novel, Tale, and Romance," *The New York Review of Books* 30 (12 May 1983), 49–54.

69. Jack B. Yeats, *Sailing, Sailing Swiftly* (London: Putnam, 1933), p. 2. All page references are to this edition.

70. Brian O'Doherty, "Jack B. Yeats: Promise and Regret," in *A Centenary Gathering*, pp. 84–85.

71. Pyle, *Biography*, p. 141.

72. Mays, p. 40.

73. Robert Scholes, *Structural Fabulation* (Notre Dame, Indiana: University of Notre Dame Press, 1975), p. 29.

74. Robert Scholes, *Fabulation and Metafiction* (Urbana: University of Illinois Press, 1979), pp. 2–3.

75. Mays, p. 41.

76. Scholes, *Fabulation and Metafiction*, p. 8.

77. Mays, p. 41.

78. Jack B. Yeats, *The Amaranthers* (London: William Heinemann Ltd., 1936), p.183–84. All references are to this original edition.

79. Pilling, p. 57.

80. Samuel Beckett, "An Imaginative Work," *The Dublin Magazine* 11 (July-September 1936), 81.

81. Mays, p. 41.

82. Beckett, p. 81.

83. Jack B. Yeats, *The Charmed Life* (1938; rpt. London: Routledge and Kegan Paul, 1974), p. 4. All page references are to the reprint edition.

84. Pilling, p. 57.

85. Terence de Vere White, "The Personality of Jack B. Yeats," in *A Centenary Gathering*, pp. 24–25.

86. Ibid., p. 26.

87. Ibid., p. 27.

88. Pilling, p. 57.

89. W. B. Yeats, *On the Boiler* (Dublin: Cuala Press, 1939), p. 36.

90. Pilling, p. 62.

91. Pyle, *Biography*, p. 154.

92. Pilling, p. 62.

93. Jack B. Yeats, *Ah Well* (1942; rpt. London, Routledge and Kegan Paul, 1974), p. 8. All page references are to this reprint edition, which also contains *And To You Also*.

94. Scholes, *Fabulation and Metafiction*, p. 3.

95. O'Doherty, p. 78.

96. Sigmund Freud, "General Theory of Neuroses," Lecture 23 in *Introductory Lectures on Psychoanalysis*, ed. James Strachey (1928; rpt. New York: W. W. Norton and Company, 1977), p. 376.

97. John Berger, *Selected Essays and Articles* (Harmondsworth: Penguin, 1972), p. 57.

98. Hans Arp et al., "Manifesto: Poetry is Vertical," *transition* (March 1932), 148–49.

99. Quoted in Pyle, p. 146. Letter from MacGreevy dated 22 December 1930.

100. Vivian Mercier, *Beckett/Beckett* (New York: Oxford University Press, 1977), pp. 95 and 25.

101. Marilyn Gaddis Rose, "Solitary Companions in Beckett and Jack B. Yeats," *Eire-Ireland* 4 (Summer 1969), 68.

102. A card in the collection of Anne Yeats, examined July 1985.

103. Samuel Beckett, "Recent Irish Poetry," published in *Bookman*, August 1934, under the pseudonym "Andrew Belis."

104. J. B. Yeats, "Education of Jack B. Yeats," p. 5.

105. Pilling, pp. 57 and 62.

106. O'Doherty, pp. 78.

107. Mays, p. 46.

108. Jack B. Yeats, *And To You Also*, p. 96. *And To You Also* is reprinted in the same volume with *Ah Well* and begins on page 93 in the 1974 reprint edition. All page references are to this reprint edition.

109. Murphy, pp. 172–73.

110. Pyle, *Biography*, p. 155. Letter of 3 February 1944.

111. Denis Donaghue, ed., *William Butler Yeats Memoirs* (New York: Macmillan, 1972), p. 11.

112. Mays, p. 37.

113. Murphy, p. 94.

114. Loftus, p. 68.

115. Jack B. Yeats, *The Careless Flower* (London: The Pilot Press Ltd., 1947), p. 20. All page references are to this original edition.

116. J. B. Yeats, "The Education of Jack B. Yeats," p. 5.

117. Seamus Heaney, "The Fire in the Flint," in *Preoccupations* (New York: Farrar, Straus, and Giroux, 1980), p. 97.

118. Mays, p. 47.

119. Ibid., p. 43.

120. Connelly, p. 154.

Chapter 4

1. Ruby Cohn, *From Desire to Godot*, (Berkeley: University of California Press, 1987), p. 133.

2. Pyle, *Biography*, p. 154.

3. Robin Skelton, ed., "Introduction," *The Collected Plays of Jack B. Yeats* (London: Secker and Warburg, 1971), p. 11. All subsequent page references will be to this text.

4. Rose, "Mixed Metaphors," in *A Centenary Gathering*, p. 95.

5. John Butler Yeats, *John Butler Yeats, Letters to His Son W. B. Yeats and Others, 1869–1922,* ed. Joseph Hone (London: Faber & Faber Ltd., 1944), p. 68.

6. Jack B. Yeats, "How Jack B. Yeats Produced His Plays," p. 51.

7. D. J. Gordon and Ian Fletcher, *WB Yeats: Images of a Poet* (Manchester: Whitworth Art Gallery Exhibition Catalogue, 1961), pp. 57–58.

8. Skelton, p. 43.

9. Pyle, *Biography*, p. 64.

10. Jack B. Yeats, "A Theatre for Every Man," *The Music Review* (Autumn 1912), pp. 83–85.

11. Pyle, *Biography*, pp. 65–66.

12. Rose, "Mixed Metaphors," p. 98.

13. Prologue to vol. 5 of *The Mask*, July 1912.

14. Carric, "Captain Jack B. Yeats," p. 45.

15. Ernest Marriott, *Jack B. Yeats: His Pictorial and Dramatic Art* (London: Elkin Mathews, 1911), p. 21.

16. Ibid., p. 22.

17. Quoted on the title page of Jack Yeats's copy of *James Flaunty* in the collection of Miss Anne Yeats.

18. Jack B. Yeats, "Life in Manchester: The Melodrama Audience," *Manchester Guardian* (9 December 1905).

19. Christine Brooke-Rose, *A Rhetoric of the Unreal* (Cambridge: Cambridge University Press, 1981), p. 4.

20. Seamus Deane, "Irish Poetry and Irish Nationalism," in *Two Decades of Irish Writing: A Critical Survey,* ed. Douglas Dunn (Cheshire: Carcanet Press Ltd., 1975), p. 9.

21. Brooke-Rose, p. 8.

22. Pyle, *Biography*, p. 145.

23. Skelton, "Introduction," p. 5.

24. David Krause, *The Profane Spirit of Irish Comedy* (Ithaca: Cornell University Press, 1982), p. 23.

25. Deane, p. 11.

26. Rose, "Solitary Companions," p. 73.

27. Ibid., and "Sub-Rosa," p. 44.

28. Mays, p. 39.

29. Robin Skelton, "Themes and Attitudes in the Later Dramas of Jack B. Yeats," *Yeats Studies* 2 (1972), p. 105.

30. Skelton, "Introduction," p. 6.

31. Ibid.

32. Rose, "Sub-Rosa," p. 44.

33. Owen Dudley Edwards, *Conor Cruise O'Brien Introduces Ireland* (London: Andre Deutsch, 1969), p. 24.

34. Brian Friel, *Translations* (London: Faber and Faber, 1981), p. 35.

35. Ibid., p. 40.

36. Ibid.

37. Maire Cruise O'Brien, "The Two Languages," in Edwards, p. 55.

38. Skelton, "Themes and Attitudes," p. 113.

39. Pyle, *Biography*, p. 154.

40. Ibid.

41. Skelton, in "Themes and Attitudes" (p. 115), and in the "Introduction" (p. 9) finds this "portrait of questioning, fearful, speculative man" to be the play's central issue. He speaks of the "nakedness we share beneath all our pretensions and talk." He finds the play to be a "happening" and doesn't see that the nudity can be "fitted to any thematic pattern." Knowledge of *A Broadside* and the narratives reveals both a thematic pattern and a social criticism.

42. Rose, "Mixed Metaphors," p. 94.

43. Rose, "Solitary Companions," p. 74.

44. Pyle, p. 155.

45. Ibid., p. 154.

46. Skelton, "Introduction," p. 9.

47. Patrick Rafroidi, *Aspects of the Irish Theatre,* Encyclopedie Universitaire 3 (1972), p. 34.

48. Jack B. Yeats, *In Sand, A play, with The Green Wave, a one-act Conversation Piece.* Edited with a Preface by Jack Mac Gowran and with a drawing by the author (Dublin: Dolmen Press, 1964).

49. Skelton, "Introduction," p. 10.

50. Ibid., p. 11.

51. O'Doherty, p. 90.

52. Skelton, "Themes and Attitudes," p. 117.

53. Skelton also illuminates a possible source for the idea of writing in sand, in an often-anthologized poem of Landor's.

54. Skelton, "Themes and Attitudes," p. 119.

55. Brooke-Rose, p. 10.

56. Skelton, "Introduction," p. 11.

57. Ibid.

Bibliography

The Writings of Jack B. Yeats

Ah Well: A Romance in Perpetuity and *And To You Also*. Rpt. London: Routledge and Kegan Paul, 1974.

The Amaranthers. London: William Heinemann Ltd., 1936.

And To You Also. London: George Routledge and Sons Ltd., 1944.

Apparitions: Three Plays. London: Jonathan Cape, 1933.

The Bosun and the Bob-Tailed Comet. London: Elkin Mathews, 1904. Rpt. 1933.

A Broadside. Dublin: Dun Emer and Cuala Presses, 1908–15.

"A Canal Flat." *Manchester Guardian*, 31 March 1906.

The Careless Flower. London: The Pilot Press, 1947.

"The Cattle Market." *Manchester Guardian*, 19 May 1906.

The Charmed Life. Rpt. London: Routledge and Kegan Paul, 1974.

"A Cycle Drama." *The Success*, 7 September 1895.

"A Flat Iron." *Manchester Guardian*, 26 May 1906.

"For the Friends of the National Collections of Ireland" (A radio talk), 18 November 1937. Typescript in the private papers of Jack B. Yeats.

"The Glove Contest." *Manchester Guardian*, 5 May 1906.

"The Great White Elk." *Boy's Own Paper*, Christmas Number 1895.

"How Jack B. Yeats Produced His Plays for the Miniature Stage." *The Mask* 7 (July 1912): 49–54.

In Sand. A play, with The Green Wave, a one-act Conversation Piece. Edited with a Preface by Jack Mac Gowran and with a drawing by the author. Dublin: Dolmen Press, 1964.

"Ireland and Painting" (Parts 1 and 2). *Arn-Eire: New Ireland*, 18 and 25 February 1922.

"Jack B. Yeats" (Irish Authors: 36). *Eason's Bulletin* 4, no. 5 (October 1948).

James Flaunty or The Terror of the Western Seas. London: Elkin Mathews, 1901.

"The Jumpers." *Manchester Guardian*, 7 April 1906.

La La Noo. Dublin: Cuala Press, 1943.

"Life in Manchester: The Melodrama Audience." *Manchester Guardian*, 9 December 1905.

Life in the West of Ireland. Dublin: Maunsel, 1912.

A Little Fleet. London: Elkin Mathews, 1909.

Modern Aspects of Irish Art. Dublin: Cumann Leigheacht an Phobail, 1922.

"An Old Ale House." *Manchester Guardian*, 14 April 1906.

"On the Stones." *Manchester Guardian*, 26 August 1905.

"A Painter's Life." *The Listener*, September 1937, pp. 454–55.

"Racing Donkeys." *Manchester Guardian*, 26 August 1905.

Sailing, Sailing Swiftly. London: Putnam, 1933.

The Scourge of the Gulph. London: Elkin Mathews, 1903.

"Shove Halfpenny." *Manchester Guardian*, 4 October 1905.

Sligo. London: Wishart & Co., 1930.

"A Theatre for Every Man." *The Music Review*, Autumn 1912, pp. 83–85.

The Treasure of the Garden: A Play in the Old Manner. London: Elkin Mathews, 1902.

Secondary Sources

Aldous, Tony. *Book of London's Villages.* London: Secker and Warburg, 1980.

Allen, Mairin. "Jack B. Yeats: An Impression." *Capuchin Annual* (1933): 579–87.

Anonymous review. *Studies: An Irish Quarterly Review* 30 (March 1941): 75.

Archibald, Douglas N. *John Butler Yeats.* Lewisburg: Bucknell University Press, 1974.

Arensberg, Conrad. *The Irish Countryman.* Garden City, New York: The National History Press, 1968.

Arp, Hans, Samuel Beckett, Carl Einstein, Eugene Jolas, Thomas MacGreevy, Georges Pelorson, Theo Rutra, James J. Sweeney, Ronald Symond. "Manifesto: Poetry Is Vertical." *transition* 21 (March 1932): 148–49.

Arnold, Bruce. *A Concise History of Irish Art.* London: Thames and Hudson, revised ed., 1977.

Beckett, J. S. *A Short History of Ireland.* London: Hutchinson and Co., Ltd., 1979.

Beckett, Samuel. "Homage à Jack Yeats." *Les Lettres Nouvelles* (April 1954): 619–20.

———. "An Imaginative Work." (*The Amaranthers* - A review). *The Dublin Magazine* (July–September 1936): 80–81.

———. (writing under pseudonym "Andrew Belis"). "Recent Irish Poetry." *Bookman* (August 1934).

Berger, John. *Selected Essays and Articles*. Harmondsworth: Penguin, 1972.

Berger, Pamela. "Many-Shaped: Art, Archaeology, and *The Tain*." *Eire-Ireland* 17 (Winter 1982): 6–18.

Bertram, Anthony. *Sickert*. London: Studio Publications, 1955.

Boyd, Ernest. *Ireland's Literary Renaissance*. Dublin: Maunsel, 1916; rpt., Dublin: Figgis, 1964.

Brook-Rose, Christine. *A Rhetoric of the Unreal*. Cambridge: Cambridge University Press, 1981.

Browse, Lillian, ed. *Sickert*. London: Faber & Faber, 1943.

Caldwell, Martha B. "Jack Butler Yeats: Painter of Life in the West of Ireland." Ph.D. dissertation, Indiana University. Ann Arbor: University Microfilms, 1971.

Carpenter, Andrew, and Peter Fallon. *The Writers: A Sense of Ireland*. New York: George Braziller, 1980.

Carric, Allen. "Captain Jack B. Yeats: A Pirate of the Old School." *The Mask* 7 (July 1912): 44–49.

Clissman, Anne. "Brian O'Nolan." *The Macmillan Dictionary of Irish Literature*. London: Macmillan, 1979.

Cohn, Ruby. *From Desire to Godot*. Berkeley: University of California Press, 1987.

———. *Samuel Beckett: A Collection of Criticism*. New ,York: McGraw Hill, 1975.

Colum, Padraic. "Tendencies in Irish Art." *Survey Graphic* (December 1921): 342–45.

Connelly, Joseph F. "Jack Yeats: Entertaining the Common Man." *Eire-Ireland* 17 (Winter 1982): 152–58.

Costello, Peter. *The Heart Grown Brutal: The Irish Revolution in Literature from Parnell to the Death of Yeats, 1891–1939*. Dublin: Gill and Macmillan, 1977.

Cronin, Anthony. *Heritage Now: Irish Literature in the English Language*. New York: St. Martin's Press, 1982.

Curran, C. P. "Jack B. Yeats, RHA." *Studies: An Irish Quarterly Review* 30 (March 1941): 78–89.

———. "The Yeats Exhibition." *Capuchin Annual* (1945–46): 102–22.

de Paor, Liam. *Portrait of Ireland.* New York: St. Martin's Press, 1985.

de Valera, Eamon. "Introduction" to *Modern Aspects of Irish Art.* Dublin: Cumann Liegheacht an Phobail, 1922.

Deane, Seamus. "Irish Poetry and Irish Nationalism." In *Two Decades of Irish Writing: A Critical Survey.* Cheshire: Carcanet Press Ltd., 1975.

————. *A Short History of Irish Literature.* Indiana: University of Notre Dame Press, 1986.

Donaghue, Denis. "Introduction" to *William Butler Yeats Memoirs.* New York: Macmillan, 1973.

Dunn, Douglas, ed. *Two Decades of Irish Writing: A Critical Survey.* Cheshire: Carcanet Press Ltd., 1975.

Eagleton, Terry. *Criticism and Ideology.* London: Verso Editions, 1978.

Edwards, Owen Dudley, ed. *Conor Cruise O'Brien Introduces Ireland.* London: Andre Deutsch, 1969.

Ehrmann, Jacques. *Structuralism.* New York: Doubleday, 1970.

Ellmann, Richard. *Yeats, The Man and the Masks.* London: Faber and Faber, 1949.

Fallis, Richard. *The Irish Renaissance.* Syracuse: Syracuse University Press, 1977.

Foster, R. F. *Modern Ireland 1600–1972.* New York: Viking Penguin, 1989

Freud, Sigmund. *Introductory Lectures on Psychoanalysis.* Rpt. New York: W. W. Norton and Company, 1977.

Friel, Brian. *Translations.* London: Faber and Faber, 1981.

Gadamer, Hans-Georg. *Philosophical Hermeneutics.* Berkeley: University of California Press, 1976.

Genette, Gerard. *Narrative Discourse.* Ithaca: Cornell University Press, 1980.

Gittes, Katherine Slater. "The Canterbury Tales and the Arabic Frame Tradition." *PMLA* 98 (March 1983): 228–35.

Gogarty, Oliver St. John. *As I Was Going Down Sackville Street: A Phantasy in Fact.* New York: Harcourt, Brace, and World, 1937.

Gordon, D. J., and Ian Fletcher. *Exhibition Catalogue: W. B. Yeats—Images of a Poet.* Manchester: Whitworth Art Gallery, 1961.

Greene, David H. "Synge and the Irish." *Colby Library Quarterly* (February 1957): 158–67.

Gregory, Isabella Augusta (Lady). *Our Irish Theatre.* New York and London: G. P. Putnam's Sons, 1914; rpt. Gerrards Cross: Colin Smythe, 1972.

Gwynn, Stephen. *Irish Literature and Drama in the English Language: A Short History.* London: Thomas Nelson and Sons Ltd., 1936; rpt. Folcroft, Pennsylvania: Folcroft Press, Inc., 1969.

Hall, Wayne E. *Shadowy Heroes: Irish Literature of the 1890's*. Syracuse: Syracuse University Press, 1980.

Hamilton, G. H. *Painting and Sculpture in Europe 1880–1940*. Baltimore: Penguin, 1967.

Harmon, Maurice, ed. *Image and Illusion: Anglo-Irish Literature and Its Contexts*. Dublin: Wolfhound Press, 1979.

Hassan, Ihab. "The Dismemberment of Orpheus." In *Learners and Discerners*. Charlottesville: University of Virginia Press, 1964.

Hawkes, Terence. *Structuralism and Semiotics*. Berkeley: University of California Press, 1977.

Heaney, Seamus. "The Fire in the Flint." In *Preoccupations*. New York: Farrar, Strauss, and Giroux, 1980.

Hewitt, John. "Coming to Terms with Jack B. Yeats." *The Threshold* 33 (1983): 43–50.

H. M. "Book Reviews." *The Mask* 7 (July 1912): 77.

Hogan, Robert. *After the Irish Renaissance: A Critical History of the Irish Drama Since the Plough and the Stars*. Minneapolis: University of Minnesota Press, 1967.

———. *The Macmillan Dictionary of Irish Literature*. London: Macmillan, 1979.

Inglis, Brian. *The Story of Ireland*. London: Faber and Faber, 1965.

Iser, Wolfgang. *The Act of Reading*. Baltimore: The Johns Hopkins University Press, 1978.

"*Jack B. Yeats, His Pictorial and Dramatic Art* by Ernest Marriott" (A review). *The Mask* 7 (July 1912): 77–78.

Jameson, Fredric. *The Prison-House of Language*. Princeton: Princeton University Press, 1972.

Jeffares, A. Norman. *Macmillan History of Anglo-Irish Literature*. Dublin: Gill and Macmillan, 1982.

———. *W. B. Yeats*. London: Routledge and Kegan Paul, 1971.

———, ed. *Yeats, Sligo and Ireland*. Gerrards Cross: Colin Smythe, 1980.

Kilroy, Thomas. "Tellers of Tales." *The Times Literary Supplement*, 17 March 1972, pp. 301–2.

Krause, David. *The Profane Spirit of Irish Comedy*. Ithaca: Cornell University Press, 1982.

"*La La Noo* by Jack B. Yeats" (A review). *The New Alliance* (April–May 1943): 12.

Levi-Strauss, Claude. *Structural Anthropology*. London: Penguin Books, 1972.

Loftus, Richard J. *Nationalism in Modern Anglo-Irish Poetry*. Madison: University of Wisconsin Press, 1964.

Lucie-Smith, Edward. *Cultural Calendar of the 20th Century*. Oxford: Phaidon Press, Ltd., 1979.

Lucy, Sean. *Irish Poets in English*. Dublin: Mercier Press, 1973.

Lynch, David. *Yeats: The Poetics of the Self*. Chicago: University of Chicago Press, 1979.

Lyons, F. S. L. *Ireland Since the Famine*. London: Weidenfeld and Nicholson, 1971.

MacCarvill, Eileen. "Jack B. Yeats—His Books." *The Dublin Magazine* 20 (July–September 1945): pp. 47–52. (In the private papers of Jack B. Yeats.)

MacGowran, Jack, ed., *In Sand, A Play, with The Green Wave, A One-act Conversation Piece*. Dublin: Dolmen Press, 1964.

MacGreevy, Thomas. *Collected Poems*. Thomas Dillon Redshaw, ed. Dublin: New Writers' Press, 1971.

———. "Homage to Jack B. Yeats." (In the private papers of Jack B. Yeats.)

———. *Jack B. Yeats: An Appreciation and an Interpretation*. Dublin: Victor Waddington Publications, 1945.

———. "Three Historical Paintings by Jack B. Yeats." *Capuchin Annual* (1942): 238–51.

MacGreevy, Thomas, and Ernie O'Malley. *Jack B. Yeats 1871–1957*. (Exhibition Catalogue) Sligo: Sligo County Library and Museum, 1963.

MacInnes, Colin. *No Novel Reader*. London: Martin, Brian and O'Keeffe, 1975.

Maguire, William J. *Irish Literary Figures: Biographies in Miniature*. Dublin: Metropolitan Publishing Co., Ltd.; rpt. Folcroft, Pennsylvania: Folcroft Library Editions, 1974.

Marcus, Phillip L. *Yeats and the Beginning of the Irish Renaissance*. Ithaca: Cornell University Press, 1970.

Marriott, Ernest. *Jack B. Yeats: His Pictorial and Dramatic Art*. London: Elkin Mathews, 1911.

Martin, Augustine. *Anglo-Irish Literature*. Dublin: Department of Foreign Affairs, 1980.

Masefield, John. "Mr. Jack B. Yeats." *Dublin Magazine* (August 1923): 3–4.

———. *Some Memories of W. B. Yeats*. Dublin: Cuala Press, 1940; rpt. Shannon: Irish University Press, 1971.

Mason, Eugene. *Considered Writers Old and New*. London: Methuen and Co., Ltd., 1925.

———. Untitled. *Today*, 4 (June 1917): 133.

Mays, James. "Jack B. Yeats: Some Comments on His Books." *Irish University Review* 2 (Spring 1972): 34–54.

McCarthy, Mary. "Novel, Tale and Romance." *The New York Review of Books* 30 (12 May, 1983): 49–56.

McHugh, Roger. *Jack B. Yeats: A Centenary Gathering*. Dublin: Dolmen Press, 1971.

Mercier, Vivian. *Beckett/Beckett*. New York: Oxford University Press, 1977.

———. *The Irish Comic Tradition*. Oxford: Clarenden Press, 1962.

Murphy, William. "The Ancestry of William Butler Yeats." *Yeats Studies* 1 (1971): 1–20.

———. *Prodigal Father: The Life of John Butler Yeats (1839–1922)*. Ithaca: Cornell University Press, 1978.

———. *The Yeats Family and the Pollexfens of Sligo*. Dublin: National Gallery, 1971.

Neill, Kenneth. *An Illustrated History of the Irish People*. New York: Mayflower Books, 1979.

O'Brien, Maire Cruise. "The Two Languages." In *Conor Cruise O'Brien Introduces Ireland*. London: Andre Deutsch, 1969.

O'Connor, Frank. *The Backward Look: A Survey of Irish Literature*. London: Macmillan, 1967.

O'Doherty, Brian. "Jack B. Yeats: Promise and Regret." In *Jack B. Yeats: A Centenary Gathering*. Dublin: Dolmen Press, 1971.

O'Driscoll, Robert, and Lorna Reynolds, eds. "Theatre and the Visual Arts: A Centenary Celebration of Jack Yeats and John Synge." *Yeats Studies* 2 (1972).

O'Faolain, Sean. "Jack B. Yeats." *The Bell* 4 (January 1941): 33–36.

Olney, James. "Father and Son: J. B. Yeats and WBY." *South Atlantic Quarterly* 79 (1980): 321–28.

O'Malley, Ernie. "Introduction to the Catalogue for the Exhibition held in the National College of Art, Dublin, June–July 1945." In *Jack B. Yeats 1871–1957*. Sligo: Sligo County Library and Museum , 1963.

Orvell, Miles. "Entirely Fictitious: The Fiction of Flann O'Brien." *Journal of Irish Literature* 3 (January 1974): 93–103.

Pilling, John. "The Living Ginger: Jack B. Yeats's *The Charmed Life*." *Journal of Beckett Studies* 2 (Summer 1977): 55–65.

Plunkett, James. *The Gems She Wore: A Book of Irish Places*. London: Hutchinson and Company, 1972.

Power, Patrick C. *The Story of Anglo-Irish Poetry 1800–1922*. Cork: Mercier Press, 1967.

Pyle, Hilary. "Catalogue Notes." In *Jack B. Yeats 1871–1957: A Centenary Exhibition*. London: Secker and Warburg, 1971.

———. *Jack B. Yeats: A Biography*. London: Routledge and Kegan Paul, 1970.

————. *Jack B. Yeats in the National Gallery of Ireland.* Dublin: National Gallery of Ireland, 1986

Rafroidi, Patrick. *Aspects of the Irish Theatre.* Lille: Encyclopedie Universitaire, 3 (1972).

Reid, Frederick W. "Star Dreams and Pigments" (A poem). (In the private papers of Jack B. Yeats.)

Rose, Marilyn Gaddis. *Jack B. Yeats: Painter and Poet.* Berne: Herbert Lang, 1972.

————. "Jack B. Yeats: Visionary Realist." *Modernist Studies: Literature and Culture 1920–1940* 2 (1976): 27–32.

————. "The Kindred Vistas of W. B. and Jack B. Yeats." *Eire-Ireland* 5 (Spring 1970): 67–79.

————. "Solitary Companions in Beckett and Jack B. Yeats." *Eire-Ireland* 4 (Summer 1969): 66–80.

————. "The Sterne Ways of Beckett and Jack B. Yeats." *Dublin University Review* (1972): 164–71.

————. "Sub Rosa: The Writings of Jack B. Yeats." *Eire-Ireland,* 3 (Summer 1968): 37–47.

Rosenthal, T. G. *Masters of Painting #40.* London: The Studio, 1925; rpt. London: Knowledge Publications, 1966.

Rothenstein, John. "Visits to Jack Yeats." *New English Review* (July 1946): 42–44.

Russell, Ann. "Remembering Jack B. Yeats." *Colby Library Quarterly* 6 (December 1963): 354–61.

Russell, George (AE). "An Artist of Gaelic Ireland." *Freeman's Journal* (undated). (In the private papers of Jack B. Yeats.)

Saddlemyer, Ann. "The Cult of the Celt: Pan-Celticism in the Nineties." In *The World of W. B. Yeats.* Seattle: University of Washington Press, 1967.

————. "The Noble and the Beggar-man: Yeats and Literary Nationalism." In *The World of W. B. Yeats.*

————. "A Share in the Dignity of the World: J. M. Synge's Aesthetic Theory." In *The World of W. B. Yeats.*

Saddlemyer, Ann, and Robin Skelton, eds. *The World of W. B. Yeats.* Seattle: University of Washington Press, 1967

Scholes, Robert. *Fabulation and Metafiction.* Urbana: University of Illinois Press, 1979.

————. *Structural Fabulation.* Notre Dame, Indiana: University of Notre Dame Press, 1975.

————, ed. *Learners and Discerners, A Newer Criticism.* Charlottesville: University of Virginia Press, 1964.

Scholes, Robert, and Robert Kellogg. *The Nature of Narrative.* New York: Oxford University Press, 1966.

Shattuck, Roger. "Life Before Language." *New York Times Book Review* (1 April 1984), pp. 1 and 31.

Sheehy, Edward. "Jack B. Yeats." *Dublin Magazine*. (July–September 1945): 38–41.

Skelton, Robin, ed. *The Collected Plays of Jack B. Yeats*. London: Secker and Warburg, 1971.

————. "Themes and Attitudes in the Later Drama of Jack B. Yeats." *Yeats Studies* 2 (1972).

————. "Unarrangeable Reality: The Paintings and Writings of Jack B. Yeats." In *The World of W. B. Yeats*, ed. Ann Saddlemyer and Robin Skelton. Seattle: University of Washington Press, 1967.

Smith, James L. *Melodrama*. London: Methuen, 1973.

Synge, J. M. *The Autobiography of J. M. Synge: Constructed from Ms by Alan Price*. Dublin: Dolmen Press, 1965.

Torchiana, Donald T. *W. B. Yeats and Georgian Ireland*. Evanston: Northwestern University Press, 1966.

Vendler, Helen. "JBY." *The New Yorker*. 8 January 1979, pp. 66–67.

Warner, Alan. *A Guide to Anglo-Irish Literature*. New York: St. Martin's Press, 1981.

Wheeler, Mitchell, et al. "Queen's College Belfast Fete Supplement." (Monograph in the private papers of Jack B. Yeats.)

White, James, ed. *Jack B. Yeats 1871–1957: A Centenary Exhibition*. London: Secker and Warburg, 1971.

White, Terence de Vere. "The Personality of Jack B. Yeats." In *Jack B. Yeats: A Centenary Gathering*. Dublin: Dolmen Press, 1971.

Worth, Katharine. *The Irish Drama of Europe from Yeats to Beckett*. London: Athlone Press, 1978.

Yeats, Anne. *Broadside Characters*. Dublin: Cuala Press, 1971.

Yeats, John Butler. *Early Memories: Some Chapters of Autobiography*. Churchtown: Cuala Press, 1923; rpt. Shannon: Irish University Press, 1971.

————. "The Education of Jack B. Yeats." *Christian Science Monitor*, 2 November 1920, p. 5.

————. *Essays Irish and American*. Dublin: Talbot, 1918.

————. *Further Letters of John Butler Yeats: Selected by Lennox Robinson*. Dundrum: Cuala Press, 1920; rpt. Shannon: Irish University Press, 1971.

————. *Letters to His Son W. B. Yeats and Others, 1869–1922*, ed. Joseph Hone. London: Faber and Faber Ltd., 1944.

————. *Passages from the Letters of John Butler Yeats: Selected by Ezra Pound*. Dundrum: Cuala Press, 1917.

Yeats, William Butler. *The Autobiography of William Butler Yeats*. 1916; rpt. New York: Collier Books, 1965.

————. *Dramatis Personae*. Dublin: Cuala Press, 1935.

————. *Memoirs*. Transcribed and edited by Denis Donoghue. New York: Macmillan, 1973.

————. *On The Boiler*. Dublin: Cuala Press, 1939.

————. *Synge and the Ireland of his Time with a note concerning a walk through Connemara with him by Jack B. Yeats*. Dublin: Cuala Press, 1911.

Index

Abbey Theatre, 178, 231–32
AE (George Russell), 27
aesthetic principles, 49, 54–58; active role of viewer, 57; of reader, 71
aging motif, 138
Ah Well, 39, 74; discussion of, 138–50; continuity, 138–39; as fabulation, 139, 146–47; dominance of death theme, 139–40, 152; and youth, 141; suicide, 141–42; and nature of art, 143–45; and utopia, 145–46; as social criticism, 146; journey motif in, 148; ritual suicide attempt, 148; aging, 148–49; epiphany, 149; metafiction, 150
Allied Artists Association, 48
Amaranthers, 8; discussion of, 111–24; Pollexfen and Yeatsean values, 111; balance outer and inner worlds, 111, 114, 122–23, 142; artistic authenticity, 111; as fabulation, 112–13, 121; as social criticism, 113; and river motif, 114–16; acceptance of rhythms of life, 114, 117, 120; isolation, 118, 123; imagery, 120; Beckett's comments on, 120, 123–24; creative imagination, 123
An Artist of Gaelic Ireland, 27
And To You Also, 150–65; primary themes, 150; visionary states, 150–52, 162–63; death 152, 162; human isolation, 152, 157–59; paired protagonists, 153; Good Boy, 154, 156, 157, 158, 159; continuity, 156; aesthetic appeal, 156; Man-Without-A-

Shirt (the Baron), 158–59, 161, 164; Christian context, 159, 162, 165; the Squire, 160–61; nationalist ideals, 160–61; parallels to childhood, 160–61; Bowsie, 161, 162
Anglo-Irish: Yeats's appeal to, 27; Irish scorn for, 215; "social suicide" of, 217; squandering of inheritance, 217–20, 223; dream of security, 220, 233
Anglo-Irish War, 52–53
Antaeus myth, 47–48, 111, 142
Apparitions, 16; discussion of volume, 206–27; discussion of play, 206–12; as social criticism, 206, 208–11; and Irish paralysis, 210; contempt for Shaw, 210; and rejection of artist, 211; summary of volume's themes, 226–27
Archibald, Douglas, 7
art: criticism, 51; and balance, 142, 168; and poetic vision, 143; and transformative powers, 143, 168
Artist of Gaelic Ireland, 27, 59
artistic authenticity, viii, 58, 60, 107, 113, 116, 124, 138, 152, 167, 172–73, 202, 205
artists, vii; necessity of balance, 6, 39, 142; as outsiders, 30–31; and metaphors from circus life, 39, 45–48, 256; as magicians, 44–45; "true" artists, 54–55, 172; and sense of place, 56; solitude of, 58–59; and convention, 68, 108; interaction with audience, 71, 153–55, 168–69, 202; trans-

use of humor in, 212; paired protagonists in, 212–13; role of the artist in, 213, 217; Christian context,
217
oral tradition, influence on narrative
style, 91
outsider motif, 1, 29–33, 62, 100–101,
130–33, 212–13; family origins, 2,
31; and pirates, 30, 194; in *Sailing,
Sailing Swiftly,* 100–102

painting: themes, 20; symbolic qualities, 43; sub rosa, 45; use of oils,
48; "clairvoyance" and "half-memory," 49; nonlinear style, 64; relation to narrative style, 69; transformation in, 142
pantomime, 197
paralysis motif, 117, 179, 197, 210, 214,
216, 218, 227–28, 231–32, 237–39
parents: separation, 3; mother, 2, 5,
11; father's influence, 7, 9, 46, 48,
57, 58, 252
Pilling, John, viii; comments on narrative style, 61; comments on Modernism, 118; comments on imagination in *The Charmed Life,* 125, 129
pirate motif: and grandfather Pollexfen, 29–30; and nostalgia, 41, 194
Plunkett, Horace, 36
Poetry is Vertical manifesto, 143–44,
176
political prisoners: and outsider motif,
32–33
political satire, 209–10, 247–52; of political rhetoric, 229, 235
politicization of art, 15–16
Pollexfen family: instability, 4; major
traits, 8, 10; values, 8, 106–7, 111,
203; and the outsider motif, 31;
view of father, 31, 161
Pollexfen, George, 43
Pollexfen, William, grandfather, 29,
105, 141
propaganda: and art, 15–16
providence motif, 103, 108, 126, 196
provincialism, 233, 236; Yeats's ambivalence about, 236, 238–39
Purser, John, ix
Pyle, Hilary, viii, 6, 9; on Yeats's re-

serve, 11, 28; on Yeats's marriage,
12; on Yeats's patriotism, 27–28; on
Yeats's circus motif, 47; Childers's
death, 54; on *Sailing, Sailing
Swiftly,* 96; miniature theatre, 194

Quinn, John, 36, 49

rain motif: as symbol of uncontrollable forces, 87, 95
randomness motif, 19, 65, 72, 88, 92,
96, 99, 103, 124
Rattle, 8, 44; discussion of, 217–27;
and the Anglo-Irish, 217; and social
criticism, 217–23; fabulation in, 218,
223; paralysis of Irish, 218; consequences of colonialism, 221–22,
225–26, 248; color imagery, 221–22;
place names in, 223–24; Gaelic's
hermetic core, 224; utopia motif,
224–25; inheritance question, 225;
uncertainty and chance, 225–26;
principal themes, 226–27; Anglo-
Irish guilt, 227
realistic fiction, rejection of, 65–66, 69
Republicans, 12, ideals of art, 57; and
IRA, 85
Reveries Over Childhood and Youth, 27
rhythm of life motif, 98, 104, 124, 138,
191, 201, 212, 222, 225, 244, 252–53
river (stream) motif, 114–16, 145, 201,
219
romantic aesthetic: in art, 55
romantic idealism, 86
Romantic Shades, 44
romanticism, vii, x
rose motif: as symbol of artistic inspiration, 45, 221
Rose, Marilyn Gaddis, viii, 189, on
narrative style, 61, on similarity of
Yeats's characterization to Beckett's,
129; on irony and theatre of the absurd, 241
Rosses Point, 86

Sailing, Sailing Swiftly, 7, 16, 88; discussion of, 96–111; primary themes,
96; rhythms of life theme, 96, 98,
104; ballad device, 97–98; journey
motif, 99; Irish-English contrast, 99–

The Literary Universe of Jack B. Yeats was composed in 10.5/12.5 ITC Garamond Light by World Composition, Inc., Sterling, Virginia; printed and bound by Braun-Brumfield, Inc., Ann Arbor, Michigan; and designed and produced by Kachergis Book Design, Pittsboro, North Carolina.